THE **BIG** BOOK OF QUICK & HEALTHY RECIPES

KIRSTEN HARTVIG

THE **BIG** BOOK OF QUICK & HEALTHY RECIPES

365

**DELICIOUS & NUTRITIOUS
MEALS IN UNDER 30 MINUTES**

DUNCAN BAIRD PUBLISHERS

LONDON

Dedication: to Al Hart and Essie Jain

Thank you to Amanda Preston, Bob Ashby, Bob Saxton,
Catherine Frances, Charlotte Charmetant, Esther Gillett, Fiona
Gilmore, Françoise Nassivet, Geoffrey Cannon, Helouise Sarrat,
Jennifer Maughan, Joyce Thomas, Julia Charles, Kathy Mitcherson,
Nic Rowley, Paul Charmetant, Peter Firebrace, Sue Mitcherson,
Tara Firebrace and Zoë Stone for their help, inspiration and
support. Special thanks to chef François Salies for his
invaluable contribution to the recipes.

The Big Book of Quick & Healthy Recipes
Kirsten Hartvig

Conceived, created and designed
by Duncan Baird Publishers Ltd
Sixth Floor
Castle House
75–76 Wells Street
London W1T 3QH

Managing Editor: Julia Charles
Editor: Zoë Stone
Managing Designer: Manisha Patel
Designer: Sailesh Patel
Commissioned Photography: William Lingwood
Photography Assistant: Estelle Cuthbert
Stylists: Joss Herd (food) and Helen Trent

British Library Cataloguing-in-Publication Data:
A CIP record for this book is available from the British Library

ISBN-10: 1-84483-074-8
ISBN-13: 9-781844-830749

10 9 8 7 6 5 4 3 2 1

Typeset in Frutiger and MetaPlus
Colour reproduction by Scanhouse, Malaysia
Printed in China by Imago

CONTENTS

INTRODUCTION

The Big Book of Quick and Healthy Recipes is based on the concept that healthy food should be available to all, and that it is possible to create tasty, nutritious meals without spending a lot of money, time or effort.

Whatever your experience as a cook, this book will enable you to create a healthy meal in half an hour, 365 days of the year, using fresh, high-quality, varied seasonal ingredients prepared with minimal processing to ensure maximum taste and nutritional value. It offers all the choice necessary for a varied and interesting diet, and makes it possible for people of all different dietary preferences, habits and needs to eat together. The book draws on ethnic influences from all over the world, and blends modern nutritional science with tried and tested natural healthy-eating principles.

The recipes are divided into four chapters reflecting the changing seasons. All the dishes are rated and explained for health features, including calorie and cholesterol count, nutrient content and medicinal value. Every dish is a nourishing, balanced meal in itself, and most dishes give meat, vegetarian and vegan options – the basic recipe being the same for each. I have also provided serving suggestions for a number of the recipes, which are, of course, optional and may be tailored to suit your needs and preferences.

Special dietary requirements are catered for because an increasing number of people suffer from some form of food allergy, or need to avoid certain foods for health reasons. In each recipe, it is possible to see at a glance whether it contains wheat or gluten, solinaceae, or citrus, and suggestions for alternatives to dairy products are also given.

Recipes for each season are divided into seven groups; Soups, Salads and Raw Foods, Pasta Dishes, Ethnic Dishes, Omelettes, Pancakes and Pizzas, Grills, Bakes and Casseroles and Sweet Fruit Dishes. These categories are based on the old principle that recommends eating the same type of meal on the same day each week. In natural medicine, it is also thought to be good for health to have a "fruit only" day once a week, so most of the fruit recipes can be used both for main meals and desserts. All main meals can be used as starters, too.

If you don't want to choose a different category of food each day of the week, the nutritional information given with each recipe enables you to plan your meals not only by taste and ingredients, but also according to what you feel you need each day in order to maintain (or regain) maximum health.

HOW TO USE THIS BOOK

This book enables you to make a healthy meal in half an hour, 365 days a year. Every dish actively promotes health and provides a nourishing, balanced meal in itself. The recipes are arranged according to season, and make use of fresh seasonal ingredients. They are also organized into seven different categories so you can choose a different type of meal each day of the week.

There is a set of icons by each recipe that shows the health-promoting features of each dish. This makes it easy for those with special dietary requirements to choose suitable meals, and enables you to check at a glance whether the meal you choose contains ingredients you would prefer to avoid – wheat or gluten, solinaceae (tomatoes, peppers, aubergines, potatoes, paprika and Tabasco sauce), or citrus. ✪ indicates "boosts immunity"; ♥ "good for the heart or circulation"; ◑ "an aid to detox"; ✖ "low in calories"; ✍ "contains wheat or gluten"; ✪ "contains solinaceae"; and ◻ "contains citrus". The icons are present when this quality applies to the recipe. So, for example, if a dish helps to boost immunity and it contains wheat or gluten, both the star and the wheat or gluten icon will appear beneath the recipe name.

Multi-choice ingredients make it possible to cater for people with different food preferences using the same basic recipe. Every recipe has a vegan option which contains no meat, dairy or other animal products, and there is a nutritional table that gives the calorie counts for average portions of the meat or dairy version (calories) and the vegan version (vegan calories) of each recipe. The cholesterol ratings only apply to dishes containing meat and/or dairy. The vegan versions are all 100 per cent cholesterol free.

Beneath this is a star rating system for the nutrients found in each recipe to help you to choose daily meals that enhance health and help prevent disease. Three stars means the dish contains a large amount of the given nutrient, two stars a medium amount and one star a low level. All the listed nutrients are important for general well-being. For example, polyunsaturates (polyunsats) include *essential fatty acids* vital for normal hormone production and immunity, and are thought to protect against heart disease. Antioxidants such as vitamins A, C, E, zinc and selenium are all important for healthy skin, good eyesight and strong immunity. Calcium is necessary for healthy bones, iron is essential to the blood and circulation, and B vitamins are important for the nervous system. When you are feeling run-down, the book makes it simple to choose recipes high in antioxidants that give your immune system a boost. If you are under a lot of stress, you should choose recipes high in B vitamins. If you are concerned about your blood fat levels, you can choose recipes low in cholesterol and high in polyunsaturates.

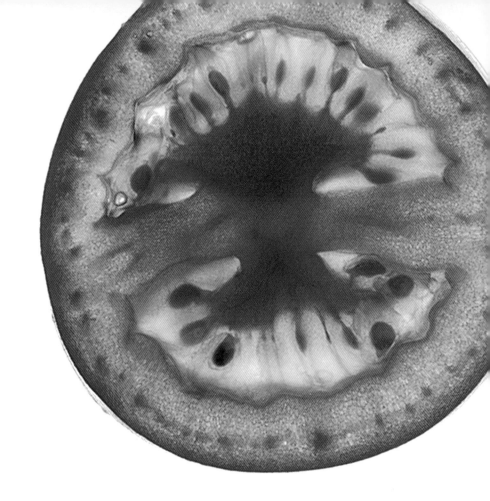

HEALTHY
EATING
BASICS

Healthy eating involves using fresh ingredients and gentle cooking methods to enhance natural flavours without the need for artificial additives. However, this doesn't have to mean spending a lot of time and effort in the kitchen, it is more a question of getting organized.

First you need to rethink your attitude toward shopping and cooking: let it be part of your daily routine instead of an inconvenience that has to be "fitted in". Planning a weekly menu and writing shopping lists makes it cheaper, quicker and easier to shop. Seeking out good local food shops and markets can pay back handsomely in terms of time and money, as well as offering the benefits of connecting you with your local environment and like-minded people.

Cooking doesn't have to be a challenge reserved for special occasions – it can be an enjoyable part of everyday life that enables you to feel better and have more energy for living. What we eat becomes part of us, and connects us to the vitality of life. So make your kitchen a playground where you relax, experiment and enjoy preparing healthy meals.

CHOOSING INGREDIENTS

Vegetables: are best eaten young before they begin to coarsen and lose their colour. Buy vegetables as fresh as possible, preferably from "box schemes" or vegetable markets. Supermarket vegetables have often travelled long distances and have been stored for longer than local market produce.

Fruit: is most tasty when picked ripe, but ripe fruit doesn't travel and keep as well as unripe fruit, so it is often picked early and artificially ripened when en route from producer to consumer. Locally-grown, naturally-ripened, organic fruits have the most flavour and are more nutritious.

Herbs and spices: keep a selection of fresh and dried herbs and spices in your kitchen. Stand bouquets of fresh herbs in a glasses of cold water, or buy individual herbs in pots and keep them on the windowsill. Spices have more flavour if you buy them whole and use them freshly ground (in a mortar or a coffee grinder). The most commonly used herbs and spices are thyme, marjoram, oregano, basil, dill, mint, tarragon, parsley, garlic, ginger, cayenne pepper, coriander, cumin, cinnamon, paprika, turmeric and bay leaf.

Cheese: taste cheese before you buy it, and buy small quantities at a time. Store in the bottom of the fridge (the least cold part), wrapped in foil or cling film.

Eggs: always use free-range eggs, and buy organic whenever possible.

Fish: really fresh fish is free of odour, but is not so easy to come by these days. If you have a local fishmonger, ask for your fish to be cleaned and boned while you wait. If you don't have access to local fresh fish, buy frozen. Remember that fish from fish farms are often fed a diet supplemented with antibiotics, hormones and other drugs.

Shellfish: fresh shellfish are heavy with seawater and their shells tightly closed. When you buy oysters or mussels, ask your fishmonger to remove the shells.

Meat: buy organic, free-range meat to avoid hormones and other drug residues in your diet. Intensive farming has made it more difficult to find natural, unspoilt meats, so make sure you know the source of your butcher's meat. Animals that live on a natural diet and have access to fresh air and sunshine have fewer illnesses than those that spend their time in cramped, indoor conditions.

Game: animals and birds that live in the wild have more meat and less fat in their flesh, and the fat is higher in polyunsaturates. Farmed game is cheaper than wild game, but inferior in terms of quality and taste.

Seitan: is a form of wheat gluten, with a high-protein, low-fat content, and no cholesterol. It is usually sold in strips, and can be used as an alternative to meat. It is available from most health food shops.

Soya beans: are a versatile and extremely nutritious food that can be turned into textured meat substitutes, such as **soya chunks, tempeh** and **tofu. Soya milk, soya yoghurt, soya cheese** and **soya cream** are good alternatives to dairy products. Soya beans are also used to make **miso** and **soya sauce. Tamari** is a wheat free type of soya sauce.

Tempeh: is a form of bean curd, originating in Indonesia but now popular all over the world. A fine source of protein, it contains no saturated fats, and is one of the few vegetable products to contain vitamin B12. It resembles chicken in taste and texture, and is available from health food and ethnic shops.

Tofu: is also a soya bean curd. Another alternative to meat, it is widely available from health food shops and supermarkets. Tofu originated in China and has been eaten in the Far East for more than 2000 years. It is low in calories, high in protein and calcium, low in fat, and contains no cholesterol.

Grains, flour, pasta and bread: wholemeal products have a higher nutritional value than refined products because many important nutrients are contained in the outer layers of the kernel, which are removed in the refining process. However, some refined foods (for example, pasta) have a finer texture than their wholemeal counterparts, and are easier to cook and digest, so you may want to experiment with white/wholemeal blends.

Rice: white rice is quicker to cook than whole grain, but less nutritious because, as with other grains, the important nutrients are found just under the skin.

Oils: cold-pressed extra virgin olive oil is best to use for stir-frying because it is not affected as much by heat as polyunsaturated oils such as **grapeseed** or **sunflower oil**. However, in some recipes the thinner polyunsaturated oils give better results. French dressing is easier to whisk into an even texture when made with olive oil, but polyunsaturated oils contain more essential fatty acids and are therefore healthier. I prefer to use a mixture of both.

Margarine/butter: choose unhydrogenated polyunsaturated vegetable margarine. If you use butter, buy organic.

Stock: read the ingredient list on the packet of ready-made stocks and stock cubes to make sure you know what they contain. Avoid flavour enhancers, such as mono-sodium-glutamate. Many also contain tomatoes, which you should avoid if you are allergic to solinaceae. Choose meat, fish or vegetable stock according to your preference where no particular type is specified.

Vinegar: choose red or white wine vinegar for use in cooked dishes and dressings. Balsamic vinegar gives a rich caramel flavour, but should be used sparingly as it can be overpowering.

Lemon juice: is an excellent addition to salad dressings, providing both flavour and vitamin C. It prevents discolouration (for example, of avocados, artichokes or apple slices) and gives dressings a lighter colour.

Salt: grey unrefined sea salt is not as pretty as white refined table salt, but it contains valuable trace elements and is less concentrated and thus better for health.

Black pepper: freshly ground black pepper gives a much more peppery flavour than pre-ground pepper.

Sugar: raw cane sugar is preferable to white refined sugar because it contains small amounts of minerals and is less concentrated.

Brewer's yeast flakes: are high in protein, calcium, iron and B vitamins. They have a nut-like flavour and make a useful alternative to Parmesan.

HOT SHOPPING TIPS

You can improve the quality of what you eat without it adding extra to your food budget. For example, buying fresh products is more cost effective than buying "ready meals" because processed foods are usually prepared from poor quality ingredients, plus some additives to give longer shelf life, brighter colours and a stronger taste. With fresh foods, what you see is what you get, and by cutting out the middle man you can create your own naturally fresh and healthy diet, reaping all the benefits of unadulterated ingredients without having to bear the cost of processing, packing and storing.

As consumers we have real power to influence the economic, social and technological processes that affect how food is produced and prepared by making active choices about what we eat and where our food comes from. By choosing ingredients that are produced in ways we agree with, we can help create an agricultural and food distribution system that supports gentle, ecologically sensitive, organic growing methods, both locally and in other parts of the world. By expressing a preference for natural, unadulterated, organically-grown foods, we can contribute to the growth of sustainable agriculture worldwide.

Research has shown that the nutrient content of fruits and vegetables was considerably higher before the widespread adoption of chemicals in food growing. Luckily, the tide is turning as more incentives are offered to farmers to convert to organic production by governments responding to consumer pressure. The cumulative effect is that more local and imported organic foods are becoming available at lower prices, thus creating a sustainable, balanced, happier lifestyle for food producers and consumers alike.

In summary, to ensure that you purchase high-quality, fair trade foods for maximum taste and nutritional value, follow the practical and simple shopping tips outlined below:

• Select ingredients that are organically grown, seasonal and local.
• When buying products from further afield (such as spices and tropical fruits), choose organic, fair trade foods wherever possible. That way you support local producers in other parts of the world too.
• Avoid genetically modified foods. Organic produce is not genetically engineered, and expressing a preference for natural foods reduces the incentive to develop more GMOs.
• Choose fresh, unprocessed ingredients when available.
• When buying processed foods, read the list of ingredients on the label and make sure you know what you are buying.

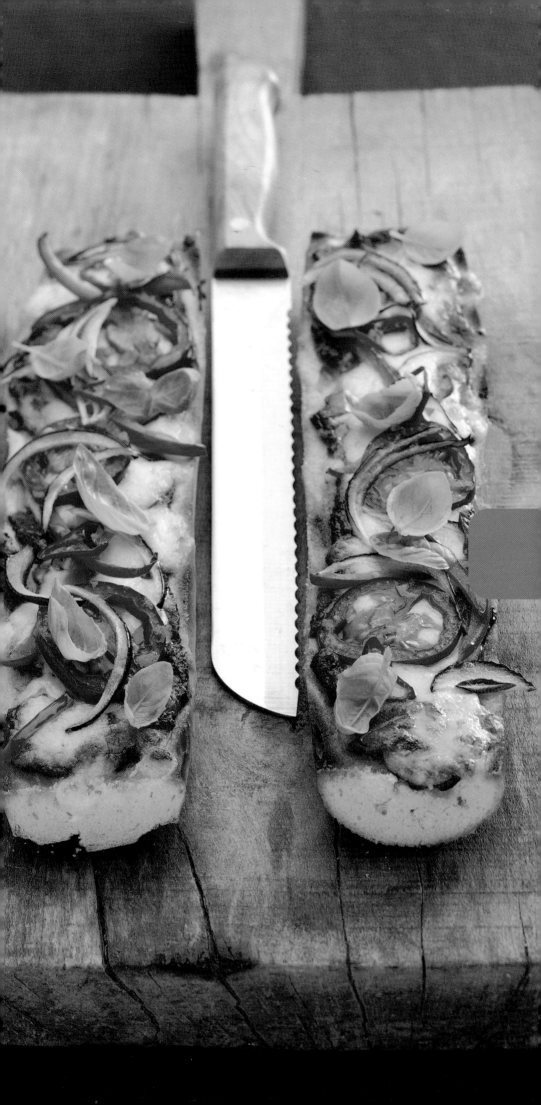

HOT COOKING TIPS

• **Read your chosen recipe** through before you start cooking, then collect all the ingredients and prepare them as described in the ingredients list (for example, "2 carrots, chopped") before you start cooking. The amounts in each recipe are for two people, so you can easily halve them to cook for one, or double them to cook for four.

• **Cooking soup**: the trick is to get as much of the taste as possible out of the ingredients and into the water. Sauté the ingredients before adding the preheated liquid or, alternatively, place all the ingredients in a pot with cold water and salt, and let them all heat up together.

• **Cooking fish**: fish are fragile and should be gently cooked to avoid them drying out and disintegrating.

• **Cooking meat**: meat usually needs to be "sealed" at the beginning of the cooking process. Sauté it first, set aside and add to the dish later on.

• **To sauté** means to gently stir-fry over a relatively low heat thus avoiding high-temperature frying, which destroys nutrients and is generally bad for health. Prepare all the ingredients and place them in separate piles. Heat a little oil in a pan, then add ingredients to the pan, one pile at a time, starting with the hardest (which will take the longest to cook), and finishing with the most watery.

• *Al dente* is an Italian expression and means "slightly chewy". Pasta loses its taste and texture if over-cooked and so is best served al dente. Vegetables cooked al dente are slightly crisp with their flavour and bright colours intact.

• **Blanching** means to cook in boiling water for just a few minutes. Use plenty of boiling water and quickly rinse in cold water afterwards to stop the cooking process.

• **Blend whole fresh tomatoes** instead of peeling them or using tinned ones. This will improve the flavour of your dish and conserve important nutrients found in the skins.

• **Use olive oil** as it is more stable than other fats and oils and does not form trans fats (found in hydrogenated oils, margarines and butter) when heated.

• **Fresh herbs**: rosemary, thyme, sage, marjoram, oregano and bay leaf all have strong flavours and can withstand cooking. More delicate herbs, such as chives, tarragon, mint and basil, should be added at the last moment to preserve their flavour. Use fresh herbs because, as well as contributing flavour, they add medicinal value to your diet. Garnish salads and cooked dishes with freshly chopped herbs.

• **Salads**: discard the coarsest leaves, cut off the base and wash lettuce and other green leaves in cold water. Gently dry, then wrap in a cloth (or a plastic bag) and store in the fridge until ready to use. Add dressing to salads just before serving.

• **Mushrooms**: cut off the base of the stalks, place in a colander, briefly rinse in cold water and pat dry before using. Clean wild mushrooms by very gently scraping the stems and cups with a small, sharp knife. Morels should be washed and carefully checked for small insects and worms before cooking.

• **Rice**: wholegrain brown rice takes longer to cook than white rice (up to approximately 40 minutes), so put it on before you start preparing the rest of the ingredients.

• **Stock**: vegetable cooking water makes a quick and useful stock. Cool it down and keep it in a clean jar in the fridge for up to three days.

• **Heat stock** before you add it to a dish, thereby keeping the temperature of your dish even and speeding up cooking time.

• **Avoid frying** at very high temperatures to guard against the production of harmful chemicals.

• **Peel or scrub?** The highest concentration of taste and nutrients in fruit and vegetables is found just under the skin, and is lost with peeling. Scrubbing with a hard brush is just as quick, and is all that is needed for most organic foods. However, if you are not able to use organic ingredients, it is advisable to peel your fruit and vegetables because most chemical residues (for example, pesticides, herbicides and antibiotics) are found in the peel.

• **Blending**: using an electric hand blender is the quickest and easiest way to blend as it avoids removing the dish from the pan, then pouring it back into the pan and reheating. Hand blenders are also easy to clean.

• **Nuts and seeds:** lightly toasting nuts and seeds brings out their flavour. Toast in a dry, heavy-based frying pan over a medium–low heat. Remove the pan from the heat as soon as the first seeds start to brown or pop. Add a little salt or soya sauce to enhance the taste.

• **Preheat the oven** to reduce cooking time. Make sure your oven is set at the right temperature before you put anything in it.

• **Baking blind:** to avoid a pastry-based dish turning soggy, place the rolled-out pastry in a baking dish, cover with dried butter beans or lentils and bake "blind" in a preheated oven for 10–15 minutes while you prepare the remaining ingredients. Remove the beans and leave to cool.

• **Weights and measures:** both metric and imperial weights and measurements are given for the recipes. You should follow either set of measures, not a mixture of both, as they are not interchangeable.

• **Cooking temperatures:** oven temperatures are given in degrees Celsius, degrees Fahrenheit and gas mark for each recipe. Remember if you have a fan-assisted oven that you need to reduce the temperature slightly (usually by approximately 20 degrees) and/or adjust the cooking times. Please refer to manufacturer's guidelines for more specific information on adjusting the temperature and time of your oven, if applicable.

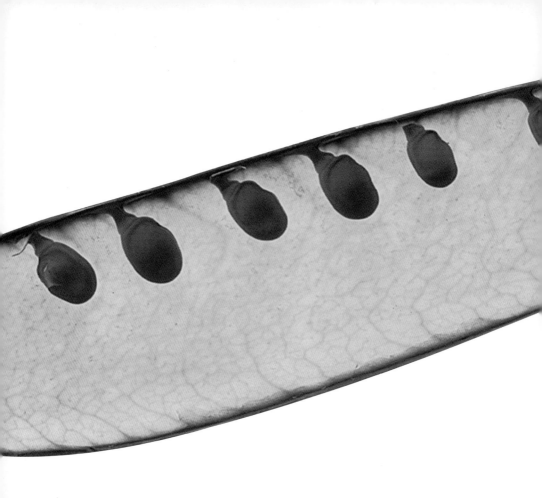

SPRING
RECIPES

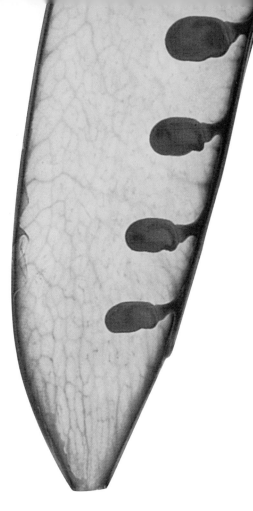

Spring is the time of waking up after the still winter. In nature, energy rises and green shoots appear everywhere and, as the light grows stronger, so does our need to recharge our batteries and have a good clean out. Young nettle shoots, dandelion leaves, sorrel and cress are bursting with vitamins and minerals to replenish the body, and they are also excellent remedies for detoxifying.

Spring is the best time to go on detox cures and regimes, because the various spring greens are full of new nourishment, antioxidants and phytochemicals that help us shed the winter cold. It is a time of new life and new beginnings, and the pastel-coloured flowers all around bear witness to the fruits to come.

What a joy to cook with sparkling fresh ingredients after a winter using stored roots! The first asparagus is followed by a myriad of sunny spring feasts of strawberries, cherries, mushrooms, new carrots and potatoes, green beans, fresh herbs and tender courgettes. Colourful meals, high in nutrients and lower in calories, replace heavier winter meals. The sun is back, and with it come the plentiful foods and enthusiasm we need to enjoy the delights of the new season.

001 ARTICHOKE HEART SOUP

CALORIES	314
CHOLESTEROL	7
VEGAN CALORIES	285
POLYUNSATS	★★☆
ANTIOXIDANTS	★★★
CALCIUM	★★☆
IRON	★★☆
B VITAMINS	★★☆

4 artichokes
2 tbsp lemon juice
2 tbsp olive oil
1 shallot, sliced
1 small potato, diced
100g (3½oz) tomatoes, blended

850ml (1½pts) vegetable stock
2 tbsp small pasta shapes
sea salt and black pepper to taste
1 handful fresh parsley, finely
    chopped

Peel the leaves off the artichokes, cut them into quarters and remove the choke and any remaining leaf edges with a sharp knife. Plunge the artichoke hearts into cold water with the lemon juice. Heat the oil in a saucepan and gently soften the shallot. Add the potato and the artichoke hearts, stir-fry for 2 minutes, then add the tomatoes, heat through and pour in the stock. Bring to the boil, then add the pasta and simmer for 10–15 minutes. Season with salt and pepper, garnish with fresh parsley and serve with bread and cheese or soya cheese.

002 ASPARAGUS SOUP

CALORIES	305
CHOLESTEROL	7
VEGAN CALORIES	285
POLYUNSATS	★★☆
ANTIOXIDANTS	★★☆
CALCIUM	★★☆
IRON	★★☆
B VITAMINS	★★☆

1 bunch asparagus
2 tbsp olive oil
1 small onion, chopped
1 small carrot, chopped
2 medium potatoes, chopped
850ml (1½pts) vegetable stock

1 small bunch fresh parsley,
    chopped
100ml (3½fl oz) milk/soya milk
sea salt and black pepper to taste
fresh parsey to garnish, finely
    chopped

Chop the ends off the asparagus, and peel off any coarse outer skin with a potato peeler. Cut off the tips and steam them separately for 5–6 minutes. Chop the remaining asparagus into chunks. Gently heat the oil in a large saucepan and sweat the onion, carrot, potatoes and aspargus chunks for a couple of minutes before adding the vegetable stock and the parsley. Bring to the boil and gently simmer for 15 minutes. Remove from the heat, pour in the milk, blend and season. Add the asparagus tips, gently reheat and serve garnished with fresh parsley.

003 CATALAN THYME AND GARLIC SOUP

CALORIES	149
CHOLESTEROL	0
VEGAN CALORIES	149
POLYUNSATS	★★☆
ANTIOXIDANTS	★★☆
CALCIUM	★☆☆
IRON	★☆☆
B VITAMINS	★☆☆

500ml (18fl oz) water
2 tsp fresh thyme
2 cloves garlic, chopped

sea salt and black pepper to taste
olive oil for drizzling
1 handful croutons

Bring the water to the boil in a saucepan with the thyme, garlic and a little salt and pepper. Simmer for 2–3 minutes, check the seasoning, drizzle with a little oil and garnish with croutons before serving.

004 CHINESE GREEN ASPARAGUS SOUP

CALORIES	265
CHOLESTEROL	0
VEGAN CALORIES	265
POLYUNSATS	★★★
ANTIOXIDANTS	★★★
CALCIUM	★★☆
IRON	★★☆
B VITAMINS	★★☆

2 tbsp olive oil
100g (3½oz) green asparagus, sliced
1 small stick celery (with leaves), sliced
4 red radishes, sliced
1 clove garlic, finely chopped
1 tsp fresh ginger, finely chopped
125g (4½oz) spinach leaves, chopped
2 tsp tamari (soya sauce)
1 tbsp sesame oil
700ml (1¼pts) vegetable stock
sea salt and black pepper to taste

Stir-fry the asparagus, celery, radishes, garlic and ginger in a casserole dish with the olive oil for 2 minutes. Add the spinach, tamari and sesame oil and fry for another 30 seconds. Pour in the stock, bring to the boil and simmer for 15 minutes. Season and serve hot.

005 SAVOY CABBAGE SOUP

CALORIES	369
CHOLESTEROL	0
VEGAN CALORIES	369
POLYUNSATS	★★☆
ANTIOXIDANTS	★★★
CALCIUM	★★☆
IRON	★★☆
B VITAMINS	★★☆

1ltr (1¾pts) vegetable stock
2 tbsp olive oil
1 small leek, sliced
2 potatoes, cubed
1 carrot, cubed
1 slice celeriac, cubed
¼ Savoy cabbage, shredded
1 bay leaf
1 tsp paprika
a few sprigs each of parsley, sage, rosemary and thyme, chopped
1 handful small pasta shapes
sea salt and black pepper to taste

Bring the stock to the boil in a casserole dish with the other ingredients and simmer for 15 minutes. Season and serve with wholemeal bread.

006 HARISSA SOUP

CALORIES	498
CHOLESTEROL	0
VEGAN CALORIES	498
POLYUNSATS	★☆☆
ANTIOXIDANTS	★★★
CALCIUM	★★☆
IRON	★★★
B VITAMINS	★★☆

½ hot chilli pepper, chopped
2 cloves garlic, crushed
1 tsp coriander seeds
1 tsp ground cumin
2 tbsp olive oil
2 spring onions, sliced
1 carrot, diced
1 stick celery, sliced
100g (3½oz) green beans, sliced
450g (1lb) ripe tomatoes, blended
250g (9oz) flageolet beans, cooked or canned
250g (9oz) chick peas, cooked or canned
850ml (1½pts) vegetable stock
sea salt and black pepper to taste
1 handful fresh mint, chopped

In a mortar, pound the chilli, garlic, coriander and cumin with a little oil. Then gently heat the remaining oil in a large casserole dish and add the onion and the vegetables. Heat through, add the tomatoes, beans, chick peas and chilli paste. Stir for 1 minute before adding the stock and a little salt. Bring to the boil and simmer for 15 minutes. Season with salt and pepper, garnish with fresh mint and serve.

007 HOT NETTLE SOUP

★ ♡ ◊ ✕ ⊘

CALORIES	258
CHOLESTEROL	0
VEGAN CALORIES	258
POLYUNSATS	★☆☆
ANTIOXIDANTS	★★★
CALCIUM	★★☆
IRON	★★★
B VITAMINS	★★☆

1ltr (1¾pts) vegetable stock
200g (7oz) fresh nettle tips, washed
2 tbsp olive oil
½ tsp cayenne pepper
1 pinch saffron
1 bay leaf
1 clove garlic, crushed

1 red onion, halved and sliced
1 potato, diced
1 carrot, sliced
1 stick celery, finely chopped
3 tbsp white beans, cooked
   or canned
sea salt and black pepper to taste

Bring the stock to the boil in a casserole dish with the nettles and the rest of the ingredients. Heat through and simmer for 15 minutes. Blend, adjust the seasoning and serve with croutons.

008 PORTUGUESE SPRING GREEN SOUP

★ ◊ ⊘

CALORIES	461
CHOLESTEROL	25
VEGAN CALORIES	394
POLYUNSATS	★★☆
ANTIOXIDANTS	★★★
CALCIUM	★★☆
IRON	★★★
B VITAMINS	★★☆

850ml (1½pts) vegetable stock
300g (10½oz) new potatoes,
   quartered and thinly sliced
½ spanish onion, thinly sliced
150g (5½oz) spring greens,
   shredded

1 tsp mustard seeds
1 tsp paprika
2 tbsp olive oil, plus some for frying
sea salt and black pepper to taste
100g (3½oz) spicy sausage
   (pork/soya), sliced

Bring the stock to the boil in a casserole dish with the potatoes, onion, spring greens, mustard seeds, paprika, olive oil and some salt and pepper. Heat through and simmer for 15 minutes. Meanwhile, fry the sausage slices in a frying pan with a little oil. When the soup is ready, check the seasoning, garnish with the fried sausage slices and serve.

009 FRENCH ONION SOUP

♡ ✕ 🌿

CALORIES	368
CHOLESTEROL	0
VEGAN CALORIES	368
POLYUNSATS	★★☆
ANTIOXIDANTS	★☆☆
CALCIUM	★☆☆
IRON	★☆☆
B VITAMINS	★★☆

2 tbsp olive oil
150g (5½oz) onions, finely chopped
1 tbsp wheat flour
1ltr (1¾pts) vegetable stock

1 tbsp port
sea salt and black pepper to taste
2 thin slices bread, toasted

Heat the oil in a casserole dish over a low–medium heat and stir-fry the onions until soft. (Don't let them brown too much.) Sprinkle with the flour and stir for 1 minute. Slowly add the stock and the port, bring to the boil, simmer for 20 minutes and season. Place a thin slice of toasted bread in the bottom of each bowl and pour the soup on top. Serve immediately.

010 ▼ SPICY BEETROOT SOUP

★◐✖◪

CALORIES	296
CHOLESTEROL	28
VEGAN CALORIES	368
POLYUNSATS	★★★
ANTIOXIDANTS	★★★
CALCIUM	★☆☆
IRON	★★☆
B VITAMINS	★★☆

1 tbsp grapeseed oil
1 tsp ground cumin
1 cinnamon stick
½ tsp ground cloves
1 tsp freshly ground black pepper
250g (9oz) raw beetroot, diced

250g (9oz) tomatoes, diced
½ltr (18fl oz) vegetable stock
 or water
sea salt to taste
50ml (2fl oz) crème fraîche/coconut
 cream

Heat the oil in a saucepan, add the spices and stir for 10 seconds. Add the beetroot, stir for a further 30 seconds, then add the tomatoes. Stir-fry for 1 minute before adding the stock or water. Bring to the boil and simmer for 15 minutes, then season. Take off the heat, remove the cinnamon stick, blend and add the cream. Serve with croutons or toast.

011 SPRING VEGETABLE SOUP

CALORIES	298
CHOLESTEROL	0
VEGAN CALORIES	298
POLYUNSATS	★☆☆
ANTIOXIDANTS	★★★
CALCIUM	★☆☆
IRON	★★☆
B VITAMINS	★★☆

2 tbsp olive oil
2 spring onions, sliced
100g (3½oz) new potatoes, sliced
100g (3½oz) young carrots, chopped
450g (1lb) fresh tomatoes, blended
the tips from a small bunch of
    asparagus
100g (3½oz) shelled peas

3 red radishes, sliced
½ltr (18fl oz) vegetable stock
1 tsp maple syrup
1 tbsp fresh tarragon, finely
    chopped
sea salt and black pepper to taste
a little Parmesan/brewer's yeast
    flakes (optional)

Heat the oil in a casserole dish. Gently sweat the spring onions, potatoes and carrots for 5 minutes. Add the tomatoes. Heat through, then add the asparagus, peas and radishes. Add the stock, maple syrup and a little salt. Bring to the boil and simmer for 10 minutes. Add the tarragon, season, sprinkle with Parmesan or brewer's yeast flakes (if using) and serve.

012 HIMALAYAN NETTLE SOUP

CALORIES	93
CHOLESTEROL	0
VEGAN CALORIES	93
POLYUNSATS	★☆☆
ANTIOXIDANTS	★★★
CALCIUM	★★☆
IRON	★★★
B VITAMINS	★★☆

250g (9oz) young nettle tips
1ltr (1¾pts) vegetable stock
½ tsp black pepper
1 tsp fresh ginger, chopped

1 tbsp wheat flour mixed with a little
    milk/soya milk
sea salt to taste

Pick and wash the nettles using gloves. Bring the stock to the boil in a saucepan. Add the nettle tips, pepper, ginger and a little salt. Simmer for 15 minutes. Blend and thicken with the flour, while stirring continuously. Check the seasoning and serve with rice.

013 TIBETAN BOETUK

CALORIES	502
CHOLESTEROL	55
VEGAN CALORIES	416
POLYUNSATS	★★☆
ANTIOXIDANTS	★★☆
CALCIUM	★★☆
IRON	★★☆
B VITAMINS	★★☆

100g (3½oz) wheat flour
2 tbsp olive oil
3 spring onions, sliced
1 clove garlic, crushed
1 tsp fresh ginger, chopped
1 pinch asafoetida
1 pinch grated nutmeg
1 pinch saffron

100g (3½oz) lean lamb chunks/
    25g (1oz) soya chunks
    (dry weight), rehydrated
1 tbsp tamari (soya sauce)
2 tomatoes, chopped
4 red radishes, sliced
150g (5½oz) green peas
1ltr (1¾pts) vegetable stock

Mix the flour with a little salt and enough water to make a stiff dough. Roll the dough into a thin snake and cut into 1cm (½in) dumplings. Set aside. Heat the oil in a saucepan, add 2 spring onions, followed by the garlic and ginger and fry for 1 minute. Then add the spices and the lamb or soya chunks and fry for a further 5 minutes. Add the tamari, heat through, then add the tomatoes. Turn down the heat and simmer for a few minutes before adding the radishes, peas and stock. Bring to the boil and add the dumplings. Simmer for 8–10 minutes. Finely chop the remaining spring onion, sprinkle over the soup and serve.

014 SPROUTING SPRING SALAD
🟊♥🜄✗🌰

CALORIES	316
CHOLESTEROL	0
VEGAN CALORIES	316
POLYUNSATS	★★☆
ANTIOXIDANTS	★★★
CALCIUM	★★☆
IRON	★★★
B VITAMINS	★★☆

1 large handful Iceberg lettuce
1 handful rocket
1 chicory (Belgian endive), sliced
   lengthways
100g (3½oz) fresh green peas
1 small courgette, finely sliced
1 handful alfalfa sprouts

Basic French dressing:
1 tbsp lemon juice
1 clove garlic, crushed
2 tsp Dijon mustard
sea salt and black pepper to taste
3 tbsp olive oil

To make a basic French dressing, mix the lemon juice, garlic, mustard, salt and pepper in a large salad bowl. Slowly add the oil and whisk until smooth and creamy. Shred the lettuce and place it in the bowl along with the other ingredients. Add the dressing, toss well and serve immediately.

015 SALADE PRINTANIÈRE
🟊✗🍞🌰

CALORIES	260
CHOLESTEROL	168
VEGAN CALORIES	371
POLYUNSATS	★★☆
ANTIOXIDANTS	★★★
CALCIUM	★★☆
IRON	★★★
B VITAMINS	★★☆

100g (3½oz) green beans,
   cooked and halved
½ bunch radishes, sliced
8 mushrooms, sliced
juice of 1 lemon
2 tbsp olive oil

1 tbsp fresh tarragon, chopped
sea salt and black pepper to taste
10 cherry tomatoes, halved
12 scampi, cooked and shelled/
   50g (1¾ oz) Brazil nuts, halved

Mix the green beans, radishes and mushrooms in a salad bowl. Make a vinaigrette by whisking the lemon juice, oil, tarragon, salt and pepper in a bowl. Pour two-thirds of the vinaigrette over the mixed vegetables and gently toss, then divide between two large plates. Dip the tomatoes in the remaining vinaigrette and arrange them around the edge of each plate. Garnish with scampi or Brazil nuts and serve with French baguette.

016 SMOKY SWEDISH SALAD
🟊♥🜄✗🌰

CALORIES	390
CHOLESTEROL	22
VEGAN CALORIES	382
POLYUNSATS	★★★
ANTIOXIDANTS	★★★
CALCIUM	★★☆
IRON	★☆☆
B VITAMINS	★★★

oil for frying (optional)
100g (3½oz) smoked herring
   fillets/smoked tempeh, cubed
1 raw beetroot, chopped into
   thin sticks
1 carrot, chopped into thin sticks
1 dessert apple, quartered, cored
   and finely chopped

1 spring onion, finely sliced
2 tbsp light almond butter
1 tbsp tarragon vinegar
1 tbsp lemon juice
1 tsp Dijon mustard
½ tsp ground coriander
½ tsp thyme
sea salt and black pepper to taste

If you are using tempeh, stir-fry in a frying pan with a little oil until golden. Mix the beetroot, carrot, apple and spring onion in a salad bowl. Make a dressing by mixing the almond butter with the vinegar, lemon juice, mustard, coriander, thyme, salt and pepper in a bowl. Add a little water to get a smooth and creamy consistency. Gently mix the dressing with the salad and garnish with the herring or tempeh. Serve with a bowl of green lettuce or curly endive (frisée) and slices of wholemeal or rye bread.

017 ◄ SALMON WITH MANGO AND ASPARAGUS SALAD

CALORIES	615
CHOLESTEROL	96
VEGAN CALORIES	349
POLYUNSATS	★★☆
ANTIOXIDANTS	★★★
CALCIUM	★★☆
IRON	★★☆
B VITAMINS	★★★

1 tbsp olive oil
300g (10½oz) salmon fillet, boned
   and flaked/100g (3½oz) seitan,
   cubed
200g (7oz) asparagus spears,
   trimmed and chopped
2 handfuls lamb's lettuce

½ Florence fennel bulb, sliced
1 mango, pitted, peeled and cubed
1 spring onion, finely chopped
100ml (3½fl oz) plain/soya yoghurt
1 tsp Dijon mustard
sea salt and black pepper to taste

Stir-fry the salmon or seitan in a frying pan with the oil for 2–3 minutes, until it begins to brown. Blanch the asparagus in a saucepan of boiling water with a little salt for 2–3 minutes, drain and set aside. Divide the lamb's lettuce between two large plates. Add the fried salmon or seitan, asparagus, fennel, mango and spring onion. To make the dressing, place the yoghurt in a small bowl, add the mustard and salt and pepper. Mix well and pour over the two salads. Serve with crusty bread.

018 FRENCH BEAN SALAD

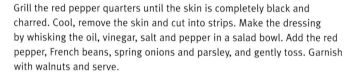

CALORIES	393
CHOLESTEROL	0
VEGAN CALORIES	393
POLYUNSATS	★★★
ANTIOXIDANTS	★★☆
CALCIUM	★★☆
IRON	★★★
B VITAMINS	★★☆

1 red pepper, quartered and
   deseeded
250g (9oz) French beans, blanched
2 spring onions, sliced
1 handful fresh parsley

2 tbsp walnut oil
2 tsp balsamic vinegar
sea salt and black pepper to taste
1 handful walnuts, shelled

Grill the red pepper quarters until the skin is completely black and charred. Cool, remove the skin and cut into strips. Make the dressing by whisking the oil, vinegar, salt and pepper in a salad bowl. Add the red pepper, French beans, spring onions and parsley, and gently toss. Garnish with walnuts and serve.

019 SPRING CRUDITÉS WITH RAVIGOTE

CALORIES	397
CHOLESTEROL	0
VEGAN CALORIES	397
POLYUNSATS	★★☆
ANTIOXIDANTS	★★★
CALCIUM	★★☆
IRON	★★★
B VITAMINS	★★★

2 chicory (Belgian endive), sliced
lengthways
100g (3½oz) shiitake mushrooms,
   sliced and fried
1 bunch asparagus tips
1 large handful fresh broad beans,
   shelled
¼ cauliflower, cut into small florets
1 beetroot, cut into thin sticks
1 tbsp red wine vinegar

1 pinch salt
1 tsp mustard
½ tsp each of chopped tarragon
   and fine herbs
1 tsp each of chopped parsley
   and chervil
1 spring onion, finely chopped
2 tsp capers, chopped
3 tbsp olive oil

Divide the crudités between two large plates. To make the dressing, blend the vinegar, salt, mustard, herbs, spring onion and capers. Slowly add the oil and blend to an even consistency. Sprinkle the dressing onto the crudités and serve with toasted bread.

020 TARAMASALATA AND GREEK SALAD

CALORIES	199
CHOLESTEROL	382
VEGAN CALORIES	201
POLYUNSATS	★★★
ANTIOXIDANTS	★★★
CALCIUM	★★★
IRON	★★★
B VITAMINS	★★☆

125g (4½oz) red caviar/smoked tofu, crumbled
2 tbsp lemon juice
1 tsp grated lemon rind
3 tbsp water
1 small shallot, finely chopped
1 clove garlic, finely chopped
2 tbsp breadcrumbs

1 tbsp tomato ketchup (optional)
sea salt and black pepper to taste
1 small lettuce, shredded
1 carrot, grated or cut into peelings
1 large ripe tomato, sliced into boats
1 tbsp capers
10 Greek olives, pitted
2 tbsp fresh parsley, chopped

Make the taramasalata by blending the red caviar or smoked tofu with the lemon juice, lemon rind and water. Add the shallot, garlic, breadcrumbs and tomato ketchup (if using). Season and keep in the fridge until needed. Place the lettuce in a salad bowl and top with the carrot, tomato, capers, olives and parsley. Serve with the taramasalata and warm pitta bread.

021 ASPARAGUS AND TOMATO SALAD

CALORIES	264
CHOLESTEROL	0
VEGAN CALORIES	264
POLYUNSATS	★★☆
ANTIOXIDANTS	★★☆
CALCIUM	★☆☆
IRON	★☆☆
B VITAMINS	★★☆

1 bunch white asparagus, peeled and ends cut off
2 tomatoes, sliced
1 pinch sea salt and black pepper

1 tbsp lemon juice
3 tbsp olive oil
1 small bunch chives, chopped

Boil the asparagus in a saucepan with salted water for approximately 10 minutes. Then chop the asparagus into 3cm (1¼in) pieces, place on a serving plate and cover with the tomato slices. To make the vinaigrette, whisk the salt, pepper, lemon juice and olive oil in a bowl, and spoon over the tomatoes. Garnish with chives and serve immediately.

022 FLORENCE FENNEL SALAD

CALORIES	249
CHOLESTEROL	0
VEGAN CALORIES	249
POLYUNSATS	★★★
ANTIOXIDANTS	★★★
CALCIUM	★★☆
IRON	★☆☆
B VITAMINS	★★☆

2 Florence fennel bulbs, halved lengthways and finely sliced (reserve the tops to garnish)
6 radishes, sliced
1 carrot, cut into fine sticks
1 dessert apple, quartered, cored and cubed

1 spring onion, finely sliced
1 tbsp light almond butter
1 tbsp tarragon vinegar
1 tbsp lemon juice
1 tsp Dijon mustard
sea salt and black pepper to taste

Mix the fennel, radishes, carrot, apple and spring onion in a salad bowl. Make the dressing by mixing the almond butter with the vinegar, lemon juice, mustard, salt and pepper in a bowl. Add a little water to get a smooth and creamy consistency. Gently toss the dressing with the salad, garnish with fennel tops and serve with bread and pâté.

023 ▲ KIMCHEE SALAD

★♥◊✗∅

CALORIES	97
CHOLESTEROL	0
VEGAN CALORIES	97
POLYUNSATS	★☆☆
ANTIOXIDANTS	★★★
CALCIUM	★☆☆
IRON	★★☆
B VITAMINS	★★☆

1 small Chinese cabbage, finely chopped
1 small white radish, finely chopped
1 tsp sea salt
½ tsp cayenne pepper
1 clove garlic, finely chopped
1 tsp fresh ginger, finely chopped
2 spring onions, finely chopped
1 carrot, grated
100g (3½oz) green peas, fresh or frozen, blanched

Place the Chinese cabbage and the white radish in a salad bowl, sprinkle with salt and cayenne pepper. Mix well, then add the garlic, ginger, spring onions, carrot and peas. Mix again and serve with toasted bread and pâté.

024 AVOCADO, SPINACH AND GREEN PEA SALAD

★♥◊🌾

CALORIES	411
CHOLESTEROL	0
VEGAN CALORIES	411
POLYUNSATS	★★★
ANTIOXIDANTS	★★★
CALCIUM	★★★
IRON	★★★
B VITAMINS	★★☆

250g (9oz) fresh spinach leaves, sliced
1 avocado, diced
200g (7oz) green peas, fresh or defrosted
1 tbsp tarragon vinegar

½ tsp maple syrup
1 clove garlic, crushed
sea salt and black pepper to taste
2 tbsp wheatgerm oil
1 small bunch watercress, chopped
1 tbsp pumpkin seeds

Mix the spinach, avocado and peas in a large salad bowl. To make the dressing, whisk the vinegar, maple syrup, garlic, salt and pepper in a bowl. Slowly add the oil, whisk to a smooth consistency, then toss with the salad. Garnish with watercress and pumpkin seeds and serve with bread.

025 SALADE D'ASPERGE

♥◊

CALORIES	430
CHOLESTEROL	120
VEGAN CALORIES	226
POLYUNSATS	★★☆
ANTIOXIDANTS	★★☆
CALCIUM	★★☆
IRON	★★☆
B VITAMINS	★★☆

1 bunch white asparagus, peeled and ends cut off
2 chicken breasts/125g (4½oz) tofu, sliced
2 handfuls mixed salad leaves

1 tbsp white wine vinegar
2 tbsp olive oil, plus some for frying
sea salt and black pepper to taste
1 tbsp chives, chopped

Cook the asparagus in a saucepan with boiling water and a little salt until tender (5–10 minutes, depending on size). Fry the chicken or tofu in a frying pan with a little oil and set aside. Make a vinaigrette by whisking the vinegar, oil, salt and pepper in a bowl. Divide the salad leaves between two large plates and garnish them with the fried chicken or tofu slices and the cooked asparagus. Drizzle with the vinaigrette and garnish with chives. Serve with toasted bread.

026 MESCLUN SALAD

★♥◊✗🌰

CALORIES	315
CHOLESTEROL	19
VEGAN CALORIES	289
POLYUNSATS	★★☆
ANTIOXIDANTS	★★☆
CALCIUM	★★☆
IRON	★★☆
B VITAMINS	★★☆

1 curly endive (frisée), sliced
1 handful lamb's lettuce
1 handful young dandelion leaves
1 handful rocket
1 handful oakleaf lettuce
1 tbsp sorrel, chopped
2 tbsp chervil, chopped

3 tbsp olive oil
1 tbsp lemon juice
1 clove garlic, crushed
1 pinch raw cane sugar
sea salt and black pepper to taste
10 anchovy fillets/20 olives, pitted

Make the vinaigrette in a salad bowl by whisking the olive oil, lemon juice, garlic, sugar, salt and pepper. Add the salad ingredients and gently toss. Garnish with anchovies or olives and serve.

027 ▲ SPAGHETTI WITH ARTICHOKES, BEANS AND SPINACH

CALORIES	599
CHOLESTEROL	0
VEGAN CALORIES	599
POLYUNSATS	★★☆
ANTIOXIDANTS	★★★
CALCIUM	★★☆
IRON	★★★
B VITAMINS	★★★

150g (5½oz) spaghetti pasta
2 tbsp olive oil
1 spring onion, sliced
1 clove garlic, chopped
1 red pepper, halved and sliced
100g (3½oz) broad beans, fresh or frozen

125g (4½oz) fresh spinach, chopped
4 artichoke hearts, sliced
2 tbsp tomato paste (purée)
½ tsp raw cane sugar
1 tbsp fresh marjoram
sea salt and black pepper to taste

Boil the spaghetti in plenty of salted water with a little oil. Meanwhile, gently heat the oil in a large saucepan. Add the onion, garlic and red pepper and gently fry for 2 minutes. Stir in the beans, spinach and artichoke hearts. Add the tomato paste (purée), sugar and marjoram, and a little water if necessary. Cover and very gently simmer for 10 minutes. Season and serve with the cooked spaghetti.

PASTA WITH SAUSAGE AND ITALIAN TOMATO SAUCE
⭐🖤💧🌿🌾

CALORIES	705
CHOLESTEROL	13
VEGAN CALORIES	671
POLYUNSATS	★★☆
ANTIOXIDANTS	★★★
CALCIUM	★★☆
IRON	★★★
B VITAMINS	★★★

200g (7oz) tricolor fusilli pasta
150g (5½oz) sausage (meat/soya)
2 tbsp olive oil
1 spring onion, chopped
200g (7oz) fresh peas, shelled
1 small pickled red pepper, sliced

200ml (⅓pt) passata (sieved tomato)
2 handfuls rocket or 2 curly endive (frisée)
sea salt and black pepper to taste
1 handful fresh parsley, chopped

Cook the pasta in plenty of boiling water with a little salt and oil. Chop the sausage into chunks. Heat the oil in a heavy-based frying pan, add the chunks of sausage and the spring onion. Stir-fry over a medium heat until the sausage begins to brown. Add the peas, pickled pepper and passata, bring to the boil and simmer for 10 minutes. Arrange the salad leaves on two large plates. Drain the cooked pasta and place in the middle of each plate. Top with the sauce, season, garnish with parsley and serve.

LINGUINI WITH BEETROOT SAUCE
⭐🖤🌿

CALORIES	507
CHOLESTEROL	8
VEGAN CALORIES	519
POLYUNSATS	★☆☆
ANTIOXIDANTS	★★☆
CALCIUM	★★☆
IRON	★★★
B VITAMINS	★★☆

200g (7oz) linguini pasta
1 tbsp olive oil
1 small red onion, halved and sliced
1 medium raw beetroot, diced
2 tbsp red wine
2 tbsp water or vegetable stock

1 tbsp balsamic vinegar
1 small bunch flat-leaf parsley, chopped
sea salt and black pepper to taste
50g (1¾oz) parma ham/smoked tempeh, diced

Cook the pasta in plenty of boiling water with a little salt and oil. Heat the oil in a casserole dish. Add the onion and the beetroot and gently stir-fry for 5 minutes. Add the red wine, water or stock, vinegar and parsley and bring to the boil. Simmer until the beetroot is soft, then season. Mix the drained pasta into the sauce. Garnish with ham or tempeh and serve hot.

FETTUCCINE WITH TUSCAN SAUCE
⭐🖤🌿

CALORIES	762
CHOLESTEROL	53
VEGAN CALORIES	707
POLYUNSATS	★★★
ANTIOXIDANTS	★★☆
CALCIUM	★★☆
IRON	★★☆
B VITAMINS	★★☆

2 tbsp olive oil
150g (5½oz) boned hare (or rabbit) saddle/seitan, diced
1 small red onion, finely chopped
1 clove garlic, finely chopped
1 tbsp pine kernels
½ Florence fennel bulb, sliced

100ml (3½fl oz) vegetable stock
20g (¾oz) dark chocolate
1 tbsp red wine vinegar
1 tbsp fresh oregano, chopped
sea salt and black pepper to taste
200g (7oz) fettuccine pasta

Heat the oil in a casserole dish, add the hare (or rabbit) or seitan, onion, garlic, pine kernels and fennel, one by one, and stir-fry over a medium–high heat for 5 minutes. Add the stock and the chocolate, bring to the boil, cover and simmer for 10 minutes. Add the vinegar and oregano, heat through and season. Cook the pasta in plenty of boiling water with a little salt and oil. Drain and serve with the sauce and a green salad.

CORN PASTA WITH ROCKET AND SUN-DRIED TOMATOES

CALORIES	659
CHOLESTEROL	5
VEGAN CALORIES	646
POLYUNSATS	★★★
ANTIOXIDANTS	★★★
CALCIUM	★★☆
IRON	★★☆
B VITAMINS	★★☆

200g (7oz) corn pasta
1 bunch rocket, chopped
10–12 black olives, pitted
   and chopped
10–12 sun-dried tomatoes, chopped

2 tbsp safflower oil
1 tbsp lime juice
sea salt and black pepper to taste
1–2 tbsp Parmesan/soya cheese,
   freshly grated

Cook the pasta in plenty of boiling water with a little salt and olive oil. Meanwhile, mix the rocket with the olives, sun-dried tomatoes, safflower oil, lime juice, salt and pepper in a large serving bowl. Drain the cooked pasta and add to the salad. Check the seasoning, sprinkle with Parmesan or soya cheese and serve.

TAGLIATELLE WITH BROAD BEANS

CALORIES	599
CHOLESTEROL	0
VEGAN CALORIES	599
POLYUNSATS	★★☆
ANTIOXIDANTS	★★★
CALCIUM	★★☆
IRON	★★★
B VITAMINS	★★★

200g (7oz) tagliatelle pasta
1 tbsp olive oil
1 spring onion, finely chopped
1 clove garlic, finely chopped
1 handful fresh parsley, finely
   chopped

150g (5½oz) small broad beans
   (shelled weight), fresh or frozen
100ml (3½fl oz) water
sea salt and black pepper to taste
a little Parmesan/brewer's yeast
   flakes (optional)

Cook the pasta in plenty of boiling water with a little salt and oil. Meanwhile, heat the oil in a separate saucepan, add the spring onion, garlic and parsley and very gently stir-fry for 5 minutes until soft. Add the beans and the water. Season, bring to the boil and cook for 5 minutes. Remove from the heat, mash half the bean mixture to a coarse paste and return to the pan with the whole beans. Check the seasoning and heat through. Drain the cooked pasta, then add to the sauce and stir. Sprinkle with Parmesan or brewer's yeast flakes (if using) and serve immediately.

PENNE WITH ASPARAGUS AND MUSHROOM SAUCE

CALORIES	543
CHOLESTEROL	0
VEGAN CALORIES	543
POLYUNSATS	★★☆
ANTIOXIDANTS	★★☆
CALCIUM	★☆☆
IRON	★☆☆
B VITAMINS	★★★

200g (7oz) penne pasta
1 bunch green asparagus, trimmed
2 tbsp olive oil
1 shallot, finely chopped
100g (3½oz) mushrooms, sliced

100ml (3½fl oz) vegetable stock
1 tsp cornflour dissolved in a little
   cold water
1 tbsp tamari (soya sauce)
sea salt and black pepper to taste

Cook the pasta in plenty of boiling water with a little salt and oil. Cut the asparagus into penne-sized lengths, then stir-fry them in the olive oil together with the shallot and the mushrooms for 5 minutes. Add the stock, bring to the boil and simmer for 2–3 minutes, or until the asparagus is tender. Pour in the dissolved cornflour and the tamari and cook until the sauce thickens. Season with salt (if necessary) and plenty of black pepper. Drain the cooked pasta and add to the sauce. Serve immediately.

PASTA PRIMAVERA

⭐ 🖤 💧 🌾 ▢

CALORIES	563
CHOLESTEROL	0
VEGAN CALORIES	563
POLYUNSATS	★★☆
ANTIOXIDANTS	★★★
CALCIUM	★★☆
IRON	★★☆
B VITAMINS	★★☆

200g (7oz) tricolor fusilli pasta
2 tbsp olive oil
2 spring onions, chopped
100g (3½oz) young carrots, cut into
    thin sticks
100g (3½oz) celeriac, cut into thin
    sticks
100g (3½oz) mangetout

100g (3½oz) young nettle tips or
    baby spinach leaves, chopped
100ml (3½fl oz) vegetable stock or
    water
1 tbsp lemon juice
1 tsp Dijon mustard
sea salt and black pepper to taste
1 handful watercress, chopped

Cook the pasta in plenty of boiling water with a little salt and oil.
Meanwhile, heat 1 tablespoon of oil in a casserole dish and gently
stir-fry the spring onions for 30 seconds, then add the carrots, celeriac,
mangetout and nettle tips or spinach leaves. (Only touch raw nettles
with gloves on. Once cooked they lose their sting.) Stir-fry for a further
2 minutes then add the stock or water. Bring to the boil and simmer for
5 minutes. Add the lemon juice, mustard and the remaining 1 tablespoon
of oil, and season. Drain the cooked pasta and mix with the vegetables.
Garnish with watercress and serve immediately.

PENNINI WITH HORN-OF-PLENTY MUSHROOMS

CALORIES	884
CHOLESTEROL	525
VEGAN CALORIES	647
POLYUNSATS	★★★
ANTIOXIDANTS	★★★
CALCIUM	★★☆
IRON	★★☆
B VITAMINS	★★☆

300g (10½oz) chicken livers/150g (5½oz) seitan, cut into chunks
1 tbsp wheat flour
grapeseed oil for (stir-)frying
200g (7oz) pennini pasta
1 shallot, chopped
100g (3½oz) horn-of-plenty mushrooms (craterellus)
3 tbsp dry white wine
4 tbsp chicken/vegetable stock
3 tbsp crème fraîche/soya cream
sea salt and black pepper to taste
1 small bunch chives, finely chopped

Coat the chicken livers or seitan in the flour and a little salt and pepper, then place them in a frying pan and fry with some oil over a high heat until brown. Remove and set aside. Meanwhile, boil the pennini in plenty of salted water with a little oil. Add a little more oil to the frying pan and stir-fry the shallot and the mushrooms, then remove and set aside. Add the wine to the pan and reduce to half the volume, then add the stock and let it reduce, too. Add the cream, followed by the fried shallot and mushrooms. Leave to simmer until the sauce thickens. Add the fried livers or seitan, check the seasoning and serve with the cooked pennini, garnished with chopped chives.

SALADE DE PÂTES

CALORIES	663
CHOLESTEROL	86
VEGAN CALORIES	634
POLYUNSATS	★★☆
ANTIOXIDANTS	★★★
CALCIUM	★★☆
IRON	★★☆
B VITAMINS	★★★

200g (7oz) fresh linguini pasta
300g (10½oz) fresh tuna fillets/150g (5½oz) tempeh and 1 sheet of nori seaweed, toasted and crushed
juice of ½ lemon
10 salted anchovy fillets (soaked for 10 minutes)/10 black olives, pitted
1 dash red wine vinegar
2 tbsp olive oil
black pepper to taste
100g (3½oz) Florence fennel, finely sliced
5 cherry tomatoes
1 tbsp fresh parsley, finely chopped

Cook the pasta in plenty of boiling water with a little salt and oil. Cool the pasta under running water, drain and set aside. Place the tuna or tempeh on a baking tray, add the crushed nori (if using), drizzle with oil and lemon juice and bake in a preheated oven at 220°C/425°F/gas mark 7 for 5–10 minutes. Meanwhile, blend the anchovies or olives, vinegar, oil and pepper to a smooth consistency (and pass through a sieve afterwards if you are worried about the fishbones). Mix the fennel with the cooked pasta and the sauce. Divide between two plates, top with the baked tuna or tempeh slices and cherry tomatoes, and serve garnished with parsley.

037 VERMICELLI WITH CURRIED OYSTER MUSHROOMS

CALORIES	335
CHOLESTEROL	0
VEGAN CALORIES	335
POLYUNSATS	★★☆
ANTIOXIDANTS	★★☆
CALCIUM	★☆☆
IRON	★★☆
B VITAMINS	★★☆

200g (7oz) vermicelli pasta
2 tbsp olive oil
1 tsp curry powder
2 spring onions, sliced
1 tsp fresh ginger, finely chopped

250g (9oz) oyster mushrooms, sliced
1 tbsp fresh coriander leaves, chopped
sea salt and black pepper to taste

Cook the pasta in plenty of salted water with a little oil. Heat the oil in a frying pan or wok, add the curry powder and the spring onions and stir-fry for 30 seconds, then add the ginger and the mushrooms and stir-fry over a medium heat for a further 5 minutes. Add the coriander, season and serve with the cooked, drained pasta and a green salad.

038 CHINESE FIVE-SPICE NOODLES

CALORIES	358
CHOLESTEROL	182
VEGAN CALORIES	341
POLYUNSATS	★★☆
ANTIOXIDANTS	★★☆
CALCIUM	★★☆
IRON	★★☆
B VITAMINS	★★☆

2 tbsp safflower oil
1 clove garlic, finely chopped
4 spring onions, sliced
125g (4½oz) prawns, cooked and shelled/125g (4½oz) marinated tofu, cubed
125g (4½oz) fresh spinach, chopped
1 tsp fresh ginger, grated

1 tbsp tamari (soya sauce)
1 tsp Chinese Five-Spice
1 tbsp Chinese rice wine or dry sherry
1 tsp raw cane sugar
200g (7oz) Chinese rice noodles
1 tbsp salted sesame seeds (gomasio), toasted

Heat the oil in a wok or large pan and stir-fry the garlic, spring onions and prawns or tofu over a medium heat for 3 minutes. Add the spinach, ginger and tamari and stir-fry for a further minute, then add the Five-Spice, wine or sherry and sugar. Lower the heat and very gently simmer for 3–4 minutes. Check the seasoning. Cook the noodles as indicated on the packet. Serve topped with the sauce and garnished with sesame seeds.

039 TAGLIATELLE AUX MORILLES

CALORIES	826
CHOLESTEROL	166
VEGAN CALORIES	623
POLYUNSATS	★★☆
ANTIOXIDANTS	★★☆
CALCIUM	★★☆
IRON	★★☆
B VITAMINS	★★☆

200g (7oz) fresh tagliatelle pasta
300g (10½oz) turbot fillets/150g (5½oz) tofu
oil for frying
10 small morel mushrooms
juice of ½ lemon

20ml (⅔fl oz) old Rivesaltes wine or dry sherry
100ml (3½fl oz) fish/vegetable stock
100ml (3½fl oz) crème fraîche/soya cream
sea salt and black pepper to taste

Cook the pasta in boiling water with a little salt and oil. Cut the tofu into strips (if using). Fry the fillets or tofu in a pan with the oil and set aside (keep warm). Clean and halve the morels, then fry them in the same pan for 3 minutes. Add the lemon juice and reduce until almost evaporated, then add the wine or sherry and the stock and reduce to half the volume. Add the cream and very gently simmer until the sauce thickens, then season. Divide the cooked pasta between two plates, arrange the fillets or tofu strips next to the pasta and top with the sauce. Serve immediately.

040 CHENG MAI STIR-FRY

CALORIES	338
CHOLESTEROL	0
VEGAN CALORIES	338
POLYUNSATS	★★★
ANTIOXIDANTS	★★★
CALCIUM	★★☆
IRON	★★☆
B VITAMINS	★★★

200g (7oz) cauliflower
200g (7oz) purple sprouting broccoli
100g (3½oz) oyster mushrooms
2 tbsp grapeseed oil
1 clove garlic, crushed

100g (3½oz) mangetout
150g (5½oz) baby sweetcorn
2 tbsp tamari (soya sauce)
50g (1¾oz) bean sprouts

Chop the cauliflower into florets and cut the broccoli and mushrooms into slices and set aside. Heat the oil in a wok or a heavy-based pan. Add the garlic and fry for 10 seconds, then add the mangetout, cauliflower florets and broccoli slices, one by one, stirring continuously. Stir-fry for a further 2 minutes, then add the mushroom slices and the sweetcorn. Heat through, add the tamari and stir. Turn down the heat, cover and simmer for 5 minutes (adding a little water if necessary). Add the bean sprouts, heat through and serve hot with rice or noodles.

041 LEBANESE SPINACH

CALORIES	553
CHOLESTEROL	11
VEGAN CALORIES	547
POLYUNSATS	★★★
ANTIOXIDANTS	★★★
CALCIUM	★★★
IRON	★★★
B VITAMINS	★★★

olive oil for frying
1 onion, halved and sliced
500g (1lb 2oz) fresh spinach,
    roughly chopped
2 large slices bread, chopped
    into cubes

200ml (⅓pt) plain/soya yoghurt
1 clove garlic, crushed
1 tbsp fresh mint, chopped
2 tbsp pine kernels, toasted
sea salt and black pepper to taste

Gently sweat the onion in a large casserole dish with a little oil until soft. Add the spinach, heat through, cover and very gently simmer until soft (approximately 10 minutes), then season. Make the dressing by whisking together the yoghurt, garlic and mint. Season and set aside. Fry the bread in a frying pan with a little oil until golden to make croutons, then place half of them in a serving bowl, add the cooked spinach, followed by the yoghurt dressing. Top with the remaining croutons and garnish with toasted pine kernels. Serve immediately.

042 ASIAN ASPARAGUS

CALORIES	263
CHOLESTEROL	0
VEGAN CALORIES	263
POLYUNSATS	★★☆
ANTIOXIDANTS	★★★
CALCIUM	★★☆
IRON	★★☆
B VITAMINS	★★☆

1 bunch green asparagus, trimmed
    and peeled
2 tbsp olive oil
½ tsp ground cumin
1 stalk lemon grass, finely sliced
2 tsp fresh ginger, finely chopped
2 medium carrots, cut into sticks
3 spring onions, sliced

1 tbsp tamarind paste dissolved in
    200ml (⅓pt) hot water
1 handful bean sprouts
1 tbsp tamari (soya sauce)
1 tsp maple syrup
1 tbsp lemon juice
sea salt and black pepper to taste
    (optional)

Cut the asparagus into 5cm (2in) pieces. Heat the oil in a wok. Add the spices, then the asparagus, carrots and spring onions and stir-fry for 5 minutes. Add the dissolved tamarind paste. Simmer until the asparagus is tender, then add the bean sprouts, tamari, maple syrup and lemon juice. Heat through, season (if using), and serve with rice or noodles.

043 PROVENÇAL LEMON POTATOES

CALORIES	300
CHOLESTEROL	0
VEGAN CALORIES	300
POLYUNSATS	★★☆
ANTIOXIDANTS	★★★
CALCIUM	★★☆
IRON	★★☆
B VITAMINS	★★☆

500g (1lb 2oz) small new potatoes, kept whole and unpeeled
2 tbsp olive oil

½ lemon (unpeeled), chopped
1 tsp herbes de Provence
sea salt and plenty of black pepper

Boil the potatoes in lightly salted water until tender (approximately 10 minutes). Drain and set aside. Heat the oil in a large pan, add the boiled potatoes, lemon and herbs. Stir continuously until the potatoes are well coated with herbs. Season and serve on a bed of fresh rocket.

044 ◀ INDONESIAN TEMPEH AND VEGETABLES

CALORIES	440
CHOLESTEROL	0
VEGAN CALORIES	440
POLYUNSATS	★★★
ANTIOXIDANTS	★★☆
CALCIUM	★★☆
IRON	★★☆
B VITAMINS	★★★

4 tempeh rashers, cut into sticks
2 tbsp tamari (soya sauce)
2 tbsp olive oil
1 clove garlic, sliced
1 tbsp fresh ginger, chopped
1 green chilli, deseeded and sliced
100g (3½oz) baby corn, kept whole

100g (3½oz) mangetout, kept whole
100g (3½oz) oyster mushrooms, kept whole
2 spring onions, sliced
1 tbsp toasted sesame oil
sea salt and black pepper to taste

Marinate the tempeh in the tamari while you prepare the other ingredients. Then stir-fry the marinated tempeh with the olive oil in a large pan or wok, add the remaining ingredients (except for the sesame oil), one by one, and stir-fry for a few more minutes. Add the sesame oil, season and serve with noodles.

045 GERMAN SALAD

CALORIES	487
CHOLESTEROL	48
VEGAN CALORIES	508
POLYUNSATS	★★★
ANTIOXIDANTS	★★★
CALCIUM	★★☆
IRON	★★☆
B VITAMINS	★★☆

200g (7oz) new potatoes, boiled and coarsely chopped
1 red apple, cored and chopped
1 tbsp mayonnaise/soya mayonnaise
1 large gherkin, diagonally sliced
2 small herring fillets/60g (2¼oz) walnut halves, shelled

2 tbsp fresh parsley, chopped
1 beetroot, cooked and sliced
½ small red onion, finely sliced
2 tsp white wine vinegar
½ tsp mustard
1 tbsp walnut oil
sea salt and black pepper to taste

Place the boiled potatoes and the apple in a salad bowl and mix in the mayonnaise. Top with the gherkin and herring or walnuts. Garnish with fresh parsley, cooked beetroot and red onion. Make the dressing by whisking the vinegar, mustard, oil, salt and pepper, and sprinkle over the salad just before serving.

046 BAKED CHICORY AND BEETROOT

CALORIES	659
CHOLESTEROL	34
VEGAN CALORIES	568
POLYUNSATS	★★★
ANTIOXIDANTS	★★☆
CALCIUM	★★★
IRON	★★★
B VITAMINS	★★☆

2 large chicory (Belgian endive),
   quartered lengthways
1 medium beetroot, sliced
6 sun-dried tomatoes, sliced
50g (1¾oz) chopped walnuts
2 tbsp olive oil

1 tbsp lemon juice
sea salt and black pepper to taste
1 handful Gouda/soya cheese,
   grated
2 tbsp breadcrumbs

Preheat the oven to 200°C/400°F/gas mark 6. Place the quartered chicory and the beetroot slices in a shallow ovenproof dish. Scatter the sun-dried tomato slices and the chopped walnuts on top, drizzle with oil and lemon juice, and season. Top with the grated cheese and the breadcrumbs. Bake in the oven for 20 minutes (adding a little water if necessary) and serve.

047 SENGALESE YASSA

CALORIES	400
CHOLESTEROL	120
VEGAN CALORIES	277
POLYUNSATS	★★★
ANTIOXIDANTS	★★★
CALCIUM	★★★
IRON	★★★
B VITAMINS	★★★

250g (9oz) chicken breast/seitan,
   sliced
1 tbsp groundnut (peanut) oil or
   grapeseed oil
1 large onion, grated

juice of 2 limes
1 tsp Tabasco sauce
2 tbsp water
sea salt and black pepper to taste

Make a marinade of the oil, onion, lime juice and Tabasco sauce. Brush the chicken or seitan with the marinade and grill (or barbecue) until well browned. Pour the remaining marinade into a frying pan, heat through, add the cooked chicken or seitan and the water, cover and simmer until tender (approximately 15 minutes). Season and serve with boiled rice and steamed spring greens, Swiss chard, curly kale or cabbage.

048 AFRICAN-STYLE BROAD BEANS

CALORIES	178
CHOLESTEROL	0
VEGAN CALORIES	178
POLYUNSATS	★☆☆
ANTIOXIDANTS	★★★
CALCIUM	★★☆
IRON	★★☆
B VITAMINS	★★★

2 tbsp olive oil
2 tsp ground cumin
2 cloves garlic, chopped
250g (9oz) fresh broad beans,
   shelled

3 tbsp lemon juice
2 tbsp fresh parsley, chopped
sea salt and cayenne pepper
   to taste
1 tsp paprika

Gently heat the oil in a casserole dish, add the cumin and the garlic and stir-fry for 15 seconds. Add the fresh broad beans and stir for a further 15 seconds, then add enough water to cover the beans, bring to the boil and simmer for approximately 10 minutes until the beans are soft. Add the lemon juice and the fresh parsley. Mash some of the cooked beans with a spoon. Season and serve garnished with paprika on a bed of millet or couscous.

SPRING MASALA

★ ⊘

CALORIES	421
CHOLESTEROL	210
VEGAN CALORIES	490
POLYUNSATS	★★★
ANTIOXIDANTS	★★★
CALCIUM	★★☆
IRON	★★★
B VITAMINS	★★☆

1 tbsp grapeseed oil
1 small red onion, chopped
1 clove garlic, chopped
1 tsp turmeric
1 small fresh or dried green chilli, chopped
1 tsp fresh ginger, chopped
2 medium carrots, chopped
150g (5½oz) prawns, cooked and peeled/50g (1¾oz) cashew nuts
approximately 200ml (⅓pt) coconut milk
1 tsp garam masala
sea salt to taste
100g (3½oz) green peas, shelled
1 handful fresh coriander leaves, chopped

Heat the oil in a heavy-based pan and gently stir-fry the onion and garlic for a few minutes until they begin to soften. Add the turmeric, chilli, ginger and carrots and stir-fry for a further 2 minutes before adding the prawns or cashews. Stir for a further minute, then add the coconut milk and the garam masala and simmer for 5–10 minutes until the carrots are cooked (adding more coconut milk if necessary). Season, add the peas and heat through. Garnish with fresh coriander leaves and serve with rice.

GREEK RAGOUT

050

CALORIES	401
CHOLESTEROL	0
VEGAN CALORIES	401
POLYUNSATS	★☆☆
ANTIOXIDANTS	★★☆
CALCIUM	★★☆
IRON	★★☆
B VITAMINS	★★☆

2 tbsp olive oil
1 leek, sliced
500g (1lb 2oz) new potatoes, chopped
200g (7oz) fresh green beans
400ml (14fl oz) vegetable stock, heated

1 tbsp tomato paste (purée)
1 dash honey
1 tsp fresh or dried oregano, plus some to garnish
sea salt and black pepper to taste
1 tbsp lemon juice

Heat the oil in a medium casserole dish and sauté the leek for 3 minutes. Add the potatoes and the trimmed beans and sauté for a further 2 minutes, then add the heated stock, tomato paste, honey and oregano, and season. Bring to the boil and cook until the potatoes are tender (approximately 15 minutes). Add the lemon juice, check the seasoning, garnish with a sprinkle of oregano and serve.

KOREAN SALAD

051

CALORIES	352
CHOLESTEROL	0
VEGAN CALORIES	352
POLYUNSATS	★★★
ANTIOXIDANTS	★★★
CALCIUM	★★☆
IRON	★★☆
B VITAMINS	★★☆

2 medium carrots, cut into thin diagonal sticks
200g (7oz) white radish, cut into thin diagonal sticks
½ cucumber, cut into diagonal sticks
½ tsp sea salt
1 tbsp (rice) vinegar

1 dash tamari (soya sauce)
1 pinch raw cane sugar
1 dash Tabasco sauce
1 tbsp toasted sesame oil
2 tbsp almonds, chopped and toasted

Place the carrots, radish and cucumber sticks in a salad bowl. Sprinkle with the salt and mix well. To make the dressing, whisk the vinegar, tamari, sugar and Tabasco sauce. Then add the oil and whisk again. Pour the dressing over the salad, garnish with toasted almonds and serve with pan bread.

MEXICAN CASSEROLE

052

CALORIES	820
CHOLESTEROL	165
VEGAN CALORIES	552
POLYUNSATS	★★☆
ANTIOXIDANTS	★★★
CALCIUM	★★☆
IRON	★★★
B VITAMINS	★★☆

oil for frying
300g (10½oz) loin of lamb, diced/ 60g (2¼oz) soya chunks (dry weight), rehydrated
1 onion, sliced
½ red pepper, sliced
½ green pepper, sliced
1 clove garlic, crushed
1 small hot chilli, kept whole

1 tomato, chopped
200ml (⅓pt) white wine
1 pinch thyme
1 bay leaf
400g (14oz) kidney beans, cooked or canned
sea salt and cayenne pepper to taste

Heat a little oil in a casserole dish and fry the lamb or soya chunks over a high heat. Set aside. Fry the onion, red and green peppers and garlic in the same pan with a little more oil. Add the chilli, tomato, white wine, thyme and bay leaf. Bring to the boil, cover and simmer for 10 minutes. Add the beans and cook for 5 minutes. Add the cooked lamb or soya chunks, heat through and season. Serve with corn bread.

053 EGGLESS OMELETTE PRINTANIÈRE

CALORIES	350
CHOLESTEROL	0
VEGAN CALORIES	350
POLYUNSATS	★★★
ANTIOXIDANTS	★★☆
CALCIUM	★★☆
IRON	★★☆
B VITAMINS	★★☆

basic eggless omelette batter:
100g (3½oz) wheat flour
½ tsp sea salt
1 tsp baking powder
1 phial saffron
200ml (⅓pt) water
black pepper to taste

filling:
2 tbsp fresh green peas, blanched
1 tbsp fresh mint, finely chopped
oil for frying

To make the basic eggless batter, mix the flour, salt, baking powder and saffron in a bowl. Add the water, whisk to a smooth batter and season. Heat a little oil in a frying pan. Pour in the batter and spread it evenly to form a thin pancake. Turn down the heat and cook slowly until the topside begins to firm. Spread the peas and mint over half of the omelette, fold and fry on each side for 30 seconds. Remove from the heat and serve.

054 TOFU OMELETTE AUX FINE HERBES

CALORIES	248
CHOLESTEROL	0
VEGAN CALORIES	248
POLYUNSATS	★★★
ANTIOXIDANTS	★★☆
CALCIUM	★★★
IRON	★★☆
B VITAMINS	★★☆

batter:
125g (4½oz) tofu, crumbled
100ml (3½oz) soya/rice milk
1 tbsp wheat flour
1 tsp baking powder
sea salt and black pepper to taste

filling:
2 tsp each of finely chopped chives,
  parsley and chervil or tarragon
oil for frying

Blend the tofu with the milk. Transfer to a mixing bowl, add the flour and the baking powder and season. Add the herbs and mix again. Heat a little oil in a frying pan. Pour in the tofu batter and spread it evenly over the pan. Turn down the heat and gently cook until the topside is firm. Sprinkle with oil, turn and cook the other side. Remove from the heat and serve.

055 SPICY SPRING OMELETTE

CALORIES	376
CHOLESTEROL	408
VEGAN CALORIES	399
POLYUNSATS	★★★
ANTIOXIDANTS	★★☆
CALCIUM	★★★
IRON	★★☆
B VITAMINS	★★☆

omelette:
4 eggs
½ tsp sea salt
1 clove garlic, crushed
or 1 portion basic eggless omelette
  batter (see above)

filling:
oil for frying
100g (3½oz) ham/tempeh, diced
200g (7oz) fresh spinach, chopped
1 tsp hot chilli sauce (optional)
sea salt and black pepper to taste

Heat a little oil in a frying pan and fry the ham or tempeh. Add the spinach, turn down the heat and simmer until the spinach is wilted, then add the chilli sauce (if using) and season. Beat the eggs with the salt, add the garlic and season. Alternatively, prepare the eggless batter. Heat a little oil in a frying pan and pour in your chosen batter. Push back the edges of the mixture to let any uncooked egg run underneath the omelette. Repeat until the omelette has set and the underside is brown. Cover with the filling, fold in half, cook for 30 seconds, remove from the heat and serve.

056 · OMELETTE À LA JARDINIÈRE
★✕🌿

CALORIES	397
CHOLESTEROL	391
VEGAN CALORIES	406
POLYUNSATS	★★★
ANTIOXIDANTS	★★★
CALCIUM	★★☆
IRON	★★☆
B VITAMINS	★★★

omelette:
4 eggs, beaten
sea salt and black pepper to taste
or 1 portion basic eggless omelette
 batter (see p.41)

filling:
1 handful green beans
1 carrot, cut into thin sticks
1 small cauliflower, cut into florets
100g (3½oz) green peas

Cook the trimmed beans, carrot and cauliflower in a saucepan with a little salted water until just tender. Drain and set aside. Prepare your chosen batter and set aside. Heat a little oil in a frying pan, add the cooked vegetables and the peas and gently stir-fry for 2–3 minutes. Pour the batter over the vegetables and cook like a thick pancake. Serve hot.

057 · CRÊPES WITH MUSHROOM FILLING
★🌿

CALORIES	614
CHOLESTEROL	238
VEGAN CALORIES	544
POLYUNSATS	★★☆
ANTIOXIDANTS	★★☆
CALCIUM	★★☆
IRON	★★☆
B VITAMINS	★★★

basic egg pancake batter:
125g (4½oz) wheat flour
2 eggs, beaten
125ml (4fl oz) milk/soya milk
125ml (4fl oz) water
1tbsp grapeseed oil (or butter)
1 pinch sea salt
or 1 portion basic eggless pancake
 batter (see below)

filling:
a little olive oil, plus some for frying
 crêpes
250g (9oz) mushrooms, sliced
1 shallot, chopped
1 clove garlic, chopped
1 tbsp plain flour
1 pinch nutmeg
150ml (¼pt) milk/soya milk

To make the basic egg batter, mix the batter ingredients and set aside. Alternatively, prepare the eggless batter and set aside. Stir-fry the mushrooms, shallot and garlic in a casserole dish with oil. Sprinkle with flour and nutmeg, lower the heat and stir for 1 minute. Add milk to make a thick sauce, and season. Pour the batter into an oiled frying pan. Fry the crêpes for 2 minutes on each side. Top with the filling, roll and serve hot.

058 · PANCAKES WITH SPINACH FILLING
★♥◗🌿

CALORIES	642
CHOLESTEROL	57
VEGAN CALORIES	642
POLYUNSATS	★★★
ANTIOXIDANTS	★★★
CALCIUM	★★☆
IRON	★★★
B VITAMINS	★★☆

basic eggless pancake batter:
125g (4½ oz) wheat flour
1 tsp baking powder
1 pinch salt
100ml (3½oz) soya milk
100ml (3½oz) water
2 tbsp grapeseed oil
oil for frying

filling:
200g (7oz) fresh spinach
1 tbsp wheat flour
100ml (3½fl oz) soya cream/crème
 fraîche
1 pinch nutmeg and sea salt to taste
a little soya/Gruyère cheese
(optional)

To make the basic eggless batter, mix the batter ingredients and set aside. Gently cook the spinach in a saucepan of water until soft. Add the flour and stir for 30 seconds, then add the cream, heat and season. Heat a little oil in a frying pan, pour in the batter and fry the pancakes for 2 minutes on each side. Top with 1 tablespoon of filling, roll and place in an ovenproof dish. Sprinkle with soya or Gruyère cheese and grill or bake at 230°C/ 450°F/gas mark 8 for a few minutes until the cheese melts. Serve hot.

CHEESY POTATO AND ROCKET PANCAKES

★ ○ ◗ ✿ ◎

CALORIES	732
CHOLESTEROL	242
VEGAN CALORIES	667
POLYUNSATS	★★☆
ANTIOXIDANTS	★★★
CALCIUM	★★☆
IRON	★★☆
B VITAMINS	★★☆

pancakes:
1 portion basic pancake batter (see opposite page)
olive oil for frying

filling:
500g (1lb 2oz) potatoes, chopped

2 cloves garlic, crushed
1 small fresh or dried red chilli, chopped or crumbled
200g (7oz) fresh rocket, chopped
50g (1¾oz) Gruyère/soya cheese, grated
sea salt to taste

Boil the potatoes in salted water until soft. Meanwhile, mix all the batter ingredients and set aside. Heat 1 tablespoon of oil in a large casserole dish and fry the garlic and chilli for 30 seconds. Add half the rocket and stir. Remove from the heat. Stir in the cooked potatoes, the Gruyère or soya cheese and the remaining rocket. Mash, mix and season. Heat a little more oil in a frying pan and fry the pancakes for 2 minutes on each side. Top with 1–2 tablespoon of filling. Roll the pancakes and serve as you go.

060 CORN PANCAKES WITH SPICY PEAS

CALORIES	749
CHOLESTEROL	0
VEGAN CALORIES	749
POLYUNSATS	★★★
ANTIOXIDANTS	★★☆
CALCIUM	★★☆
IRON	★★☆
B VITAMINS	★★☆

pancakes:
125g (4½oz) cornflour
125g (4½oz) wheat flour
1 tbsp baking powder
½ tsp sea salt
2 tbsp corn oil, plus some for frying
300ml (½pt) water

filling:
1 spring onion, sliced
1 tsp ground cumin
1 clove garlic, crushed
250g (9oz) chick peas, cooked or canned
100g (3½oz) fresh green peas
100ml (3½fl oz) vegetable stock
1 dash Tabasco sauce
sea salt and black pepper to taste

Mix the two flours with the baking powder, salt, corn oil and water, and whisk to a smooth consistency. Set aside. Stir-fry the spring onion in a casserole dish with 1 tablespoon of oil, then add the cumin and the garlic. Heat through, add the chick peas and stir for 1 minute. Add the green peas, stock and Tabasco sauce, and season. Leave the peas to simmer while you heat a little more oil in a frying pan and fry approximately six pancakes. Divide the filling between the pancakes and serve.

061 PIZZA CASSUOLA

CALORIES	524
CHOLESTEROL	57
VEGAN CALORIES	406
POLYUNSATS	★★☆
ANTIOXIDANTS	★★☆
CALCIUM	★★☆
IRON	★★☆
B VITAMINS	★★☆

1 pizza base
2 fresh tomatoes, chopped
sea salt to taste
6 anchovy fillets/12 black olives, pitted and chopped

1 tbsp capers
1 tbsp fresh oregano
100g (3½oz) mozzarella/soya cheese, grated
black pepper to taste

Preheat the oven to 240°C/475°F/gas mark 9 and warm up the pizza tray. Cover the prepared base with the chopped tomatoes. Sprinkle with salt. Top with the anchovies or olives, capers and oregano. Sprinkle with grated cheese and bake in a hot oven for approximately 15 minutes. Garnish with black pepper and serve hot with a side salad.

062 ◄ PIZZA PEPPERONI

CALORIES	609
CHOLESTEROL	54
VEGAN CALORIES	489
POLYUNSATS	★★☆
ANTIOXIDANTS	★★☆
CALCIUM	★★☆
IRON	★★☆
B VITAMINS	★★☆

1 pizza base
2–3 tbsp tomato sauce (passata) or sauce tomate concassé (see p.115)
100g (3½oz) fresh spinach, sautéed
1 clove garlic, crushed

100g (3½oz) spicy sausage (pork/soya), sliced and fried
1 tsp each of thyme and oregano
sea salt and black pepper to taste
100g (3½oz) mozzarella/soya cheese, grated

Preheat the oven to 240°C/475°F/gas mark 9 and warm up the pizza tray. Spread the tomato sauce over the prepared base and top with the sautéed spinach, garlic and spicy sausage. Sprinkle with the herbs, season and sprinkle with the grated cheese. Bake in a hot oven for approximately 15 minutes. Serve hot with a side salad.

063 SPRING SPECIAL

CALORIES	592
CHOLESTEROL	38
VEGAN CALORIES	515
POLYUNSATS	★★☆
ANTIOXIDANTS	★★★
CALCIUM	★★★
IRON	★★★
B VITAMINS	★★★

1 pizza base
2–3 tbsp tomato sauce (passata) or
    sauce tomate concassé
    (see p.115)
1 handful rocket leaves, chopped
100g (3½oz) mozzarella/soya
    cheese, grated
1 clove garlic, crushed

8 green asparagus, trimmed
    and blanched
1 tbsp grated Parmesan/brewer's
    yeast flakes
fresh oregano to taste
sea salt and black pepper to taste
1 tbsp olive oil

Preheat the oven to 240°C/475°F/gas mark 9 and warm up the pizza tray. Spread the tomato sauce over the prepared base. Add the rocket and the mozzarella or soya cheese, then the garlic and asparagus. Sprinkle with Parmesan or brewer's yeast flakes, and season. Drizzle with oil and bake in a hot oven for approximately 15 minutes. Serve hot.

064 SPICY VEGAN PIZZA

CALORIES	467
CHOLESTEROL	0
VEGAN CALORIES	467
POLYUNSATS	★☆☆
ANTIOXIDANTS	★★☆
CALCIUM	★★★
IRON	★★★
B VITAMINS	★★☆

1 pizza base
2–3 tbsp tomato sauce (passata) or
    sauce tomate concassé
    (see p.115)
1 tsp hot chilli paste
1 clove garlic, crushed
125g (4½oz) smoked tofu, crumbled
1 handful fresh rocket, chopped
oil for stir-frying

100g (3½oz) tiny cauliflower florets
100g (3½oz) fresh peas, shelled
1 carrot, grated
2 spring onions, sliced
1 tbsp tamari (soya sauce)
sea salt and black pepper to taste
1 tbsp fresh parsley or dill
oregano to taste

Preheat the oven to 220°C/425°F/gas mark 7 and warm up the pizza tray. Cover the prepared base with the tomato sauce and the chilli paste. Sprinkle with the garlic. Add the crumbled tofu and the rocket. Stir-fry the vegetables in a wok with a little oil, then stir in the tamari. Add to the pizza and season. Bake in a hot oven for approximately 15 minutes. Garnish with fresh herbs and serve hot with a side salad.

065 SICILIAN PIZZA

CALORIES	716
CHOLESTEROL	45
VEGAN CALORIES	641
POLYUNSATS	★★★
ANTIOXIDANTS	★★★
CALCIUM	★★★
IRON	★★★
B VITAMINS	★★☆

1 pizza base
10 sun-dried tomato halves
1 tbsp olive oil
1 Florence fennel bulb, chopped
100g (3½oz) fresh peas, shelled
1 clove garlic, crushed

50g (1¾oz) anchovies/black
    olives, pitted
1 tbsp fresh oregano
sea salt and black pepper to taste
100g (3½oz) mozzarella/soya
    cheese, grated

Preheat the oven to 240°C/475°F/gas mark 9 and warm up the pizza tray. Cover the prepared base with the sun-dried tomato halves. Sprinkle with the oil and top with the fennel, fresh peas, garlic, anchovies or olives and fresh oregano. Season and sprinkle with the grated mozzarella or soya cheese and bake in a hot oven for approximately 15 minutes. Serve hot with a side salad.

066 QUICK CHESTNUT BOURGUIGNONNE

CALORIES	469
CHOLESTEROL	0
VEGAN CALORIES	469
POLYUNSATS	★★☆
ANTIOXIDANTS	★★☆
CALCIUM	★★☆
IRON	★★☆
B VITAMINS	★★☆

2 tbsp olive oil
200g (7oz) bottled sweet chestnuts, drained
1 shallot, quartered
200g (7oz) button mushrooms, kept whole
1 clove garlic, chopped
1 tbsp wheat flour

100ml (3½fl oz) red wine
1 bay leaf
1 tsp thyme
1 tbsp fresh parsley, finely chopped
2 tsp tomato paste (purée)
100ml (3½fl oz) vegetable stock, heated
sea salt and pepper to taste

Gently heat the oil in a large pan and stir-fry the chestnuts and shallot for 3 minutes. Add the mushrooms and garlic, turn up the heat and stir-fry for a further 2 minutes. Stir in the flour and add the remaining ingredients. Bring to the boil, cover and simmer for 20 minutes. Serve with rice.

067 SPRING GREEN RISOTTO

CALORIES	690
CHOLESTEROL	0
VEGAN CALORIES	690
POLYUNSATS	★★☆
ANTIOXIDANTS	★★★
CALCIUM	★★☆
IRON	★★☆
B VITAMINS	★★☆

4 tbsp olive oil
1 small leek, sliced
200g (7oz) risotto rice
125g (4½oz) fresh curly kale leaves

½ltr (18fl oz) vegetable stock, heated
3 tbsp white wine
sea salt and black pepper to taste

Heat the oil in a large pan or wok and gently soften the leek for 2–3 minutes. Add the rice and stir-fry for 2 minutes, then add the curly kale leaves and let them wilt for 1 minute. Add the stock and the wine, season, cover and very gently simmer until the rice is cooked. Check from time to time (and add a little water if necessary). Serve with walnut bread.

068 CHICORY CASSOLETTES

CALORIES	558
CHOLESTEROL	286
VEGAN CALORIES	359
POLYUNSATS	★★★
ANTIOXIDANTS	★★★
CALCIUM	★★★
IRON	★★★
B VITAMINS	★★★

500g (1lb 2oz) chicory (Belgian endive), quartered lengthways
100g (3½oz) young dandelion leaves, chopped
3 tbsp lemon juice
1 tsp maple syrup
sea salt and black pepper to taste
2 tbsp grapeseed oil, plus some for cooking

500g (1lb 2oz) small fresh scallops, shelled and trimmed / 200g (7oz) marinated tofu, diced
1 pinch cayenne pepper
1 tbsp port
2 tbsp vegetable margarine or butter
1 tsp lemon zest
1 tbsp fresh parsley

Place the chicory and dandelion leaves in a large casserole dish, add 2 tablespoons of the lemon juice, the maple syrup, salt and pepper, and gently soften in a little oil for 8–10 minutes. Meanwhile, heat the oil in a frying pan over a low heat and fry the scallops or tofu cubes until they begin to brown. Add the cayenne pepper with the port, the remaining tablespoon of lemon juice and the margarine or butter. Place the cooked chicory in a heated serving dish and arrange the fried scallops or tofu on top. Garnish with lemon zest and parsley and serve with rice or bread.

069 ▲ SPICY BEAN BURGERS

⭐❤️🌾🥜

CALORIES	541
CHOLESTEROL	0
VEGAN CALORIES	541
POLYUNSATS	★★★
ANTIOXIDANTS	★★☆
CALCIUM	★☆☆
IRON	★★☆
B VITAMINS	★★☆

200g (7oz) red kidney beans, cooked or canned and drained
1 shallot, finely chopped
50g (1¾oz) hazelnuts, finely chopped
1 tsp fresh ginger, finely chopped

1 pinch cayenne pepper
2 tsp tamari (soya sauce)
2 tbsp breadcrumbs
2 tbsp soya flour
sea salt to taste
oil for grilling or frying

Mash or blend the kidney beans (with a little water if necessary) to a coarse paste, add the shallot, hazelnuts, ginger, cayenne pepper, tamari, breadcrumbs and soya flour, and mix well. Season and shape into approximately four 70g (2½oz) flat burgers. Brush the burgers with oil and grill over hot embers. Alternatively, fry the burgers in hot oil. Serve on a toasted bun with all the usual burger trimmings.

FENNEL, SEAFOOD AND POTATO BAKE

CALORIES	474
CHOLESTEROL	53
VEGAN CALORIES	402
POLYUNSATS	★★★
ANTIOXIDANTS	★★★
CALCIUM	★★☆
IRON	★★☆
B VITAMINS	★★★

1 tbsp olive oil
500g (1lb 2oz) trimmed monkfish, cut into chunks and seasoned/ 50g (1¾oz) soya chunks (dry weight), soaked with 2 tbsp mixed seaweed
250g (9oz) potatoes, quartered and parboiled
1 Florence fennel bulb, sliced
1 red onion, sliced
4 sun-dried tomato halves, chopped
1 lemon, thinly sliced
100ml (3½fl oz) vegetable/fish stock, heated
1 small handful fresh parsley, chopped
sea salt and black pepper to taste

Preheat the oven to 220°C/425°F/gas mark 7. Heat the oil in a large frying pan over a high heat and fry the monkfish or soya chunks for 2 minutes. Grease an ovenproof dish and arrange the parboiled potatoes on the bottom. Add the slices of fennel, onion, tomato and lemon, in layers, and finish with the fried monkfish or soya chunks. Then add the heated stock, garnish with chopped parsley and season. Cover and bake in a hot oven for 20 minutes. Serve with rice or French baguette.

CÔTELETTES PRINTANIÉRE

CALORIES	721
CHOLESTEROL	176
VEGAN CALORIES	396
POLYUNSATS	★★☆
ANTIOXIDANTS	★★★
CALCIUM	★★☆
IRON	★★★
B VITAMINS	★★★

6 small spring carrots, kept whole
2 artichoke bottoms
1 courgette, chopped into fine sticks
100g (3½oz) green beans, chopped
6 long red radishes, kept whole
2 tbsp olive oil
6 lamb chops/150g (5½oz) seitan, sliced
6 mushrooms, finely chopped
juice of 1 lemon
1 tbsp fresh parsley, finely chopped
1 clove garlic, chopped
sea salt and black pepper to taste
300g (10½oz) small new potatoes, steamed

Blanch the carrots, artichokes, courgette, beans and radishes in a saucepan of boiling water until just tender. Drain and set aside. Sauté the chops or seitan with 1 tablespoon of oil in a frying pan until just cooked, add the mushrooms and sauté until they give off their juices. Add the lemon juice and half the parsley. In a separate pan, stir-fry the cooked vegetables in 1 tablespoon of oil with the garlic, and season. Place the chops or seitan and the mushrooms on a warmed plate. Arrange the cooked vegetables and the steamed potatoes in a fan next to them. Garnish with the remaining parsley and serve.

072 FILLETS WITH MUSTARD AND SAGE SAUCE

CALORIES	544
CHOLESTEROL	110
VEGAN CALORIES	433
POLYUNSATS	★☆☆
ANTIOXIDANTS	★★☆
CALCIUM	★☆☆
IRON	★★★
B VITAMINS	★★★

oil for roasting
200g (7oz) loin of lamb/tempeh,
　sliced
1 shallot, chopped
1 sprig sage, chopped
100ml (3½fl oz) white wine

100ml (3½fl oz) stock
1 tbsp wholegrain mustard
1 tsp Maizena (corn starch)
　dissolved in a little cold water
　(optional)
sea salt and black pepper to taste

Heat a little oil in a pan over a high heat and roast the lamb or tempeh for
3 minutes on each side. Add the shallot and the sage and gently fry them
without letting them brown. Pour in the wine and let it reduce to half its
volume, then add the stock and the mustard and simmer for 5 minutes.
Season, and add the dissolved Maizena if the sauce is too thin. Heat
through. Place the roasted fillet or tempeh and the sauce on a warmed
plate, and serve with steamed new potatoes and French beans.

073 BRAISED BRUSSELS SPROUTS

CALORIES	213
CHOLESTEROL	13
VEGAN CALORIES	177
POLYUNSATS	★☆☆
ANTIOXIDANTS	★★★
CALCIUM	★★☆
IRON	★★☆
B VITAMINS	★★☆

250g (9oz) Brussels sprouts, halved
1 tbsp olive oil
juice and zest of ½ orange
50g (1¾oz) smoked bacon/

tofu, diced
1 medium carrot, diced
1 tsp wholegrain mustard
sea salt and black pepper to taste

Place the Brussels sprouts in a heavy-based casserole dish with the rest
of the ingredients. Bring to the boil, cover and very gently simmer until the
Brussels sprouts are tender (approximately 20 minutes). Stir from time to
time (adding a little water if necessary). Season and serve with rice.

074 SPINACH BOUILLABAISSE

CALORIES	337
CHOLESTEROL	196
VEGAN CALORIES	309
POLYUNSATS	★★☆
ANTIOXIDANTS	★★★
CALCIUM	★★★
IRON	★★★
B VITAMINS	★★★

1 tbsp olive oil
1 leek, sliced
2 potatoes, chopped
2 cloves garlic, chopped
250g (9oz) fresh spinach, chopped
175ml (6fl oz) vegetable stock,
　heated

½ tsp ground coriander
½ tsp turmeric
sea salt and cayenne pepper
　to taste
1 handful fresh parsley, chopped
2 eggs/125g (4½oz) marinated
　tofu, diced

Gently stir-fry the leek and potatoes in a large saucepan or casserole dish
with the olive oil for 5 minutes. Add the garlic and the spinach and stir-fry
for 5 minutes, then add the stock and the spices, and season. Bring to
the boil, add the parsley and simmer. Crack the eggs on top or add the
marinated tofu, and continue to simmer for 10 minutes. Serve immediately
with bread and cheese or soya cheese.

075 SHIITAKE STIR-FRY

CALORIES	339
CHOLESTEROL	0
VEGAN CALORIES	339
POLYUNSATS	★★★
ANTIOXIDANTS	★★★
CALCIUM	★★☆
IRON	★★★
B VITAMINS	★★☆

oil for stir-frying
250g (9oz) shiitake mushrooms,
    sliced
1 clove garlic, finely chopped
2 spring onions, chopped
1 small Chinese cabbage, chopped
1 medium carrot, cut into thin sticks
250g (9oz) broccoli, cut into florets
12 baby corn cobs

2cm (¾in) cube fresh ginger,
    finely chopped
200g (7oz) mangetout
2 tbsp tamari (soya sauce)
200ml (⅓pt) vegetable stock
1 tbsp maple syrup
1 tbsp cornflour dissolved in a
    little water

Heat a little oil in a wok. Add the mushrooms, garlic and onions. Stir-fry for
1 minute then add the Chinese cabbage, carrot, broccoli, baby corn and
fresh ginger. Heat through and add the mangetout. Stir-fry for a further
2 minutes, then add the tamari, stock, maple syrup and dissolved
cornflour. Stir until the sauce thickens. Serve with rice or noodles.

076 ASPARAGUS TART

CALORIES	618
CHOLESTEROL	31
VEGAN CALORIES	559
POLYUNSATS	★★★
ANTIOXIDANTS	★★☆
CALCIUM	★★☆
IRON	★★☆
B VITAMINS	★★☆

1 packet ready-made shortcrust
    pastry, rolled out
1 bunch green asparagus, trimmed
    and blanched
125g (4½oz) tofu, crumbled

75ml (2½fl oz) milk/soya milk
sea salt and black pepper to taste
25g (1oz) cheddar/soya cheese,
    grated

Place the rolled-out pastry in a 20cm (8in) pie dish, scatter with a handful
of beans and bake blind at 220°C/425°F/gas mark 7 for 10–15 minutes.
Allow to cool and remove the beans. Place the cooked asparagus in the
pastry shell. Blend the tofu with the milk, season and pour over the
asparagus. Top with cheddar or soya cheese and return to the oven.
Bake for 10–15 minutes until it begins to brown. Serve with a salad.

077 CELERIAC SCHNITZEL

CALORIES	316
CHOLESTEROL	98
VEGAN CALORIES	323
POLYUNSATS	★★★
ANTIOXIDANTS	★★☆
CALCIUM	★★☆
IRON	★★☆
B VITAMINS	★★☆

1 large celeriac, cut into thick slices
    and peeled
2 tbsp grapeseed oil
1 egg, beaten/1 tbsp soya flour
    dissolved in a little cold water

2 tbsp seasoned breadcrumbs
1 lemon, sliced
2 tbsp grated horseradish
1 handful fresh parsley, chopped
1 tbsp capers

Blanch the celeriac in a saucepan of boiling salted water for 3 minutes.
Heat the oil in a large frying pan. Dip the celeriac slices first into the egg
or dissolved soya flour, then into the breadcrumbs before frying them until
golden. Place a slice of lemon, a little grated horseradish and a few capers
on each schnitzel to garnish. Serve with boiled potatoes, melted butter or
vegetable margarine and chopped parsley.

078 ▲ CHOPS WITH HONEY AND THYME
⭐🌿◐

CALORIES	693
CHOLESTEROL	176
VEGAN CALORIES	368
POLYUNSATS	★★☆
ANTIOXIDANTS	★★☆
CALCIUM	★★☆
IRON	★★★
B VITAMINS	★★☆

1 tbsp olive oil
4 lamb chops/200g (7oz) seitan
sea salt and black pepper to taste
2 tsp honey

1 tsp thyme
juice of ½ lemon
100ml (3½oz) dry white wine
1 tbsp tamari (soya sauce)

Preheat the oven to 250°C/500°F/gas mark 10. Sauté the lamb or seitan in the oil in a large casserole dish, then remove from the dish, season, paint with 1 teaspoon of honey and sprinkle with thyme. Replace the lamb or seitan in the dish and bake in a hot oven for 10 minutes. Remove the lamb or seitan from the dish (discard the lamb cooking fat) and set aside. Make a sauce by browning 1 teaspoon of honey in the dish and adding the lemon juice, white wine and tamari. Bring to the boil and reduce to half the volume. Place the lamb or seitan on two plates and cover with the sauce. Serve with boiled potatoes and braised chicory (Belgian endive).

079 ▼ FRUIT JELLY
★ ✖

CALORIES	195
CHOLESTEROL	0
VEGAN CALORIES	195
POLYUNSATS	★☆☆
ANTIOXIDANTS	★★☆
CALCIUM	★☆☆
IRON	★☆☆
B VITAMINS	★☆☆

1 banana, peeled and chopped
1 sweet apple, cored and chopped
25g (1oz) dates, pitted

100ml (3½fl oz) apple juice
1 tsp agar-agar

Blend the banana, apple, dates and apple juice, and pour into a saucepan. Whisk in the agar-agar until it is dissolved. Bring to the boil, then pour the mixture into two small serving bowls and refrigerate until set. Serve with crème fraîche or soya cream.

080 RUBY-RED SALAD

★◆✖◉

CALORIES	152
CHOLESTEROL	0
VEGAN CALORIES	152
POLYUNSATS	★☆☆
ANTIOXIDANTS	★★★
CALCIUM	★★☆
IRON	★★☆
B VITAMINS	★★☆

1 ruby-red grapefruit, peeled
  and chopped
1 papaya, peeled, deseeded
  and cubed

1 small bunch fresh mint, chopped
1 tsp ground cinnamon
1 tsp maple syrup (optional)

Divide the grapefruit and papaya between two plates, garnish with fresh mint, sprinkle with cinnamon and maple syrup (if using), and serve.

081 APPLE, CHERRY AND WALNUT CRÊPES

★◉

CALORIES	676
CHOLESTEROL	227
VEGAN CALORIES	592
POLYUNSATS	★★★
ANTIOXIDANTS	★★☆
CALCIUM	★★☆
IRON	★★☆
B VITAMINS	★★☆

crêpes:
1 portion basic pancake batter
  (see p.42)

filling:
1 apple, quartered, cored
  and thinly sliced
200g (7oz) fresh cherries,
  pitted and halved
2 tbsp chopped walnuts
maple syrup
grapeseed oil for frying

Mix all the batter ingredients and set aside. Combine the apple, cherries and walnuts in a bowl with a little maple syrup. Heat a little oil in a frying pan, pour in the batter and fry the crêpes for 2 minutes on each side. Top with a couple of tablespoons of filling, roll the crêpes and serve hot.

082 EXOTIC FRUIT SALAD

★♡✖◉

CALORIES	279
CHOLESTEROL	0
VEGAN CALORIES	279
POLYUNSATS	★☆☆
ANTIOXIDANTS	★★★
CALCIUM	★★☆
IRON	★☆☆
B VITAMINS	★☆☆

1 orange, peeled and sliced
1 banana, peeled and sliced
1 pear, cored and sliced
1 apple, cored and sliced
1 kiwi, peeled and sliced
½ ruby-red grapefruit, peeled
  and chopped

6 lychees, peeled, halved and pitted
4 slices dried mango, cut into strips
1 tsp honey
juice of ½ lime
2 tsp fresh ginger, finely chopped
1 star fruit, sliced

Mix the fresh fruit (except for the star fruit) in a glass bowl. Add the dried mango strips. Melt the honey in a saucepan with the lime juice and ginger, and pour over the fruit. Gently toss, garnish with star fruit and serve.

083 APPLE TART

❌🌿🍋

CALORIES	356
CHOLESTEROL	0
VEGAN CALORIES	356
POLYUNSATS	★★★
ANTIOXIDANTS	★★☆
CALCIUM	★☆☆
IRON	★☆☆
B VITAMINS	★☆☆

1 packet ready-made shortcrust
  pastry, rolled out
400g (14oz) cooking apples, cored
  and finely sliced

a little lemon juice
a little grapeseed oil
1 pinch raw cane sugar
1 pinch cinnamon

Preheat the oven to 220°C/425°F/gas mark 7. Place the rolled-out pastry
in a 20cm (8in) round baking tin. Sprinkle the apple slices with a little
lemon juice to prevent discolouration and add them in concentric circles to
cover the whole pastry base. Sprinkle with a little oil, sugar and cinnamon.
Bake in a hot oven for 15–20 minutes until the apples begin to golden.
Serve with crème fraîche or soya cream.

084 BAKED PEARS WITH HONEY AND BRAZIL NUTS

⭐❌🍋

CALORIES	336
CHOLESTEROL	0
VEGAN CALORIES	336
POLYUNSATS	★★★
ANTIOXIDANTS	★★★
CALCIUM	★☆☆
IRON	★☆☆
B VITAMINS	★☆☆

1 tbsp grapeseed oil
2 large, sweet, ripe pears, halved,
  cored and sliced

1 tbsp liquid honey
1 tbsp lemon juice
50g (1¾oz) Brazil nuts, sliced

Preheat the oven to 200°C/400°F/gas mark 6. Grease a small ovenproof
pie dish with the oil, and cover the bottom with the pear slices. Mix the
honey with the lemon juice and pour over the pears. Sprinkle with sliced
Brazil nuts and a dash of oil. Bake in a hot oven for approximately 15
minutes until the nuts begin to brown. Serve with plain or soya yoghurt.

085 APRIL FOOL

⭐❤️❌

CALORIES	255
CHOLESTEROL	6
VEGAN CALORIES	252
POLYUNSATS	★★☆
ANTIOXIDANTS	★★☆
CALCIUM	★★☆
IRON	★☆☆
B VITAMINS	★★☆

250g (9oz) rhubarb, sliced
1 pinch cinnamon
1 tsp honey
2 tsp almond butter

1 frozen banana, peeled and
  chopped
3 large dates, pitted and chopped
100ml (3½fl oz) plain/soya yoghurt

Cook the rhubarb with the cinnamon and a little water in a casserole dish
until soft. Add the honey and continue to cook for 2 minutes. Then place
the cooked rhubarb in a glass bowl and cool in a water bath. Meanwhile,
blend the almond butter with the frozen banana, dates and yoghurt.
Gently fold the cooked and cooled rhubarb into the yoghurt blend.
Spoon into two glass bowls and chill before serving.

086 SWEET CHERRY SOUP

CALORIES	202
CHOLESTEROL	0
VEGAN CALORIES	202
POLYUNSATS	★★☆
ANTIOXIDANTS	★★★
CALCIUM	★★☆
IRON	★★☆
B VITAMINS	★★☆

250g (9oz) fresh ripe cherries, pitted
juice of 2 oranges
1 tbsp maple syrup

200ml (⅓pt) hot water
4 Brazil nuts, chopped
2 slices lime
2 tbsp fresh mint, chopped

Blend the cherries with the orange juice, maple syrup and water. Cool, and garnish with Brazil nuts, slices of lime and fresh mint just before serving.

087 PINEAPPLE COCKTAIL

CALORIES	163
CHOLESTEROL	0
VEGAN CALORIES	163
POLYUNSATS	★☆☆
ANTIOXIDANTS	★★★
CALCIUM	★★☆
IRON	★★☆
B VITAMINS	★★☆

½ pineapple, peeled, cored and cut into chunks
juice of 1 orange
juice of 1 pomelo

1 pear, cored and cut into chunks
1 tsp fresh ginger, finely chopped
2 slices lemon
2 tsp fresh mint, finely chopped

Blend the pineapple chunks with the orange juice, pomelo juice, pear chunks and chopped fresh ginger. Pour the mix into tall glasses, garnish with slices of lemon and chopped fresh mint, and serve.

088 SPRING BERRY SALAD

CALORIES	226
CHOLESTEROL	6
VEGAN CALORIES	226
POLYUNSATS	★★☆
ANTIOXIDANTS	★★★
CALCIUM	★★☆
IRON	★☆☆
B VITAMINS	★★☆

150g (5½oz) cherries, pitted and halved
150g (5½oz) strawberries, hulled and halved
150g (5½oz) raspberries

plain/soya yoghurt to taste
grated (or desiccated) coconut to taste
grated dark chocolate to taste (optional)

Divide the berries between two glass bowls. Top with yoghurt, grated coconut and grated chocolate (if using), and serve.

089 DRIED FRUIT WITH FRESH STRAWBERRIES

CALORIES	486
CHOLESTEROL	0
VEGAN CALORIES	486
POLYUNSATS	★☆☆
ANTIOXIDANTS	★★☆
CALCIUM	★★☆
IRON	★★☆
B VITAMINS	★★☆

2 dried bananas, chopped
4 dates, pitted and chopped
4 dried figs, chopped
1 handful raisins

1 pear, cored and chopped
1 apple, cored and chopped
20 strawberries, halved

Place all the fruit (except for the strawberries) in a bowl and gently mix. Spoon the mixed fruit onto two plates, garnish with strawberries and serve with plain yoghurt or soya yoghurt.

090 SPICY APPLE SALAD
★♥◐✖

CALORIES	214
CHOLESTEROL	6
VEGAN CALORIES	211
POLYUNSATS	★☆☆
ANTIOXIDANTS	★★★
CALCIUM	★★☆
IRON	★★☆
B VITAMINS	★★☆

2 red apples, cored and sliced
6 red radishes, sliced
1 small mango, peeled and diced

100ml (3½fl oz) plain/soya yoghurt
1 tsp horseradish, freshly grated

Arrange the apples, radishes and mango on two plates. Mix the yoghurt with the horseradish, then place a spoonful on each plate and serve.

091 ▼ MINTY STRAWBERRIES
♥◐✖◖

CALORIES	176
CHOLESTEROL	0
VEGAN CALORIES	176
POLYUNSATS	★☆☆
ANTIOXIDANTS	★★★
CALCIUM	★☆☆
IRON	★☆☆
B VITAMINS	★☆☆

250g (9oz) strawberries, halved
1 pear, cored and diced
1 tsp lemon juice

1 tbsp fresh mint, finely chopped
1 tbsp maple syrup
grated dark chocolate (optional)

Place the strawberries and the pear in a glass bowl. Sprinkle with the lemon juice, fresh mint, maple syrup and a little grated chocolate (if using). Serve with crème fraîche or soya cream.

SUMMER
RECIPES

Summer is the season of warmth, strong colours and ripening, sun-burnt abundance. In Chinese tradition, summer is yang – the outgoing life force – and offers us the chance to absorb energy into our hearts to use with love and warmth. There is a feeling of plenty, and an almost overwhelming choice of fresh ingredients filled with light and rich flavours.

In the healing traditions, summer is a time for eating foods rich in essential nutrients to boost immunity and strength. The season of fire and heat also inspires us to eat easily-digestible meals, full of vitality, that enable us to use the plenty that surrounds us for creativity and activity.

Trees and bushes are heavy with red fruits and berries. Gardens overflow with green vegetables and fields are filled with golden grains. They all gather energy as they ripen in the sun, and with this energy they make all the nutrients that they – and we – need to be healthy. Create your own high-energy fresh summer diet, full of antioxidants, vitamins, minerals and essential polyunsaturates. Bon appetit!

092 MINTY MELON SOUP

CALORIES	160
CHOLESTEROL	0
VEGAN CALORIES	160
POLYUNSATS	★☆☆
ANTIOXIDANTS	★★★
CALCIUM	★★☆
IRON	★★☆
B VITAMINS	★★☆

1 cantaloupe melon, deseeded, peeled and chopped
½ cucumber, chopped
1 tbsp maple syrup
2 tsp lemon zest, grated
100ml (3½fl oz) water
1 small bunch fresh mint, finely chopped
sea salt and black pepper to taste
2 tsp lemon juice

Heat the melon and the cucumber in a saucepan with the maple syrup, lemon zest and water. Simmer for 10 minutes, stirring from time to time. Add the mint. Remove from the heat, blend, season and add the lemon juice. Allow to cool, then refrigerate before serving.

093 TROPICAL AVOCADO SOUP

CALORIES	492
CHOLESTEROL	6
VEGAN CALORIES	489
POLYUNSATS	★★★
ANTIOXIDANTS	★★★
CALCIUM	★★☆
IRON	★★☆
B VITAMINS	★★☆

1 avocado, peeled and pitted
1 clove garlic
1 small fresh green chilli
1 small bunch chives, chopped, plus some to garnish
300ml (½pt) coconut milk
100g (3½fl oz) plain/soya yoghurt
100ml (3½fl oz) vegetable stock
2 tbsp lemon juice
sea salt and black pepper to taste

Blend the avocado with the rest of the ingredients and season. Chill well before serving, garnished with chives.

094 MINESTRONE

CALORIES	456
CHOLESTEROL	0
VEGAN CALORIES	456
POLYUNSATS	★★☆
ANTIOXIDANTS	★★★
CALCIUM	★★★
IRON	★★★
B VITAMINS	★★★

2 tbsp olive oil
1 small onion, chopped
1 carrot, chopped
¼ Florence fennel bulb or 1 stick celery, chopped
1 courgette, chopped
1 handful white cabbage, finely shredded
250g (9oz) ripe tomatoes, blended
500ml (18fl oz) vegetable stock
1 glass dry white wine (optional)
sea salt and black pepper to taste
2 tbsp small pasta shapes
50g (1¾oz) white beans, cooked or canned
1 small bunch parsley and basil, finely chopped
1 clove garlic, crushed
a little Parmesan/brewer's yeast flakes (optional)

Heat the oil in a large casserole dish and gently stir-fry the onion, carrot, fennel, courgette and cabbage (don't let them brown). Add the tomatoes, stock and white wine (if using), and season. Bring to the boil, add the pasta, cover and simmer for 10 minutes. Add the beans, parsley, basil and garlic. Heat through, check the seasoning, sprinkle with Parmesan or brewer's yeast flakes (if using) and serve.

095 SUMMER TOMATO SOUP

⭐♥✖️🫘

CALORIES	60
CHOLESTEROL	0
VEGAN CALORIES	60
POLYUNSATS	★☆☆
ANTIOXIDANTS	★★★
CALCIUM	★☆☆
IRON	★★☆
B VITAMINS	★★☆

500g (1lb 2oz) fresh ripe tomatoes, quartered
1 spring onion, finely chopped

1 small bunch fresh basil, finely chopped
sea salt and black pepper to taste

Blend the tomatoes, then gently heat them in a saucepan. Add the spring onion and the basil, and season. Serve hot or cold.

096 RUBY RED SOUP

⭐♥💧✖️🫘🌿

CALORIES	203
CHOLESTEROL	0
VEGAN CALORIES	203
POLYUNSATS	★★☆
ANTIOXIDANTS	★★★
CALCIUM	★★☆
IRON	★★☆
B VITAMINS	★★☆

1 tbsp olive oil
500g (1lb 2oz) red peppers, deseeded and sliced
sea salt to taste

zest and juice of 3 organic blood oranges
1 tbsp chopped dill

Heat the oil in a saucepan and gently fry the pepper slices together with a little salt and the orange zest. Cover and simmer for 15 minutes, stirring from time to time and allowing the peppers to cook in their own juices. Remove from the heat and blend the peppers with the orange juice. Reheat, garnish with dill and serve.

097 MONGOLIAN SOUP WITH DUMPLINGS

⭐♥🌾🌿

CALORIES	680
CHOLESTEROL	0
VEGAN CALORIES	680
POLYUNSATS	★★☆
ANTIOXIDANTS	★★★
CALCIUM	★★☆
IRON	★★★
B VITAMINS	★★★

300g (10½oz) wheat flour
½ tsp salt
2 tbsp olive oil
½ tsp fenugreek seeds
1 clove garlic, crushed
1 small red onion
2 tomatoes, chopped
1 tbsp fresh ginger, finely chopped

1 pinch saffron
2 tbsp tamari (soya sauce)
1 small bunch red radishes, sliced
50g (1¾oz) green peas
700ml (1¼pts) vegetable stock
2 spring onions, sliced
sea salt and black pepper to taste

Mix the flour and salt in a bowl. Add enough water to make a stiff dough. Roll the dough on a floured surface into a finger-thick snake. Cut the dough into 1cm (½in) dumplings and sprinkle with flour. Gently heat the oil in a saucepan. Add the fenugreek seeds, garlic and onion. Stir for 2 minutes, then add the tomatoes, spices and tamari. Stir, cover and simmer for 5 minutes. Add the radishes and peas. Heat through, pour in the stock and bring to the boil. Add the dumplings. Boil for 5–6 minutes until the dumplings are cooked. Add the spring onions, season and serve.

098 SOUP WITH PASTA AND SUN-DRIED TOMATOES

CALORIES	401
CHOLESTEROL	0
VEGAN CALORIES	401
POLYUNSATS	★★★
ANTIOXIDANTS	★★★
CALCIUM	★★☆
IRON	★★☆
B VITAMINS	★★☆

1ltr (1¾pts) vegetable stock
1 handful pasta shapes
1 handful sun-dried tomatoes, finely chopped
1 spring onion, finely chopped
1 small courgette, finely chopped

4–5 mushrooms, sliced
1 tbsp parsley, finely chopped
1 tbsp fresh basil, finely chopped
sea salt and black pepper to taste
½ lemon, sliced

Bring the stock to the boil in a saucepan with the pasta and the rest of the ingredients (except for the lemon). Simmer until the pasta is cooked. Garnish with slices of lemon and serve with thick slices of bread.

099 COURGETTE SOUP

CALORIES	181
CHOLESTEROL	0
VEGAN CALORIES	181
POLYUNSATS	★★☆
ANTIOXIDANTS	★★☆
CALCIUM	★☆☆
IRON	★☆☆
B VITAMINS	★☆☆

2 tbsp olive oil
1 small onion, chopped
1 potato, thinly sliced
500g (1lb 2oz) courgettes, sliced
½ltr (18fl oz) vegetable stock

juice of ½ lemon
1 tsp thyme
1 tsp marjoram
sea salt and black pepper to taste

Heat the oil in a casserole dish and gently soften the onion (don't let it brown). Add the potato and the courgettes and stir-fry for 1 minute, then add the stock. Bring to the boil and simmer for 10 minutes. Add the lemon juice and the herbs. Remove from the heat, blend and season. Serve with wholemeal bread and cheese or soya cheese.

100 SPANISH AVOCADO SOUP

CALORIES	307
CHOLESTEROL	21
VEGAN CALORIES	280
POLYUNSATS	★★☆
ANTIOXIDANTS	★★★
CALCIUM	★★☆
IRON	★★☆
B VITAMINS	★★☆

250ml (9fl oz) plain/soya yoghurt
100ml (3½fl oz) milk/soya milk
150ml (¼pt) tomato juice
1 clove garlic, finely chopped
1 ripe tomato, finely chopped
5cm (2in) cucumber, finely chopped

1 large avocado, pitted and peeled
1 tbsp lemon juice
sea salt and black pepper to taste
1 sprig fresh tarragon, finely chopped

Mix the yoghurt in a bowl with the milk and the tomato juice. Add the garlic, tomato and cucumber. Mash the avocado in a separate bowl, mixing in the lemon juice as you mash. Then add the avocado to the soup and season. Garnish with tarragon and serve cool with a couple of ice cubes in each bowl.

101 ORIENTAL SHIITAKE SOUP
🟦🟦🟦🟦

CALORIES	220
CHOLESTEROL	0
VEGAN CALORIES	220
POLYUNSATS	★★☆
ANTIOXIDANTS	★★★
CALCIUM	★★☆
IRON	★★☆
B VITAMINS	★★☆

2 tbsp olive oil
100g (3½oz) fresh shiitake
   mushrooms, sliced
1 spring onion, sliced
1 clove garlic, crushed
1 small carrot, finely chopped
1 tbsp fresh ginger, finely chopped

1 small bunch watercress, chopped
1 tbsp tamari (soya sauce)
1 tsp maple syrup
1ltr (1¾pts) vegetable stock or water
   with miso to taste
sea salt and black pepper to taste
1 handful fresh coriander, chopped

Gently heat the oil in a saucepan and stir-fry the shiitake mushrooms
with the onion, garlic and carrot for 3 minutes. Add the fresh ginger,
watercress, tamari, maple syrup and stock or water with miso. Bring
to the boil, cover and gently simmer for 5 minutes. Season, garnish
with fresh coriander and serve.

102 SPICY RED LENTIL AND TOMATO SOUP
🟦🟦🟦🟦🟦

CALORIES	290
CHOLESTEROL	0
VEGAN CALORIES	290
POLYUNSATS	★★☆
ANTIOXIDANTS	★★★
CALCIUM	★☆☆
IRON	★★☆
B VITAMINS	★★☆

2 tbsp olive oil
2 shallots, chopped
2 cloves garlic, crushed
55g (2oz) red lentils, rinsed and
   drained
450g (1lb) fresh tomatoes, blended

½ltr (18fl oz) vegetable stock
1 tsp maple syrup
1 pinch asafoetida
1 pinch cayenne pepper
1 tbsp fresh basil, chopped
sea salt and black pepper to taste

Gently heat the oil in a large casserole dish. Add the shallots and fry over
a low heat until soft. Then add the garlic and the lentils and stir-fry for 1
minute before adding the tomatoes. Stir and heat through. Add the stock,
maple syrup, spices and half the basil. Bring to the boil, cover and simmer
for 15 minutes, or until the lentils are soft. Season, garnish with the
remaining basil and serve with crusty bread and cheese or soya cheese.

103 MINT AND CUCUMBER SOUP
🟦🟦🟦🟦

CALORIES	158
CHOLESTEROL	17
VEGAN CALORIES	149
POLYUNSATS	★☆☆
ANTIOXIDANTS	★★★
CALCIUM	★★☆
IRON	★★☆
B VITAMINS	★★☆

1 handful fresh mint, finely
   chopped, plus some to garnish
1 cucumber, coarsely grated

300g (10½oz) plain/soya yoghurt
1 tbsp lemon juice
sea salt and black pepper to taste

Mix the fresh mint and the cucumber in a bowl. Stir in the yoghurt and the
lemon juice, and season. Chill well. Garnish with fresh mint and serve with
a few ice cubes in each bowl.

104 ▼ GAZPACHO DEL CAMPO

CALORIES	267
CHOLESTEROL	0
VEGAN CALORIES	267
POLYUNSATS	★★☆
ANTIOXIDANTS	★★★
CALCIUM	★★☆
IRON	★★☆
B VITAMINS	★★☆

½ cucumber
250g (9oz) tomatoes
1 small red onion
½ green pepper
1 clove garlic

3 tbsp olive oil
1 tbsp lemon juice
2 tbsp red wine vinegar
sea salt and black pepper to taste
1 handful fresh dill, finely chopped

Finely chop a quarter of each of the vegetables and set aside. Blend the remaining vegetables with the garlic, oil, lemon juice and vinegar to a thick, smooth consistency. Season and chill well. Garnish with the finely chopped vegetables and fresh dill. Serve with a few ice cubes in each bowl, and croutons.

105 ▲ AVOCADO AND SEAFOOD SALAD
★♥▨▨

CALORIES	286
CHOLESTEROL	6
VEGAN CALORIES	578
POLYUNSATS	★★☆
ANTIOXIDANTS	★★★
CALCIUM	★★☆
IRON	★★★
B VITAMINS	★★☆

1 avocado, halved, pitted, peeled and sliced
2 beef tomatoes, sliced
¼ cucumber, sliced
2 tbsp mixed seaweed, soaked for 10 minutes and boiled
100g (3½oz) prawns, cooked and peeled/100g (3½oz) walnut halves

juice of ½ lemon
100g (3½oz) plain/soya yoghurt
1 small bunch chives, finely chopped
1 tsp tomato ketchup
a few drops Tabasco sauce
sea salt and black pepper to taste

Arrange the avocado slices on two plates. Pile the tomato and cucumber slices on top. Sprinkle with the boiled seaweed and garnish with prawns or walnuts. Make the dressing by mixing the lemon juice, yoghurt, chives, tomato ketchup and Tabasco sauce in a bowl. Season and spoon over the salad. Serve with French baguette.

106 COOL BULGUR TABOULEH

CALORIES	495
CHOLESTEROL	18
VEGAN CALORIES	485
POLYUNSATS	★★★
ANTIOXIDANTS	★★★
CALCIUM	★★☆
IRON	★★★
B VITAMINS	★★☆

100g (3½oz) bulgur wheat
100g (3½oz) smoked salmon, diced/ chick peas, cooked or sprouted
2 spring onions, chopped
1 small lemon, peeled and diced
1 tbsp each of fresh parsley, mint and dill, chopped
2 tomatoes, diced

100g (3½oz) green peas, fresh or defrosted
1 Little Gem lettuce
2 tsp red wine vinegar
1 pinch raw cane sugar
1 pinch sea salt and black pepper
1 tsp Dijon mustard
2 tbsp wheatgerm oil

Put the bulgur in a small saucepan with twice its volume of water and a little salt. Bring to the boil and simmer for 8–10 minutes, or until soft. Drain in a sieve. Add the smoked salmon or chick peas, spring onions, lemon, herbs, tomatoes and peas. Mix well. Divide the lettuce leaves between two plates and cover with the bulgur mixture. To make the dressing, mix the vinegar, sugar, salt, pepper and mustard in a bowl, and slowly whisk in the oil. Sprinkle the dressing over the salads and serve.

107 SUMMER SALAD

CALORIES	241
CHOLESTEROL	0
VEGAN CALORIES	241
POLYUNSATS	★★★
ANTIOXIDANTS	★★★
CALCIUM	★★☆
IRON	★★☆
B VITAMINS	★★☆

1 Little Gem lettuce, shredded
½ small cauliflower, cut into small florets
1 green pepper, sliced
½ Florence fennel bulb, finely chopped
1 carrot, cut into peelings
5 red radishes, sliced

100g (3½oz) broad beans, chopped
¼ cucumber, finely sliced
1 small bunch watercress, chopped
1 tbsp walnut oil
1 tsp balsamic vinegar
1 tsp Dijon mustard
sea salt and white pepper to taste

To make the dressing, whisk the oil, vinegar, mustard, salt and pepper in a salad bowl. Add the salad ingredients and gently toss. Serve with bread.

108 STUFFED TOMATO SALAD

CALORIES	480
CHOLESTEROL	51
VEGAN CALORIES	284
POLYUNSATS	★★☆
ANTIOXIDANTS	★★★
CALCIUM	★★☆
IRON	★★☆
B VITAMINS	★★☆

200g (7oz) fresh tuna, diced/200g (7oz) butter beans, cooked or canned
juice of 1 lemon
1 tbsp olive oil
6 medium tomatoes, hollowed out
½ cucumber, finely diced

½ red pepper, finely diced
50g (1¾oz) red onion, chopped
12 black olives, halved and pitted
juice of ½ lemon
1 tbsp fresh basil, finely chopped
3 tbsp olive oil
sea salt and black pepper to taste

Cook the tuna or butter beans with the juice of 1 lemon and 1 tablespoon of oil in a small baking dish in a preheated oven at 220°C/425°F/gas mark 7 for 5–8 minutes. To make the dressing, blend the scooped-out tomato flesh with the lemon juice, basil, oil, salt and pepper to a thick consistency and set aside. Place the cooked tuna or butter beans in a bowl with the cucumber, red pepper, red onion and olives. Mix in the dressing. Spoon the salad mixture into the hollowed tomatoes. Serve on a bed of green lettuce.

109 A PLATE OF SUMMER CRUDITÉS
★♡◐∅

CALORIES	406
CHOLESTEROL	0
VEGAN CALORIES	406
POLYUNSATS	★★★
ANTIOXIDANTS	★★★
CALCIUM	★★☆
IRON	★★☆
B VITAMINS	★★☆

1 red pepper, halved
2 carrots
1 small raw beetroot
2 sticks celery
¼ cucumber
100g (3½oz) chanterelle
    mushrooms, stir-fried in a little oil

4 artichoke hearts, sliced
10 red radishes, kept whole
1 tbsp red wine vinegar
1 pinch sea salt and black pepper
3 tbsp walnut oil
2 tsp fresh tarragon, chopped
1 tbsp pumpkin seeds, toasted

Grill or toast the pepper until the skin becomes black and charred. Cover with a damp tea towel and leave to cool. Cut the carrots, beetroot, celery and cucumber into thin 10cm (4in) long sticks. Skin the cooled pepper and cut the flesh into long sticks, too. Arrange the crudités on two large plates. To make the dressing, dissolve the salt and pepper in the vinegar, add the walnut oil and the tarragon and whisk. Drizzle the dressing over the crudités and garnish with toasted pumpkin seeds. Serve with toast.

110 BABA GANOUSH
★♡◐∅◉

CALORIES	718
CHOLESTEROL	0
VEGAN CALORIES	718
POLYUNSATS	★★★
ANTIOXIDANTS	★★★
CALCIUM	★★★
IRON	★★☆
B VITAMINS	★★☆

1 medium aubergine
2 tbsp lemon juice
1 tbsp tahini
1 avocado, quartered and pitted
1 carrot, cut into peelings
1 large tomato, chopped

1 small Florence fennel bulb, finely
    chopped
1 bunch watercress, chopped
1 tbsp balsamic vinegar
2 tbsp walnut oil
sea salt and black pepper to taste

Prick the skin of the aubergine with a fork and grill it on all sides until it is soft and the skin charred. Cool under running water, halve and scoop out the flesh with a spoon. Blend the flesh with the lemon juice, tahini and a pinch of salt. Peel and slice the avocado and mix with the carrot, tomato, fennel and watercress in a salad bowl. Make the dressing by whisking the vinegar and oil with salt and pepper, pour over the salad and gently toss. Serve immediately with the baba ganoush and warm pitta bread.

111 CHANTERELLE SALAD
★♡◐☒

CALORIES	208
CHOLESTEROL	0
VEGAN CALORIES	208
POLYUNSATS	★★★
ANTIOXIDANTS	★★★
CALCIUM	★★☆
IRON	★★☆
B VITAMINS	★★☆

200g (7oz) chanterelle mushrooms
1 shallot, finely chopped
2 tbsp flat-leaf parsley, chopped
1 handful radicchio, shredded
1 handful curly endive (frisée)
125g (4½oz) French beans, blanched

1 small yellow courgette, sliced
1 tbsp white wine vinegar
1 tbsp walnut oil
3 tbsp olive oil, plus some for frying
sea salt and black pepper to taste
1 small bunch chives, chopped

Make the vinaigrette by mixing the vinegar, oils, salt and pepper and set aside. Heat a little oil in a saucepan and gently stir-fry the seasoned chanterelles with the shallot and the parsley for 2 minutes. Remove from the heat and drizzle with half the vinaigrette. Divide the radicchio and the curly endive between two large plates, add the blanched French beans and the courgette. Drizzle with the remaining vinaigrette. Spoon the warm chanterelles on top of the salad and serve garnished with chives.

112 ▲ AUBERGINE AND OLIVE PÂTÉ
★✕∅

CALORIES	146
CHOLESTEROL	0
VEGAN CALORIES	146
POLYUNSATS	★★☆
ANTIOXIDANTS	★★★
CALCIUM	★★☆
IRON	★★☆
B VITAMINS	★★☆

1 tbsp olive oil
1 small red onion, finely chopped
1 medium aubergine, diced
2 cloves garlic, crushed
2 tsp tamari (soya sauce)

12 grape tomatoes, blended
1 handful fresh basil
1 tsp Dijon mustard
10 black olives, pitted and chopped
sea salt and black pepper to taste

Sweat the onion in a frying pan with the oil. Turn up the heat, add
the aubergine and stir-fry until soft (approximately 10 minutes). Lower
the heat, add the garlic, tamari and tomatoes, followed by the basil,
mustard and olives. Very gently stir-fry for a further 5 minutes.
Season and serve on toasted French bread with plenty of crispy
green lettuce and French dressing (see p.23).

113 CATALAN ROAST PEPPER SALAD WITH WALNUT PÂTÉ

★♥◊◎◪

CALORIES	625
CHOLESTEROL	0
VEGAN CALORIES	625
POLYUNSATS	★★★
ANTIOXIDANTS	★★★
CALCIUM	★★☆
IRON	★★☆
B VITAMINS	★★☆

1 yellow pepper, quartered
   and deseeded
1 red pepper, quartered
   and deseeded
1 tbsp red wine vinegar
1 tbsp lemon juice
sea salt and black pepper to taste
1 tsp maple syrup
3 tbsp olive oil, plus some

for blending
1 small hot green chilli, deseeded
   and finely chopped
2 spring onions, finely sliced
100g (3½oz) walnuts, shelled
1 clove garlic, crushed
½ tsp sea salt
1 green lettuce

Grill or toast the peppers until the skins become black and charred. Cover with a damp tea towel and leave to cool. To make the dressing, whisk the vinegar, lemon juice, salt, pepper, maple syrup and oil in a bowl, then add the chilli and the spring onions. Skin the cooled peppers and cut the flesh into long strips. Mix the peppers with the dressing. To make the pâté, blend the walnuts with the garlic, salt and enough oil to easily blend to a slightly crunchy consistency. Serve the pepper salad with the walnut pâté on a bed of green lettuce and with fresh country bread.

114 SCANDINAVIAN POTATO AND SAUSAGE SALAD

★♥◿◎

CALORIES	613
CHOLESTEROL	50
VEGAN CALORIES	478
POLYUNSATS	★★☆
ANTIOXIDANTS	★★☆
CALCIUM	★★☆
IRON	★★☆
B VITAMINS	★★★

olive oil for stir-frying
1 red onion, halved and sliced
200g (7oz) spicy sausages
   (pork/soya), sliced
1 small courgette, finely sliced
1 tsp fresh thyme
1 tsp Dijon mustard
2 tsp wheat flour

3 tbsp red wine vinegar
1 tsp maple syrup
sea salt and black pepper to taste
1 large handful lettuce leaves
250g (9oz) new potatoes, halved
   and boiled
8 grape tomatoes, halved
10 gherkins

Gently heat 2 tablespoons of oil in a frying pan. Add the onion and the sausages and stir-fry for 3 minutes, then add the courgette and stir-fry for a further 2 minutes. Mix in the thyme, mustard and flour and cook over a low heat for 1 minute. Add the vinegar, maple syrup and a little more oil, and continue to stir while the mixture thickens. Season and turn off the heat. Arrange the lettuce leaves on two large plates and top with the halved potatoes and the sausage mixture. Garnish with grape tomatoes and gherkins, and serve immediately.

115 SEAFOOD TABOULEH
★ ♥ 🌿 🍞 ∅ ▢

CALORIES	425
CHOLESTEROL	140
VEGAN CALORIES	662
POLYUNSATS	★★☆
ANTIOXIDANTS	★★★
CALCIUM	★★☆
IRON	★★★
B VITAMINS	★★★

200g (7oz) couscous
½ tsp Tabasco sauce mixed with
  1 tbsp olive oil
100g (3½oz) green peas, fresh or
  defrosted
1 courgette, finely sliced
2 tbsp mixed seaweed, soaked for
  10 minutes and boiled

100g (3½oz) cooked prawns/
  cashew nuts
1 small spring onion, finely chopped
1 clove garlic, crushed
2 tbsp fresh mint, finely chopped
½ lemon, peeled and diced
sea salt and black pepper to taste

Put the couscous in a small saucepan with twice its volume of boiling water and a little salt. Cover and leave to stand for 10 minutes. Then mix in the Tabasco sauce, followed by the peas, courgette, seaweed, prawns or cashews, spring onion, garlic, mint and lemon. Season and serve.

116 ARTICHOKE SALAD
★ ♥ 🥛 ✖ 🍞 ∅ ▢

CALORIES	209
CHOLESTEROL	37
VEGAN CALORIES	142
POLYUNSATS	★☆☆
ANTIOXIDANTS	★★★
CALCIUM	★★☆
IRON	★★☆
B VITAMINS	★★☆

1ltr (1¾pts) water
1 lemon, quartered
1 onion, quartered
1 pinch raw cane sugar, sea salt and
  white peppercorns
2 artichokes
1 small butternut lettuce, shredded

1 carrot, finely sliced
2 tomatoes, cut into boats
¼ cucumber, finely sliced
50g (1¾oz) goat's/soya cheese, cut
  into chunks
gherkins and pickled chillies
  to garnish

Boil the water in a saucepan. Add the lemon, onion, sugar and seasoning. Meanwhile, peel the leaves from the artichokes, cut the hearts into quarters and cut off the choke and any remaining leaf edges. Place the artichoke quarters in the boiling water and simmer for 15 minutes. Arrange the salad ingredients and the cheese on two large plates. Add the cooked artichokes, garnish with gherkins and chillies, and serve with French dressing (see p.23) and baguette.

117 COLLIOURE SALAD
★ ▢

CALORIES	405
CHOLESTEROL	210
VEGAN CALORIES	367
POLYUNSATS	★★☆
ANTIOXIDANTS	★★★
CALCIUM	★★☆
IRON	★★☆
B VITAMINS	★★☆

3 red peppers
15 anchovies, desalted and bones
  removed/8 halved pieces of
  salsify and 8 black olives
3 tbsp olive oil
1 tbsp red wine vinegar

1 garlic clove, chopped
1 tbsp fresh parsley, finely chopped
black pepper to taste
2 hard-boiled eggs, quartered/100g
  (3½oz) butter beans, cooked or
  canned and drained

Brush the peppers with oil, place them in a baking tray and bake in a preheated oven at 250°C/500°F/gas mark 10, turning from time to time, until the skins are black and charred. Then peel off the skins (while they are still warm), deseed and cut into thick slices. Arrange the anchovies or salsify and olives like sun rays around the edge of a large plate and place the pepper slices in the middle of the plate. Drizzle with oil and vinegar, sprinkle with garlic, parsley and black pepper and top with hard-boiled egg quarters or butter beans. Serve with bread.

118 ▲ GREEN TAGLIATELLE
WITH RED HOT PEPPER SAUCE
⭐❤🌾🥖

CALORIES	829
CHOLESTEROL	150
VEGAN CALORIES	594
POLYUNSATS	★★☆
ANTIOXIDANTS	★★★
CALCIUM	★★☆
IRON	★★★
B VITAMINS	★★★

100ml (3½oz) chicken/vegetable
  stock, heated
1 red pepper, chopped and deseeded
300g (10½oz) chicken breast/
  150g (5½oz) seitan, sliced
2 tbsp olive oil, plus some for

frying and tossing
sea salt to taste
1 pinch cayenne pepper
200g (7oz) green tagliatelle pasta
1 tbsp fresh basil, chopped
black pepper to taste

Pour the stock into a small casserole dish, add the red pepper, bring to
the boil and simmer for 5 minutes. Meanwhile, fry the chicken or seitan
slices in a frying pan with a little oil until golden. Set aside. Blend the
red pepper with the stock, while slowly adding the oil, and season with
salt and cayenne pepper. Add the fried chicken or seitan to the sauce and
mix. Cook the pasta in plenty of boiling water with a little salt and oil.
Drain the pasta and return it to the pan. Toss with oil and fresh basil,
and season with salt and black pepper. Serve as nests on two large
plates with the sauce in the middle.

119
SPINACH FETTUCCINE
WITH FRESH TOMATO SAUCE
⭐❤🌿☕

CALORIES	538
CHOLESTEROL	29
VEGAN CALORIES	485
POLYUNSATS	★★☆
ANTIOXIDANTS	★★★
CALCIUM	★★☆
IRON	★★★
B VITAMINS	★★★

200g (7oz) spinach fettuccine
  pasta
2 ripe beef tomatoes, blended
1 tbsp fresh basil, chopped

100g (3½oz) mozzarella/soya
  cheese, cubed
1 tbsp safflower oil
sea salt and black pepper to taste

Cook the spinach pasta in plenty of boiling water with a little salt and oil.
Mix the blended tomatoes, chopped basil, cheese cubes and oil in a bowl,
and season. Drain the cooked pasta and toss with the sauce. Serve
immediately with a green side salad.

120
BUCKWHEAT NOODLES WITH
SPICY COURGETTE SAUCE
⭐❤💧☕

CALORIES	777
CHOLESTEROL	57
VEGAN CALORIES	656
POLYUNSATS	★★★
ANTIOXIDANTS	★★★
CALCIUM	★★☆
IRON	★★☆
B VITAMINS	★★☆

1 tbsp olive oil
1 small white onion, finely chopped
1 clove garlic, crushed
1 medium courgette, thinly sliced
50g (1¾oz) sun-dried tomatoes,
  chopped
1 small red chilli, deseeded and
  finely sliced

100ml (3½fl oz) crème fraîche/soya
  cream
1 tbsp fresh oregano, finely chopped
sea salt and black pepper to taste
200g (7oz) Japanese buckwheat
  noodles
a little grated cheese/soya cheese
  (optional)

Heat the oil in a casserole dish and sweat the onion and garlic for
5 minutes until soft (don't let them brown). Add the courgette and cook
for 2–3 minutes. Then add the sun-dried tomatoes and the chilli, cover
and simmer for 5 minutes, stirring from time to time. Add the cream and
fresh oregano, and season. Heat through and very gently simmer for 2–3
minutes. Cook the noodles as instructed on the packet. Drain and toss
with the sauce. Sprinkle with cheese (if using) and serve immediately.

121
FETTUCCINE WITH SHIITAKE
⭐❤💧🌿

CALORIES	406
CHOLESTEROL	0
VEGAN CALORIES	406
POLYUNSATS	★☆☆
ANTIOXIDANTS	★★★
CALCIUM	★☆☆
IRON	★★☆
B VITAMINS	★☆☆

200g (7oz) fettuccine pasta
1 tbsp olive oil
200g (7oz) fresh shiitake
  mushrooms, sliced
1 tsp fresh ginger, finely chopped
1 tbsp tamari (soya sauce)
200ml (⅓pt) vegetable stock

1 tsp mirin (Japanese rice wine) or
  dry sherry
2 tbsp fresh flat-leaf parsley, finely
  chopped
1 tsp cornflour dissolved in a little
  cold water
sea salt and black pepper to taste

Cook the pasta in plenty of boiling water with a little salt and oil. Heat the
oil in a saucepan and stir-fry the mushrooms until they begin to brown.
Add the ginger and the tamari, heat through, then add the stock. Bring
to the boil and simmer for 5 minutes. Add the mirin or dry sherry, fresh
parsley and dissolved cornflour. Continue to cook until the sauce thickens,
and season. Drain the pasta and stir into the sauce. Serve hot.

LUMACHE WITH SEAFOOD

★♥🌾🐚

CALORIES	617
CHOLESTEROL	55
VEGAN CALORIES	636
POLYUNSATS	★★☆
ANTIOXIDANTS	★★★
CALCIUM	★★☆
IRON	★★★
B VITAMINS	★★☆

200g (7oz) lumache (pasta snails)
   or use pasta shapes of choice
2 tbsp olive oil
200g (7oz) fresh tuna/marinated
   seitan, diced
1 clove garlic, finely chopped
1 small red pepper, quartered,
deseeded and sliced
4 tbsp dried mixed seaweed, soaked
2 ripe tomatoes, chopped
2 anchovy fillets, chopped/8 black
   olives, pitted and chopped
1 tbsp fresh basil, chopped
sea salt and black pepper to taste

Cook the pasta in plenty of boiling water with a little salt and oil. Heat the
oil in a casserole dish, add the tuna or seitan and fry until lightly browned.
Turn down the heat, add the garlic and red pepper and cook until soft. Add
the seaweed (with its soaking water), tomatoes, anchovies or olives and
basil and reduce for 5 minutes, then season. Drain the cooked pasta and
divide onto two heated plates. Top with the sauce and serve immediately.

PASTA WITH
CHUNKY TARRAGON SAUCE

★🌾

CALORIES	1,027
CHOLESTEROL	182
VEGAN CALORIES	734
POLYUNSATS	★★★
ANTIOXIDANTS	★★★
CALCIUM	★★☆
IRON	★★★
B VITAMINS	★★☆

150g (5½oz) pasta shapes
½ chicken, cut into chunks/
   60g (2¼oz) soya chunks (dry
   weight), rehydrated
plain flour for coating
vegetable oil for frying
1 onion, chopped
150ml (¼pt) white wine
200ml (⅓pt) chicken/vegetable stock
sea salt and black pepper to taste
1 small bunch fresh tarragon,
   chopped
100ml (3½fl oz) crème fraîche/soya
   cream
1 tsp Maizena (cornstarch) dissolved
   in a little cold water

Cook the pasta shapes in plenty of boiling water with a little salt and oil.
Flour the chicken or soya chunks and fry them in a casserole dish with
a little oil. Set aside. Fry the onion in the dish with a little more oil,
add the white wine and leave to reduce to half the volume. Then add
the stock, season and add half the tarragon. Add the fried chicken or soya
chunks and simmer for 20 minutes. Spoon in the cream, bring to the boil
and add the remaining tarragon. Thicken the sauce with the Maizena.
Check the seasoning and serve hot with the cooked and drained pasta.

PENNE WITH PESTO AND PEAS

★♥🌾

CALORIES	881
CHOLESTEROL	0
VEGAN CALORIES	881
POLYUNSATS	★★★
ANTIOXIDANTS	★★★
CALCIUM	★★☆
IRON	★★★
B VITAMINS	★★☆

200g (7oz) penne pasta
3 tbsp pine kernels
½ tsp coarse sea salt
2 tbsp fresh basil, finely chopped
4 tbsp olive oil
1 clove garlic, crushed (or more
   to taste)
200g (7oz) green peas, shelled

Cook the pasta in plenty of boiling water with a little salt and oil. Grind
the pine kernels and salt in a mortar. Add the basil, oil and garlic. Mix well.
Steam the peas in a vegetable steamer for 3–4 minutes. Drain the cooked
pasta and place in a large (heated) serving bowl. Mix in the pesto, top
with the steamed peas and serve immediately.

125 PASTA WITH GOUJONS IN PIQUANTE SAUCE

★♥🌿🥔

CALORIES	958
CHOLESTEROL	125
VEGAN CALORIES	770
POLYUNSATS	★★☆
ANTIOXIDANTS	★★☆
CALCIUM	★★☆
IRON	★★★
B VITAMINS	★★☆

3 cloves garlic, crushed
2 tbsp Dijon mustard
2 tbsp red wine vinegar
3 tbsp vegetable stock
1 tbsp tomato paste (purée)
1 tbsp tamari (soya sauce)
150g (5½oz) pasta of choice
2 tbsp olive oil
250g (9oz) chicken breast strips/

50g (1¾oz) soya chunks (dry
weight), rehydrated
½ Spanish onion, finely sliced
125ml (4fl oz) coconut milk
1 tsp cornflour diluted in a little
coconut milk
sea salt and black pepper to taste
fresh tarragon to garnish

Mix the garlic, mustard, vinegar, stock, tomato paste and tamari into a sauce in a bowl and set aside. Boil the pasta in plenty of water with a little salt and oil. Meanwhile, stir-fry the chicken or soya chunks in a casserole dish with the oil for 3–5 minutes. Add the onion, then the sauce, and bring to the boil. Cover and gently simmer for 5 minutes. Add the coconut milk and the diluted cornflour, stir and heat through until the sauce thickens. Season and serve garnished with fresh tarragon and black pepper.

126 LINGUINI WITH PANGRATTATO AND SPICY SAUCE

★♥🌿🥔🍋

CALORIES	648
CHOLESTEROL	8
VEGAN CALORIES	724
POLYUNSATS	★★★
ANTIOXIDANTS	★★★
CALCIUM	★★☆
IRON	★★★
B VITAMINS	★★☆

100ml (3½oz) olive oil, plus 1 tbsp
for frying
4 cloves garlic, chopped
2 thick slices bread, made into
coarse crumbs
1 small red chilli, chopped
8 anchovy fillets, chopped/

14 sun-dried tomato halves,
chopped
juice and zest of ½ lemon
sea salt and black pepper to taste
1 handful fresh flat-leaf parsley,
finely chopped
200g (7oz) linguini pasta

To make the pangrattato, heat the oil over a medium heat in a small saucepan, add the garlic and cook for 15 seconds, then add the breadcrumbs and cook until crisp and golden. Drain, season and set aside. To make the sauce, heat 1 tablespoon of oil in a saucepan and gently fry the chilli and the anchovies or sun-dried tomatoes for 2–3 minutes. Remove from the heat, add the lemon juice, and season. Cook the pasta in plenty of boiling water with a little salt and oil. Drain and mix with the spicy sauce. Place in a serving dish, sprinkle with the pangrattato, lemon zest and parsley, and serve immediately.

ROTINI WITH CHEESY COURGETTE

CALORIES	714
CHOLESTEROL	44
VEGAN CALORIES	635
POLYUNSATS	★★☆
ANTIOXIDANTS	★★★
CALCIUM	★★★
IRON	★★★
B VITAMINS	★★☆

200g (7oz) rotini pasta
1 tbsp olive oil
2 cloves garlic, chopped
500g (1lb 2oz) small courgettes, sliced

sea salt and black pepper to taste
150g (5½oz) ricotta/soya cheese, crumbled
1 handful fresh basil, chopped

Cook the pasta in plenty of boiling water with a little salt and oil. Meanwhile, heat the oil in a heavy-based saucepan and very gently fry the garlic until soft (don't let it brown). Add the sliced courgettes and gently stir-fry for 4–5 minutes. Season and set aside. Drain the pasta and mix with the courgettes. Add the cheese, check the seasoning, garnish with fresh basil and serve immediately.

128

SPAGHETTINI WITH
COOL HERBS AND HOT TOMATOES

■♥◆✿∅

CALORIES	554
CHOLESTEROL	0
VEGAN CALORIES	554
POLYUNSATS	★★★
ANTIOXIDANTS	★★★
CALCIUM	★★☆
IRON	★★★
B VITAMINS	★★★

200g (7oz) spaghettini pasta
2 cloves garlic
1 handful fresh mint
1 handful fresh basil
1 handful fresh oregano
2 large ripe beef tomatoes,
   quartered

1 tbsp capers
1 tsp Tabasco sauce
1 tsp maple syrup
2 tbsp olive oil
sea salt and black pepper to taste
2 tbsp chopped walnuts

Cook the pasta in plenty of boiling water with a little salt and oil. Coarsely chop the garlic and the herbs, then blend them with the tomatoes, capers, Tabasco sauce, maple syrup and oil. Season and set aside. Drain the cooked pasta and divide between two large plates. Top with the blended tomato sauce and garnish with walnuts. Serve immediately.

129

PENNE WITH BRAZIL NUT SAUCE

■♥◆✿∅

CALORIES	780
CHOLESTEROL	0
VEGAN CALORIES	780
POLYUNSATS	★★★
ANTIOXIDANTS	★★★
CALCIUM	★★☆
IRON	★★☆
B VITAMINS	★★☆

150g (5½oz) penne pasta
2 tbsp olive oil
1 shallot, chopped
50g (1¾oz) Brazil nuts
2 tbsp breadcrumbs

1 red pepper, quartered
1 tbsp tamari (soya sauce)
2 tomatoes, chopped
1 clove garlic, crushed
1 tbsp fresh oregano, chopped

Cook the pasta in plenty of boiling water with a little salt and oil. Heat the oil in a frying pan or wok and gently stir-fry the shallot for 30 seconds. Add the Brazil nuts and the breadcrumbs and stir-fry until they begin to turn brown. Deseed and finely slice the pepper quarters and add them to the pan or wok with the tamari. Stir for a further few seconds, then add the tomatoes and the garlic. Heat through. Drain the cooked pasta and mix with the Brazil nut sauce. Garnish with oregano and serve immediately.

130

RICE NOODLES WITH
ORIENTAL MANGETOUT SAUCE

■♥◆

CALORIES	502
CHOLESTEROL	0
VEGAN CALORIES	502
POLYUNSATS	★★★
ANTIOXIDANTS	★★☆
CALCIUM	★☆☆
IRON	★★☆
B VITAMINS	★★☆

1 tbsp grapeseed oil
2 spring onions, finely sliced
1 tsp fresh ginger, finely chopped
1 clove garlic, finely chopped
350g (12oz) mangetout, sliced
100ml (3½fl oz) water

1 tbsp tamari (soya sauce)
1 tsp cornflour dissolved in a little
   cold water
1 tbsp toasted sesame oil
sea salt and black pepper to taste
200g (7oz) vermicelli (rice noodles)

Gently heat the grapeseed oil in a large frying pan or wok. Add the spring onions, ginger, garlic and mangetout and stir-fry for 2 minutes. Stir in the water and the tamari. Bring to the boil and cook for 2 minutes. Add the cornflour and the sesame oil, stir and cook until the sauce thickens. Season and set aside (keep warm). Cook the rice noodles as instructed on the packet. Drain and toss with the mangetout sauce. Serve hot.

131 SPANISH PAELLA

CALORIES	606
CHOLESTEROL	50
VEGAN CALORIES	581
POLYUNSATS	★★☆
ANTIOXIDANTS	★★★
CALCIUM	★★☆
IRON	★★☆
B VITAMINS	★★★

2 tbsp olive oil
½ Spanish onion
1 clove garlic, crushed
100g (3½oz) chicken/tempeh, cut into chunks
100g (3½oz) brown mushrooms, sliced
150g (5½oz) long-grain semi-whole grain rice

1 pinch saffron
1 bay leaf
1 small red pepper, quartered, deseeded and sliced
1 stick celery (with leaves), sliced
400g (14oz) ripe tomatoes, blended
200ml (⅓pt) vegetable stock
1 tbsp fresh oregano, chopped
1 lemon (unpeeled), cut into wedges

Gently heat the oil in a paella pan (or a deep frying pan). Add the onion and garlic and stir-fry for 1 minute. Then add the chicken or tempeh and the mushrooms and continue to stir-fry until they brown. Add the rice, herbs, pepper and celery. Stir-fry for 2 minutes, then add the tomatoes and stock. Bring to the boil and very gently simmer until all the liquid is absorbed and the rice is cooked (adding more stock or a little water if necessary). Garnish with oregano and lemon wedges, and serve hot.

132 ORIENTAL STIR-FRY

CALORIES	556
CHOLESTEROL	138
VEGAN CALORIES	343
POLYUNSATS	★★☆
ANTIOXIDANTS	★★★
CALCIUM	★★☆
IRON	★★★
B VITAMINS	★★☆

2 tbsp tamari (soya sauce)
2 tbsp dry sherry or rice wine
1 tsp cornflour dissolved in a little cold water
1 tsp fresh ginger, finely chopped
250g (9oz) lamb fillet/tofu, diced
2 tbsp olive oil

2 green onions, chopped into strips
100g (3½oz) broccoli florets, cut into small pieces
100g (3½oz) sweetcorn kernels
1 small bunch watercress, chopped
sea salt and black pepper to taste
stock to taste (optional)

Mix the tamari, sherry or rice wine, dissolved cornflour and ginger in a bowl. Add the lamb or tofu cubes to the mixture. Leave to marinate while you chop and prepare the rest of the ingredients. Then heat the oil in a wok and stir-fry the lamb or tofu with the marinade until all the liquid is absorbed. Remove from the pan and set aside. Add a little more oil to the pan and stir-fry the vegetables for 3 minutes. Add the fried lamb or tofu, mix and season, adding a little stock (if using). Serve with rice or noodles.

133 PROVENÇALE KIDNEY BEANS

CALORIES	266
CHOLESTEROL	0
VEGAN CALORIES	266
POLYUNSATS	★☆☆
ANTIOXIDANTS	★★☆
CALCIUM	★★☆
IRON	★★☆
B VITAMINS	★★☆

1 small red onion, halved and sliced
1 clove garlic, sliced
250g (9oz) kidney beans, cooked or canned
2 large ripe tomatoes, chopped
1 small yellow courgette, sliced

1 tbsp olive oil
100ml (3½fl oz) vegetable stock, heated
2 tbsp fresh basil
50g (1¾oz) small Niçoise olives
sea salt and black pepper to taste

Preheat the oven to 220°C/425°F/gas mark 7. Place the first five ingredients in layers in an ovenproof dish. Drizzle with the oil and the stock, and garnish with fresh basil and pitted Niçoise olives. Season and bake in a hot oven for 15 minutes. Serve with wild rice.

134 ◄ BROCHETTES WITH PILI-PILI SAUCE

CALORIES	592
CHOLESTEROL	168
VEGAN CALORIES	576
POLYUNSATS	★★★
ANTIOXIDANTS	★★★
CALCIUM	★★☆
IRON	★★☆
B VITAMINS	★★★

2 red hot chillies, chopped
2 cloves garlic, chopped
juice of 1 lemon
1 tsp paprika
1 pinch salt
4 tbsp olive oil
10 scampi, peeled/125g (4½oz) smoked tofu, diced

1 sweet potato, cut into chunks
10 button mushrooms, kept whole
1 red onion, quartered
10 okra (lady's fingers), halved
1 red pepper, cut into chunks
10 cherry tomatoes
2 corn-on-the-cob, sliced into chunks

Blend the chillies, garlic, lemon juice, paprika, salt and oil to a coarse paste and set aside. Alternately spear the scampi or tofu, sweet potato, mushrooms, onion, okra, red pepper and cherry tomatoes onto two metal barbecue skewers, then place them on a tray with the corn chunks and brush with the pili-pili paste. Place the kebabs under a hot grill and cook until golden, brushing with more pili-pili paste as you turn them. Serve hot with rice or millet.

135 SICILIAN PAPILLOTES

CALORIES	384
CHOLESTEROL	88
VEGAN CALORIES	366
POLYUNSATS	★★★
ANTIOXIDANTS	★★★
CALCIUM	★★☆
IRON	★★☆
B VITAMINS	★★☆

2 tbsp olive oil
1 small aubergine, sliced
1 small courgette, sliced
4 sun-dried tomatoes, sliced
10 black olives, pitted and sliced
2 fish fillets (pink bream or sea bass)/250g (9oz) marinated

tofu, sliced
1 dash dry white wine
1 tbsp Florence fennel tops or ½ tsp fennel seeds
1 pinch oregano
sea salt and black pepper to taste
2 slices lemon

Preheat the oven to 220°C/425°F/gas mark 7. Quickly fry the aubergine and courgette in a saucepan with the oil, then mix them with the tomatoes and olives. Divide the mixture into two piles on a large piece of foil. Top with the fish or tofu. Sprinkle with the wine, fennel and oregano. Season and garnish with the lemon slices. Make a "tent" of the foil, tightly folded so that the fish or tofu is completely enclosed (but leaving plenty of free space over the fish). Bake in a hot oven for 10 minutes and serve hot.

136 SOCCA NIÇOISE

CALORIES	553
CHOLESTEROL	0
VEGAN CALORIES	553
POLYUNSATS	★★★
ANTIOXIDANTS	★★★
CALCIUM	★☆☆
IRON	★★☆
B VITAMINS	★★☆

250g (9oz) chick pea flour
300ml (½pt) cold water
300–550ml (½pt–1pt) hot water

sea salt and black pepper to taste
olive oil for sprinkling and frying

Preheat the oven to 250°C/500°F/gas 10. Place the chick pea flour in a heavy-based saucepan and slowly stir in the cold water until smooth. Place the saucepan over a moderate heat and gradually add the hot water and salt, stirring continuously. Lower the heat and continue to stir until the mixture starts to form a ball. Then spread out the dough evenly in an oiled, shallow baking tin. Sprinkle with the oil and black pepper. Bake in a hot oven for 10 minutes until slightly crisp. Cool and slice, and gently fry the pieces in oil. Drain on paper towels and serve hot with a tomato salad.

137 CATALAN 10-MINUTE TART

CALORIES	533
CHOLESTEROL	8
VEGAN CALORIES	529
POLYUNSATS	★★★
ANTIOXIDANTS	★★☆
CALCIUM	★★☆
IRON	★★☆
B VITAMINS	★★☆

2 tbsp olive oil
2 shallots, sliced
8 mushrooms, sliced
½ tsp ground cumin
½ tsp ground coriander
1 pinch saffron

1 packet ready-made shortcrust
   pastry, rolled out very thin
2 large tomatoes, sliced
8 anchovy fillets/12 black olives,
   pitted and sliced
celery salt and black pepper to taste

Preheat the oven to 200°C/400°F/gas mark 6. Heat the oil in a small wok or saucepan and gently stir-fry the shallots and mushrooms. Add the spices and heat through. Place the rolled-out pastry in a 20cm (8in) pie dish and add the mushroom mixture. Cover with tomato slices and anchovies or olives. Season, bake for 10 minutes, or until golden, and serve.

138 BASQUE CHICKEN FRICASSEE

CALORIES	561
CHOLESTEROL	90
VEGAN CALORIES	466
POLYUNSATS	★★★
ANTIOXIDANTS	★★★
CALCIUM	★★☆
IRON	★★☆
B VITAMINS	★★☆

2 chicken legs, cut into pieces/175g
   (6oz) seitan, cut into chunks
2 tbsp plain flour
olive oil for sautéing and stir-frying
1 large onion, halved
½ red pepper, deseeded
½ green pepper, deseeded

200ml (⅓pt) white wine
2 tomatoes, peeled and chopped
1 clove garlic, chopped
1 pinch thyme
1 bay leaf
½ tsp sugar
sea salt and black pepper to taste

Preheat the oven to 230°C/450°F/gas mark 8. Flour the chicken or seitan and sauté in a casserole dish with oil. Set aside. Slice the onion and the red and green peppers and stir-fry them in the dish with a little more oil. Add the white wine, tomatoes, garlic, herbs and sugar, and season. Return the chicken or seitan to the dish and bring to the boil. Cover and place in a hot oven for 20 minutes. Check the seasoning and serve with rice.

139 NEPALESE PANCH KOL

CALORIES	289
CHOLESTEROL	0
VEGAN CALORIES	289
POLYUNSATS	★★★
ANTIOXIDANTS	★★★
CALCIUM	★★☆
IRON	★★★
B VITAMINS	★★☆

2 tbsp grapeseed oil
150g (5½oz) cauliflower, cut into
   small florets
150g (5½oz) carrots, chopped
½ tsp turmeric
100ml (3½oz) vegetable stock or
   water
1 small green chilli, roughly
   chopped

1–2 cloves garlic, roughly chopped
2 large tomatoes, roughly chopped
100g (3½oz) fresh spinach, chopped
100g (3½oz) green peas, shelled
12 red radishes, sliced
1 tsp honey
sea salt and cayenne pepper
   to taste
fresh coriander to garnish (optional)

Heat the oil in a heavy-based pan and gently stir-fry the cauliflower and the carrots for 2–3 minutes. Add the turmeric, stir for a further minute, then add the stock or water. Gently simmer while you blend the chilli, garlic and tomatoes. Add the blended mixture and the fresh spinach to the pan. Bring to the boil and simmer for 10 minutes. Add the peas, radishes and honey. Stir, heat through and simmer for a further 3 minutes. Season, garnish with fresh coriander (if using) and serve with rice or chapati.

MIDDLE EASTERN PUFFS

CALORIES	722
CHOLESTEROL	0
VEGAN CALORIES	722
POLYUNSATS	★★★
ANTIOXIDANTS	★★☆
CALCIUM	★★☆
IRON	★★☆
B VITAMINS	★★☆

100g (3½oz) walnuts, shelled
2 tbsp breadcrumbs
2 cloves garlic, crushed

½ tsp (pomegranate) molasses
2 tbsp olive oil
1 packet filo pastry sheets

Preheat the oven to 220°C/425°F/gas mark 7. Roughly crush the walnuts in a mortar or a blender. Add the breadcrumbs, garlic, molasses and oil, mix well and season. Cut the pastry into 10cm (4in) squares and use two layers of pastry for each square. Place a spoonful of filling along one edge of each square and fold in the sides. Roll each square into a finger shape and firmly press together the edges. Place on a greased baking tray and bake in the middle of a hot oven until golden (approximately 10 minutes). Serve with a green salad.

141 INDONESIAN SATAY

CALORIES	578
CHOLESTEROL	75
VEGAN CALORIES	540
POLYUNSATS	★★★
ANTIOXIDANTS	★★★
CALCIUM	★★☆
IRON	★★☆
B VITAMINS	★★★

150g (5½oz) chicken breast/tempeh
8 cherry tomatoes
8 oyster mushrooms
8 pearl onions
1 small yellow courgette, cut
   into chunks
1 red pepper, deseeded and cut
   into triangles

juice of 1 lime
2 cloves garlic, chopped
2 fresh hot chillies, chopped
1 tsp tamarind paste dissolved
   in 1 tbsp water
tamari (soya sauce) to taste
grapeseed oil for blending
3 tbsp peanut butter

Cut the chicken or tempeh into cubes. Spear the tomatoes, mushrooms, onions, courgette chunks, chicken or tempeh cubes and pepper triangles onto two metal barbecue skewers and place them on a tray. Blend the lime, garlic, chillies, tamarind paste and tamari with enough oil to make a thick marinade. Brush the kebabs with half the marinade and cook them on a medium–hot barbecue (or under a grill). Mix the remaining marinade with the peanut butter to make a dip for the kebabs, and serve.

142 AUBERGINE CATALANE

CALORIES	737
CHOLESTEROL	126
VEGAN CALORIES	610
POLYUNSATS	★★☆
ANTIOXIDANTS	★★☆
CALCIUM	★★☆
IRON	★★☆
B VITAMINS	★★★

100ml (3½oz) olive oil
2 pieces guinea fowl breast
   (approximately 175g [6oz] each)
   /175g (6oz) tempeh, sliced
2–3 aubergines, peeled and cut
   lengthways into ½cm (¼in) slices

1 portion sauce tomate concassé
   (see p.115)
1 tbsp fresh basil, chopped
60g (2¼oz) breadcrumbs
12 olives, pitted and sliced
sea salt and black pepper to taste

Brown the guinea fowl or tempeh in a little oil in a frying pan over a high heat. Set aside. Add some more oil to the pan and brown the aubergine slices on both sides. Remove and leave to dry on a kitchen towel. Then place layers of the dried aubergine slices in an ovenproof dish, alternating with the sauce tomate concassé. Sprinkle with the basil and top with the fried Guinea fowl or tempeh. Garnish with breadcrumbs and olives, season and bake at 220ºC/425ºF/gas mark 7 for 15 minutes. Serve with rice.

143 SUMMER SAMBAL

CALORIES	409
CHOLESTEROL	0
VEGAN CALORIES	409
POLYUNSATS	★★☆
ANTIOXIDANTS	★★★
CALCIUM	★☆☆
IRON	★★☆
B VITAMINS	★★☆

2 fresh red chillies, chopped
2 cloves garlic, chopped
juice from 1 lime
25g (1oz) roasted peanuts
1 tbsp tamarind paste
1 tbsp raw cane sugar
1–2 tsp tamari (soya sauce)
   (to taste)

2 carrots, chopped into thin sticks
½ Chinese cabbage, finely shredded
100g (3½oz) baby sweetcorn, halved
   lengthways
1 mango, peeled and diced
100g (3½oz) mangetout,
   diagonally sliced
1 large handful bean sprouts

Blend the red chillies, garlic, lime juice, peanuts, tamarind paste, sugar and tamari in a bowl with enough water to make a thick, coarse sauce. Place the remaining ingredients in a salad bowl, top with the sauce (sambal), gently toss and serve.

144 YELLOW COURGETTE OMELETTE
◧✕🌿

CALORIES	363
CHOLESTEROL	11
VEGAN CALORIES	333
POLYUNSATS	★★☆
ANTIOXIDANTS	★★☆
CALCIUM	★★☆
IRON	★★☆
B VITAMINS	★★☆

batter:
100g (3½oz) wheat flour
1 tsp baking powder
1 phial saffron
150ml (¼pt) soya milk/milk
1 tbsp olive oil
sea salt and black pepper to taste

filling:
1 yellow courgette, grated
1 tbsp fresh parsley, finely chopped
oil for frying

Beat the flour and baking powder in a bowl, add the saffron, milk and olive oil, and season. Then add the grated courgette and the fresh parsley and mix well. Heat 1 tablespoon of oil in a frying pan. When the oil is quite hot, pour in the omelette batter and spread it evenly to form a thick pancake. Turn down the heat and very slowly cook for 10 minutes. Turn and gently cook the other side over a medium heat for 5–7 minutes. Serve with a dressed tomato salad.

145 BASQUE OMELETTE
★✕🌿◉

CALORIES	235
CHOLESTEROL	417
VEGAN CALORIES	254
POLYUNSATS	★☆☆
ANTIOXIDANTS	★★★
CALCIUM	★★☆
IRON	★★☆
B VITAMINS	★★☆

omelette:
4 eggs
a little milk/water
sea salt and black pepper to taste
or 1 portion basic eggless omelette
    batter (see p.41)

filling:
oil for frying
100g (3½oz) tuna/seitan, chopped
1 shallot, finely chopped
1 green pepper, deseeded and finely
    chopped
1 large ripe tomato, finely chopped
sea salt and black pepper to taste

Heat a little oil in a frying pan and sauté the tuna or seitan with the shallot until they begin to brown. Add the green pepper and the tomato, heat through, season and set aside (keep warm). Beat the eggs in a bowl, add the milk or water and season. Alternatively, prepare the eggless omelette batter. Add a little more oil to the pan, pour in your chosen batter and spread it evenly over the pan. Turn down the heat and gently cook until the omelette is set. Add the filling, fold, remove from the heat and serve.

146 OMELETTE FORESTIÈRE
♥✕

CALORIES	390
CHOLESTEROL	1
VEGAN CALORIES	387
POLYUNSATS	★★★
ANTIOXIDANTS	★★☆
CALCIUM	★☆☆
IRON	★☆☆
B VITAMINS	★★☆

batter:
500g (1lb 2oz) potatoes, grated
1 leek, finely chopped
1 tbsp soya milk/milk
sea salt and black pepper to taste

2 tbsp grapeseed oil

filling:
200g (7oz) chanterelle mushrooms,
    sliced and braised

Mix the potatoes and the leek in a bowl to form a coarse, flaky paste, add the milk, and season. Heat the oil in a frying pan, add the potato and leek mixture and spread it over the pan to form a 2cm (¾in) thick pancake. Cook until the underside is firm and golden. Spread the cooked chanterelles over one half of the mixture, fold like an omelette, remove from the heat and serve with pickled cucumber or cucumber salad.

147 ▼ SPANISH OMELETTE
★🌾🥜

CALORIES	360
CHOLESTEROL	391
VEGAN CALORIES	369
POLYUNSATS	★★☆
ANTIOXIDANTS	★★★
CALCIUM	★★☆
IRON	★★☆
B VITAMINS	★★★

omelette:
4 eggs
or 1 portion basic eggless omelette batter (see p.41)
1 small yellow courgette, grated

filling:
olive oil for frying
1 red pepper, deseeded and diced
1 tomato, chopped
1 clove garlic, crushed
1 handful parsley, finely chopped
sea salt and black pepper to taste

Beat the eggs in a bowl, or alternatively, prepare the eggless batter. Add the courgette. Stir-fry the filling ingredients in a frying pan with a little oil for 3 minutes, then add to the batter, and season. Add a little more oil to the pan and pour in the mixture. Turn down the heat and leave the mixture to cook very slowly for 10 minutes. Turn and cook over a medium heat for a further 5–7 minutes. Then fold in half and serve with spicy tomato sauce.

148 ▼ INSTANT TORTILLAS WITH PEPPER FILLING

★ ♥ 🌢 🍃

CALORIES	774
CHOLESTEROL	75
VEGAN CALORIES	678
POLYUNSATS	★★★
ANTIOXIDANTS	★★★
CALCIUM	★★☆
IRON	★★☆
B VITAMINS	★★★

tortillas:
1 packet ready-made corn tortillas

filling:
oil for frying
1 small red onion, halved and sliced
150g (5½oz) chicken breast/75g (2¾oz) tempeh, diced

1 small green chilli, deseeded and finely chopped
1 tsp ground coriander
½ each of a red, yellow and green pepper, deseeded and sliced
1 tbsp tamari (soya sauce)
2 tbsp bean sprouts
1 tbsp coriander leaves, chopped

Heat a little oil in a wok or frying pan and stir-fry the onion. Add the chicken breast or tempeh and fry until golden. Then add the chilli and coriander, together with the pepper slices, and stir-fry for 3 minutes. Add the tamari (and a little water if necessary). Turn down the heat and leave to simmer while you prepare six ready-made tortillas as indicated on the packet. Add the bean sprouts and coriander leaves to the wok or pan. Heat through. Divide the filling between the tortillas, roll and serve.

149   OYSTER MUSHROOM PANCAKES

⭐🌿🟫

CALORIES	643
CHOLESTEROL	227
VEGAN CALORIES	604
POLYUNSATS	★★★
ANTIOXIDANTS	★★☆
CALCIUM	★★☆
IRON	★★☆
B VITAMINS	★★☆

pancakes:
1 portion basic pancake batter
   (see p.42)
2 tbsp fresh mixed parsley, thyme
   and chives, finely chopped
2 tbsp cheese/soya cheese, grated
grapeseed oil for frying

filling:
1 tbsp olive oil
200g (7oz) oyster mushrooms,
   sliced
50g (1¾oz) walnut halves
sea salt and black pepper to taste
juice of ½ lemon

Mix the batter ingredients in a bowl with the fresh herbs and the cheese. Heat the olive oil in a frying pan and stir-fry the mushrooms until their moisture has evaporated. Add the walnuts, season and set aside. Heat the grapeseed oil in a separate frying pan and fry each pancake on one side, then turn and top with a spoonful of mushrooms and walnuts. Fold the pancakes, sprinkle with lemon juice and serve.

150   ASPARAGUS AND CHEESE CRÊPES

⭐💧🌿🟫

CALORIES	750
CHOLESTEROL	242
VEGAN CALORIES	684
POLYUNSATS	★★★
ANTIOXIDANTS	★★☆
CALCIUM	★★★
IRON	★★★
B VITAMINS	★★★

crêpes:
1 portion basic pancake batter
   (see p.42)
grapeseed oil for frying

filling:
1 large ripe avocado, halved

2 tsp white tahini
1 tbsp lemon juice
1 bunch fresh asparagus, steamed
50g (1¾oz) Gruyère/soya cheese/
   brewer's yeast flakes
sea salt and black pepper to taste

Mix the batter ingredients in a bowl and set aside. Scoop out the avocado flesh and mash it in a bowl with the tahini and the lemon juice. Heat a little oil in a frying pan and fry the crêpes. Spread 1 tablespoon of the avocado cream on each crêpe, add 3 cooked asparagus spears to each one and season. Roll and place in a greased ovenproof dish. Sprinkle with cheese or brewer's yeast flakes and grill or bake in a preheated oven at 220°C/425°F/gas mark 7 until the top is golden. Serve with a salad.

151   PROVENÇAL PANCAKES

⭐❤️🌿🟫

CALORIES	742
CHOLESTEROL	21
VEGAN CALORIES	682
POLYUNSATS	★★★
ANTIOXIDANTS	★★★
CALCIUM	★★☆
IRON	★★☆
B VITAMINS	★★★

pancakes:
100g (3½oz) wheat flour (spelt
   if possible)
4 tbsp soya flour
approximately 300ml (½pt)
   milk/soya milk
2 tbsp olive oil
grapeseed oil for frying

filling:
1 leek, chopped
1 green pepper, deseeded and
   sliced
2 large ripe tomatoes, chopped
12 black olives, pitted and chopped
1 tbsp fresh basil, chopped
sea salt and black pepper to taste

Whisk the two flours with the milk, olive oil and a pinch of salt. Set aside. Sweat the leek in a saucepan with a little olive oil for 2 minutes. Add the green pepper, tomatoes, olives and fresh basil. Cover and simmer for 5 minutes. Season and fry the pancakes in a frying pan with grapeseed oil. Place 2 tablespoons of filling on each pancake, fold and serve.

152 PIZZA MARGHERITA

⭐❤️🌾🌱

CALORIES	454
CHOLESTEROL	29
VEGAN CALORIES	401
POLYUNSATS	★☆☆
ANTIOXIDANTS	★★☆
CALCIUM	★★☆
IRON	★★☆
B VITAMINS	★★☆

1 pizza base
2 tbsp tomato sauce (passata) or
   sauce tomate concassé (see p.115)

2 fresh ripe plum tomatoes, sliced
oregano to taste
100g (3½oz) mozzarella/soya cheese

Preheat the oven to 240°C/475°F/gas mark 9 and warm up the pizza tray. Spread the tomato sauce over the prepared base. Add the tomatoes and plenty of oregano. Season to taste. Grate the cheese and sprinkle it over the pizza. Bake in a hot oven for 10–15 minutes. Serve hot.

153 ▼ PESTO PIZZA

⭐❤️💧🌾🌱

CALORIES	862
CHOLESTEROL	67
VEGAN CALORIES	720
POLYUNSATS	★★★
ANTIOXIDANTS	★★★
CALCIUM	★★★
IRON	★★★
B VITAMINS	★★☆

1 pizza base
2 tbsp pesto
10 cherry tomatoes, halved
100g (3½oz) spinach, sautéed
100g (3½oz) feta cheese/marinated
   tofu, cubed

10 sun-dried tomatoes, chopped
oregano, sea salt and black pepper
   to taste
100g (3½oz) mozzarella/soya
   cheese, grated

Preheat the oven to 240°C/475°F/gas mark 9 and warm up the pizza tray. Cover the prepared base with the pesto. Top with the cherry tomatoes, spinach, feta or tofu and sun-dried tomatoes. Sprinkle with oregano, season and sprinkle with mozzarella or soya cheese. Bake in a hot oven for approximately 20 minutes. Serve hot with a side salad.

PIZZA ATHENA

154

CALORIES	611
CHOLESTEROL	64
VEGAN CALORIES	469
POLYUNSATS	★☆☆
ANTIOXIDANTS	★★★
CALCIUM	★★★
IRON	★★★
B VITAMINS	★★☆

1 large handful fresh spinach
1 pizza base
2 tbsp tomato sauce (passata) or
  sauce tomate concassé
  (see p.115)
1 small red onion, chopped
100g (3½oz) feta cheese/tofu, cut
  into small chunks

10 kalamata olives, pitted
1 fresh tomato, sliced
1 tsp fresh thyme
1 tbsp fresh marjoram, chopped
sea salt and black pepper to taste
100g (3½oz) mozzarella/soya
  cheese, grated

Preheat the oven to 240°C/475°F/gas mark 9 and warm up the pizza tray. Meanwhile, chop the spinach and blanch it in a saucepan of boiling water. Drain and set aside. Cover the prepared base with the tomato sauce. Top with the red onion, followed by the cooked spinach, feta or tofu chunks, olives and fresh tomato slices. Sprinkle with the herbs, and season. Then sprinkle with the grated mozzarella or soya cheese and bake in a hot oven for approximately 15 minutes. Serve hot with a cucumber and yoghurt dip (tzatziki).

PIZZA ALLA ROMANA

155

CALORIES	527
CHOLESTEROL	45
VEGAN CALORIES	452
POLYUNSATS	★★☆
ANTIOXIDANTS	★★★
CALCIUM	★★☆
IRON	★★☆
B VITAMINS	★★☆

1 pizza base
2–3 tbsp tomato sauce (passata) or
  sauce tomate concassé
  (see p.115)
1 tsp hot chilli paste
100g (3½oz) mozzarella/soya
  cheese, grated

1 large fresh, ripe tomato, sliced
2 tbsp fresh basil, chopped
1 medium green pepper, halved,
  deseeded and sliced
50g (1¾oz) anchovies/black olives,
  pitted
sea salt and black pepper to taste

Preheat the oven to 240°C/475°F/gas mark 9 and warm up the pizza tray. Spread the tomato sauce over the prepared base and sprinkle with the hot chilli paste, followed by the grated cheese. Top with the fresh tomato slices, fresh basil, green pepper slices and anchovies or olives. Season and bake in a hot oven for approximately 15 minutes. Serve hot with a side salad.

SUMMER SPECIAL

156

CALORIES	595
CHOLESTEROL	97
VEGAN CALORIES	428
POLYUNSATS	★★☆
ANTIOXIDANTS	★★☆
CALCIUM	★★★
IRON	★★☆
B VITAMINS	★★☆

1 pizza base
2 cloves garlic, crushed and mixed
  with 1 tbsp olive oil
1 small courgette, sliced and
  sautéed
100g (3½oz) smoked chicken

breast/smoked tofu, diced
100g (3½oz) camembert/smoked
  soya cheese, thinly sliced
sea salt and black pepper to taste
2 tbsp fresh herbs (chervil, tarragon,
  basil and parsley), chopped

Preheat the oven to 240°C/475°F/gas mark 9 and warm up the pizza tray. Cover the prepared base with the garlic paste. Top with the courgette, smoked chicken or tofu and cheese. Season and bake in a hot oven for approximately 15 minutes. Garnish with more black pepper and the chopped fresh herbs. Serve hot with a side salad.

157 BASQUE PIPERADE

CALORIES	501
CHOLESTEROL	403
VEGAN CALORIES	498
POLYUNSATS	★★★
ANTIOXIDANTS	★★★
CALCIUM	★★☆
IRON	★★★
B VITAMINS	★★★

2 tbsp olive oil
500g (1lb 2oz) tomatoes, chopped
1 red and 1 green pepper, sliced
75g (2³⁄₄oz) Bayonne ham, diced/
    100g (3½oz) kidney beans,
    cooked or canned

200g (7oz) green peas, shelled
4 eggs, beaten/125g (4½oz)
    crumbled tofu and 25g (1oz)
    vegetable margarine
sea salt and black pepper to taste

Heat the oil in a large, heavy-based frying pan and gently fry the tomatoes and the peppers for 15 minutes. Add the ham or kidney beans and the peas, cover and cook for a further 5 minutes. Add the beaten eggs to the vegetables and cook until they are scrambled (but still quite soft), and season. Alternatively, scramble the tofu with the margarine in a separate pan, season and then add to the vegetables. Serve hot with toast.

158 SESAME AND HONEY GOUJONS

CALORIES	510
CHOLESTEROL	130
VEGAN CALORIES	347
POLYUNSATS	★★★
ANTIOXIDANTS	★★☆
CALCIUM	★☆☆
IRON	★★☆
B VITAMINS	★★☆

2 chicken breasts, sliced/200g (7oz)
    seitan, sliced
3 tbsp tamari (soya sauce)
1 tbsp honey
2 tbsp sesame seeds

olive oil for frying
1 clove garlic, chopped
½ tbsp red wine vinegar
black pepper to taste

Marinate the chicken or seitan slices in 1 tablespoon of tamari and half of the honey. Then dip the slices in the sesame seeds until they are completely coated, and fry them with oil in a casserole dish over a medium heat until brown. Set aside. Fry the garlic for 1 minute, then add the remaining honey and simmer for 2 minutes until the honey changes colour. Add the vinegar and the remaining tamari, heat through and season. Spoon the sauce over the goujons and serve with rice.

159 POLENTA GRATIN

CALORIES	586
CHOLESTEROL	80
VEGAN CALORIES	505
POLYUNSATS	★★☆
ANTIOXIDANTS	★★☆
CALCIUM	★★☆
IRON	★★☆
B VITAMINS	★★★

olive oil for stir-frying
1 red onion, chopped
150g (5½oz) chicken breast/seitan,
    diced
12 black olives, pitted and chopped
1 tbsp fresh coriander
sea salt and black pepper to taste

2 plum tomatoes, chopped
125g (4½oz) polenta
1 stick celery, sliced
100g (3½oz) green beans, topped
    and tailed and chopped
1 tbsp Parmesan/brewer's yeast
    flakes

Preheat the oven to 240°C/475°F/gas mark 9. Gently stir-fry the red onion and the chicken or seitan in a wok or a frying pan with oil until brown. Add the olives and coriander, stir for 30 seconds, season and set aside. Heat 2 tablespoons of oil in a frying pan, add the tomatoes and polenta and stir-fry for 2 minutes, then add the celery and beans. Simmer for 5 minutes. Place half of the chicken or seitan in a roasting tin, add half of the tomato and polenta mixture, then add another layer of chicken or seitan, finishing with a layer of tomato and polenta. Sprinkle with Parmesan or brewer's yeast flakes. Bake for 5 minutes and serve.

160 ▲ BARBECUE WITH RATATOUILLE KEBABS
★♥∅

CALORIES	403
CHOLESTEROL	56
VEGAN CALORIES	431
POLYUNSATS	★★☆
ANTIOXIDANTS	★★★
CALCIUM	★☆☆
IRON	★★☆
B VITAMINS	★★☆

1 small red onion, quartered
1 small aubergine, cut into chunks
1 small courgette, cut into thick
  slices
1 red pepper, cut into triangles
1 green pepper, cut into triangles
2 cloves garlic, halved

10 cherry tomatoes
3 tbsp olive oil
2 tsp herbes de Provence
sea salt and black pepper to taste
2 turkey/ready-made vegetable
  steaks

Alternately spear the vegetable pieces, garlic halves and tomatoes onto
two metal barbecue skewers, brush with oil, sprinkle with herbs and
season. Grill the vegetables kebabs over hot embers, turning frequently.
Meanwhile, brush the turkey or vegetable steaks with oil and grill until
they are brown and cooked through. Serve with the kebabs and chunky
cherry tomato sauce and pesto.

161 STEAK PROVENÇALE
⭐🌢🌿🥜

CALORIES	718
CHOLESTEROL	176
VEGAN CALORIES	477
POLYUNSATS	★★☆
ANTIOXIDANTS	★★☆
CALCIUM	★★☆
IRON	★★☆
B VITAMINS	★★☆

1 clove garlic, chopped
1 tbsp parsley, finely chopped
3 tbsp breadcrumbs
2 medium tomatoes, halved and deseeded
5 large mushrooms, stalks removed and set aside

olive oil for frying
1 shallot, finely chopped
½ clove garlic, finely chopped
4 lamb chops/2 ready-made soya steaks
1 tsp thyme
sea salt and black pepper to taste

Preheat the oven to 220°C/425°F/gas mark 7. Mix one clove of garlic with the parsley and breadcrumbs to make a stuffing. Season the tomatoes and fill them with some of the stuffing. Set aside. Finely chop the mushroom stalks and one of the mushrooms. Heat 1 tablespoon of oil in a casserole dish and gently fry the shallot, chopped mushroom and garlic. Mix the mushroom with the remaining stuffing and check the seasoning. Then stuff the four mushrooms and place on a greased baking tray with the stuffed tomatoes. Bake for 15 minutes. Meanwhile, sprinkle the chops or soya steaks with thyme and season, then grill on both sides. Serve on large plates garnished with the stuffed tomatoes and stuffed mushrooms.

162 SUMMER TAPAS TARTS
⭐❤🌢🌿🥜

CALORIES	607
CHOLESTEROL	23
VEGAN CALORIES	564
POLYUNSATS	★★★
ANTIOXIDANTS	★★★
CALCIUM	★★☆
IRON	★★★
B VITAMINS	★★★

150g (5½oz) spelt flour
1 tbsp dried yeast
¼ tsp salt
2 tbsp sunflower oil
100ml (3½oz) tepid water
250g (9oz) tomatoes, chopped
½ shallot, chopped
1 small red pepper, chopped
1 tbsp fresh parsley, chopped
1 tsp paprika
¼ tsp each of sugar and sea salt

1 dash Tabasco sauce
2 cloves garlic, chopped
½ aubergine, thinly sliced
8–10 brown mushrooms, thinly sliced
oregano to taste
sea salt and black pepper to taste
grated mozzarella/soya cheese to taste
2 tbsp brewer's yeast flakes

Preheat the oven to 200°C/400°F/gas mark 6. Combine the flour and yeast with the salt. Add the oil and water and knead to a soft dough. Set aside. Blend the tomatoes, shallot, red pepper, parsley, paprika, sugar, salt, Tabasco sauce and garlic. Set aside. Stir-fry the aubergine in a frying pan with a little oil until golden and set aside. Cut the dough into two halves and roll it out. Then place each of the rolled-out halves in two 10cm (4in) pie dishes. Add the blended tomato mixture, followed by a layer of aubergine and mushroom slices. Sprinkle with oregano, season and sprinkle with grated cheese and brewer's yeast flakes. Bake in the middle of a hot oven for 10–15 minutes, or until they begin to brown, and serve.

163 STUFFED MUSHROOMS
★♥🌾🥚🧀🥛

CALORIES	686
CHOLESTEROL	48
VEGAN CALORIES	542
POLYUNSATS	★★★
ANTIOXIDANTS	★★★
CALCIUM	★★☆
IRON	★★☆
B VITAMINS	★★☆

2 tbsp olive oil
6 large flat mushrooms, stalks
  removed and chopped
2 tbsp almonds, chopped
2 tbsp breadcrumbs

100g (3½oz) soft cheese/
  soya cheese
1 tbsp lemon juice
2 tbsp fresh parsley, chopped
1 tbsp paprika

Preheat the oven to 200°C/400°F/gas mark 6. Fry the mushroom stalks and the almonds in a frying pan with a little oil, then mix them with the breadcrumbs and the cheese. Season and set aside. Place the mushroom caps upside down on a baking tray and brush with the lemon juice and the oil. Add the filling and bake in a hot oven for 20 minutes. Garnish with fresh parsley and paprika, and serve with toast and salad.

164 LAMB OR TEMPEH SLICES WITH FLAGEOLET BEANS
★

CALORIES	565
CHOLESTEROL	99
VEGAN CALORIES	457
POLYUNSATS	★☆☆
ANTIOXIDANTS	★★☆
CALCIUM	★★☆
IRON	★★★
B VITAMINS	★★☆

1 tbsp olive oil
2 leg-of-lamb slices/175g (6oz)
  smoked tempeh, sliced
2 shallots, chopped
½ glass dry white wine
100ml (3½oz) chicken/vegetable
  stock

400g (14oz) flageolet beans,
  cooked or canned
1 clove garlic, chopped
1 pinch thyme
sea salt and black pepper to taste
1 tbsp fresh parsley, finely chopped

Cook the lamb or tempeh in a casserole dish with the oil for 2 minutes on each side. Set aside. Add the shallots to the pan and gently fry them until soft. Pour in the white wine and let it reduce to one-third of its volume. Add the stock, beans, garlic and thyme, and season. Gently simmer for 10 minutes. Meanwhile, reheat the lamb or tempeh under the grill. Add the parsley to the beans before serving hot with the lamb or tempeh slices.

165 AUBERGINES FARCIE
★♥🌾🥚🧀

CALORIES	544
CHOLESTEROL	38
VEGAN CALORIES	443
POLYUNSATS	★★☆
ANTIOXIDANTS	★★★
CALCIUM	★★☆
IRON	★★☆
B VITAMINS	★★☆

olive oil for frying
1 aubergine, sliced lengthways
1 small courgette, halved and sliced
  lengthways
2 small potatoes, finely sliced
1 red pepper, finely sliced
150g (5½oz) spicy sausage

(pork/soya), grated
1 thick slice bread, soaked in
  milk/soya milk and grated
1 clove garlic, grated
sea salt and black pepper to taste
250g (9oz) tomatoes, blended
1–2 tsp paprika

Preheat the oven to 220°C/425°F/gas mark 7. Fry the aubergines in a saucepan with oil until golden and place in the bottom of an oiled baking dish. Add the courgette, potatoes and pepper in layers. Mix the sausage, bread and garlic in a bowl, then season and spoon onto the vegetables. Pour the blended tomatoes over the mixture and make some holes with your finger, so that the liquid can run through each layer. Sprinkle with paprika and a little oil. Bake until it begins to brown. Serve hot or cold.

166 BAKED TOMATOES WITH WALNUTS
⭐❤️💧🚫

CALORIES	519
CHOLESTEROL	5
VEGAN CALORIES	507
POLYUNSATS	★★★
ANTIOXIDANTS	★★★
CALCIUM	★★☆
IRON	★★☆
B VITAMINS	★★☆

4 large beef tomatoes
100g (3½oz) chopped walnuts
100g (3½oz) green peas, shelled
   and blanched
1 clove garlic, crushed
1 tbsp olive oil

1 tsp balsamic vinegar
1 tbsp fresh basil, chopped
sea salt and black pepper to taste
1 tbsp Parmesan/brewer's yeast
   flakes

Preheat the oven to 220°C/425°F/gas mark 7. Slice off the tops of the tomatoes and set the tops aside. Scoop out the tomato seeds with a teaspoon. Lightly toast the walnuts in a saucepan and mix in the peas. Add the garlic, oil, vinegar and basil. Gently mix and season. Fill the tomatoes with the walnut mix and sprinkle with Parmesan or brewer's yeast flakes. Put the tops back on the tomatoes and bake on the top shelf of a hot oven for 10–15 minutes. Serve with rice or bread and salad.

167 PISSALADIÈRE
❤️🌿

CALORIES	584
CHOLESTEROL	11
VEGAN CALORIES	568
POLYUNSATS	★★★
ANTIOXIDANTS	★★☆
CALCIUM	★★☆
IRON	★★☆
B VITAMINS	★★☆

1 packet ready-made shortcrust
   pastry, rolled out very thinly
2 tbsp olive oil
500g (1lb 2oz) onions, halved
   and sliced
1 clove garlic, chopped

1 tsp thyme
1 bay leaf
sea salt and black pepper to taste
1 tbsp capers
12 anchovy fillets/12 black olives,
   pitted

Preheat the oven to 240°C/475°F/gas mark 9. Place the rolled-out pastry in a 20cm (8in) round baking tray. Gently sauté the onions in a saucepan with the oil until soft. Add the garlic, thyme and bay leaf, heat through and season. Pour the onion mixture onto the pastry shell, garnish with capers and anchovies or olives. Bake for 15 minutes. Serve with a green salad.

168 SUMMER KEBABS
⭐🚫🚫

CALORIES	676
CHOLESTEROL	138
VEGAN CALORIES	462
POLYUNSATS	★★☆
ANTIOXIDANTS	★★★
CALCIUM	★★★
IRON	★★★
B VITAMINS	★★★

10 cherry tomatoes
1 red pepper, cut into chunks
1 yellow courgette, cut into chunks
250g (9oz) lamb fillet/125g (4½oz)
   tofu, cut into cubes
1 aubergine, cut into chunks
2 shallots, halved
16 button mushrooms, kept whole
4 bay leaves, halved

marinade:
175ml (6fl oz) tomato ketchup
juice of 1 lemon
1 tbsp raw cane sugar
6 cloves garlic, crushed
2 tsp thyme
2 tbsp olive oil
1 tbsp mustard

Mix all the marinade ingredients in a bowl. Add the prepared kebab ingredients and gently mix. Cover and leave to marinate (for 2 hours, if possible, but a much shorter time will suffice). Then thread the marinated vegetables onto two metal skewers and brush with the marinade. Place the kebabs on a hot barbecue (or under a hot grill) for 10 minutes, turning from time to time. Serve hot on a bed of boiled rice cooked with saffron, salt and canned chick peas, accompanied by a green salad.

169 ▼ LEMON RISOTTO WITH FRESH BASIL
★ ♥ ◊ ▨

CALORIES	533
CHOLESTEROL	9
VEGAN CALORIES	504
POLYUNSATS	★★☆
ANTIOXIDANTS	★★★
CALCIUM	★☆☆
IRON	★★☆
B VITAMINS	★★☆

2 tbsp olive oil
1 leek (with half the top), sliced
2 sticks celery (with leaves), sliced
1 clove garlic, crushed
150g (5½oz) risotto rice
75ml (2½fl oz) dry vermouth

500ml (18fl oz) vegetable stock, heated
1 lemon, quartered and sliced
3 tbsp fresh basil, chopped
2 tbsp Parmesan/1tbsp brewer's yeast flakes

Heat the oil in a large, heavy-based casserole dish and gently stir-fry the leek and the celery until soft. Add the garlic and the rice, stir for 1 minute, then add the vermouth. Stir for a further minute, then add the stock. Bring to the boil, cover and very gently simmer until the rice is cooked. Add the lemon pieces and most of the basil, gently stir and heat through. Sprinkle with Parmesan or brewer's yeast flakes and the remaining basil, and serve immediately.

170 ▲ POACHED FIGS, APRICOTS AND CHERRIES

✪ ♥ 🌢 ❌ ▢

CALORIES	145
CHOLESTEROL	0
VEGAN CALORIES	145
POLYUNSATS	★☆☆
ANTIOXIDANTS	★★☆
CALCIUM	★☆☆
IRON	★☆☆
B VITAMINS	★☆☆

150ml (¼pt) apple juice
1 tbsp brandy (optional)
1 tsp maple syrup
4 fresh figs, quartered

4 apricots, quartered and pitted
8 cherries, halved and pitted
2 tbsp orange juice

Heat the apple juice in a casserole dish with the brandy (if using) and the maple syrup. Add the figs, apricots and cherries. Bring to the boil, cover and gently simmer for 5 minutes. Lift out the fruit with a slotted spoon and place them in a salad bowl. Bring the juice back to the boil and reduce to a thick syrup. Pour the syrup over the fruit, add the fresh orange juice and serve with vanilla ice cream, custard, crème fraîche or soya cream.

171 APRICOT TART

CALORIES	657
CHOLESTEROL	0
VEGAN CALORIES	657
POLYUNSATS	★★★
ANTIOXIDANTS	★★★
CALCIUM	★★☆
IRON	★★☆
B VITAMINS	★★☆

1 packet ready-made shortcrust
    pastry, rolled out
500g (1lb 2oz) ripe apricots, pitted
    and halved, plus 3 for blending

2 tbsp liquid honey
1 tbsp almond butter
2 dates, pitted
100ml (3½fl oz) apple juice

Preheat the oven to 220°C/425°F/gas mark 7. Place the pastry in a 10cm (4in) round baking tray and prick it in a few places. Arrange the apricot halves over the base (cut side down) and sprinkle with the honey. Bake in a hot oven for approximately 20 minutes. Blend the almond butter with the three apricots, the dates and the apple juice, and serve with the tart.

172 SPICY PEACHES

CALORIES	108
CHOLESTEROL	0
VEGAN CALORIES	108
POLYUNSATS	★☆☆
ANTIOXIDANTS	★★☆
CALCIUM	★☆☆
IRON	★☆☆
B VITAMINS	★☆☆

2 large ripe peaches, peeled,
    pitted and sliced
1 tsp ground cumin
2 tbsp maple syrup

1 tbsp lemon juice
1 pinch cayenne pepper
1 tsp fresh ginger, finely chopped

Place the peaches in a small serving bowl. Roast the cumin in a dry frying pan for 15 seconds, then mix with the remaining ingredients. Pour the dressing over the peaches. Serve with pancakes and plain or soya yoghurt.

173 WATERMELON SALAD

CALORIES	346
CHOLESTEROL	0
VEGAN CALORIES	346
POLYUNSATS	★★☆
ANTIOXIDANTS	★★★
CALCIUM	★★☆
IRON	★★☆
B VITAMINS	★★☆

½ watermelon, peeled, deseeded
    and diced
100g (3½oz) raspberries
1 nectarine, quartered and diced

4 greengages, quartered
½ honeydew melon
150ml (¼pt) apple juice
50g (1¾oz) hazelnuts, chopped

Place the prepared watermelon, raspberries, nectarine and greengages in a glass bowl. Peel, deseed and dice the honeydew melon and blend it with the apple juice, then pour over the fruit. Garnish with hazelnuts and serve.

174 RHUBARB AND STRAWBERRY COMPOTE

CALORIES	53
CHOLESTEROL	0
VEGAN CALORIES	53
POLYUNSATS	★☆☆
ANTIOXIDANTS	★★☆
CALCIUM	★★☆
IRON	★☆☆
B VITAMINS	★☆☆

300g (10½oz) rhubarb, sliced
1 tsp vanilla sugar
200g (7oz) strawberries, hulled

    and halved
1 tsp fresh ginger, finely chopped
maple syrup to taste

Place the rhubarb slices in a medium casserole dish, sprinkle with the vanilla sugar and cover with water. Bring to the boil and simmer for 10 minutes. Add the strawberries and the ginger. Heat through and simmer for a further 4–5 minutes. Season with maple syrup and serve.

175 SUMMER FRUIT SALAD

CALORIES	268
CHOLESTEROL	0
VEGAN CALORIES	268
POLYUNSATS	★☆☆
ANTIOXIDANTS	★★★
CALCIUM	★★☆
IRON	★★☆
B VITAMINS	★★☆

¼ watermelon
4 apricots, halved and sliced
1 peach, quartered and sliced
10 strawberries, hulled and halved
10 cherries, halved and pitted

20 raspberries
1 peeled banana and 1 nectarine
100ml (3½fl oz) unsweetened
   orange juice
1 pinch nutmeg

Peel, deseed and dice the watermelon and mix with the apricots, peach, strawberries, cherries and raspberries in a glass bowl. Blend the banana and the nectarine with the orange juice. Place the fruit in two large glasses, top with the sauce and garnish with nutmeg. Serve immediately.

176 BERRY SALAD

CALORIES	200
CHOLESTEROL	0
VEGAN CALORIES	200
POLYUNSATS	★★☆
ANTIOXIDANTS	★★★
CALCIUM	★★☆
IRON	★☆☆
B VITAMINS	★☆☆

100g (3½oz) strawberries, hulled
   and sliced
50g (1¾oz) each of raspberries,
   blackberries and blackcurrants

100g (3½oz) cherries, halved
   and pitted
1 tbsp almond butter
2 apricots, pitted and chopped

Mix the berries in a glass bowl. Blend the almond butter and the apricots with enough water to make a thick cream. Add the cream to the berries and gently coat. Serve immediately.

177 MELON NESTS

CALORIES	153
CHOLESTEROL	0
VEGAN CALORIES	153
POLYUNSATS	★☆☆
ANTIOXIDANTS	★★★
CALCIUM	★☆☆
IRON	★☆☆
B VITAMINS	★☆☆

1 cantaloupe melon, halved and
   deseeded
4 Little Gem lettuce leaves, shredded
10 strawberries, quartered

12 cherries, halved and pitted
2 tbsp lemon juice
2 tsp maple syrup
1 tsp fresh ginger, finely chopped

Scoop out the melon flesh with a melon baller, leaving a 1cm (½in) thick edge of flesh. Arrange the lettuce leaves in the hollowed melons. Mix the melon balls with the remaining ingredients. Divide the mixture between the two melon nests and serve immediately.

178 STRAWBERRY SALAD

CALORIES	189
CHOLESTEROL	0
VEGAN CALORIES	189
POLYUNSATS	★☆☆
ANTIOXIDANTS	★★★
CALCIUM	★☆☆
IRON	★★☆
B VITAMINS	★★☆

2 large Iceberg lettuce leaves
350g (12oz) strawberries, halved
1 peach, halved and sliced
1 pear, quartered, cored and sliced

1 banana, peeled
1 tbsp maple syrup
1 tbsp fresh mint, finely chopped

Divide the lettuce leaves between two plates and top with 250g (9oz) strawberries, and the peach and pear slices. Blend the remaining 100g (3½oz) strawberries with the banana, maple syrup and enough water to make a thick purée. Pour over the fruit, garnish with mint and serve.

179 FRUITY PANCAKES ⭐🌾

CALORIES	665
CHOLESTEROL	227
VEGAN CALORIES	581
POLYUNSATS	★★★
ANTIOXIDANTS	★★★
CALCIUM	★★☆
IRON	★★☆
B VITAMINS	★★☆

pancakes:
1 portion basic pancake batter
  (see p.42)

(see p.42)

filling:
1 banana, peeled and thinly sliced
1 nectarine, quartered and sliced
8 gooseberries, halved
3 blue plums, quartered
1 pinch cinnamon
2 tbsp hazelnuts, chopped
oil for frying

Mix the batter ingredients and set aside. Combine the fruit in a bowl. Heat a little oil in a frying pan and fry the pancakes for 2 minutes on each side. Fill each pancake with 2 tablespoons of fruit, sprinkle with cinnamon and hazelnuts, and serve immediately with lemon wedges and maple syrup.

180 FRUIT BROCHETTES ⭐♥💧🍃

CALORIES	447
CHOLESTEROL	0
VEGAN CALORIES	447
POLYUNSATS	★★★
ANTIOXIDANTS	★★★
CALCIUM	★★☆
IRON	★★☆
B VITAMINS	★☆☆

4 small figs
1 pear, cored and quartered
1 banana, peeled and cut
  into chunks
1 thick slice pineapple, peeled and
  cut into chunks

4 small apricots, halved and pitted
4 strawberries
2 tbsp maple syrup
2 tbsp lemon juice
2 tbsp toasted sesame oil

Thread the fruit onto two metal barbecue skewers. Make a marinade of the maple syrup, lemon juice and sesame oil in a bowl. Generously brush the fruit brochettes with the marinade and place on a barbecue (or under a medium–hot grill) for 2–3 minutes. Turn, brush again and grill the other side for a further 1–2 minutes. Repeat until the fruit begins to turn golden (don't let it turn soft). Serve hot with plain or soya yoghurt.

181 FRUIT PARFAIT ⭐♥💧🍃

CALORIES	531
CHOLESTEROL	0
VEGAN CALORIES	531
POLYUNSATS	★★★
ANTIOXIDANTS	★★★
CALCIUM	★★☆
IRON	★★☆
B VITAMINS	★★☆

½ cantaloupe melon, deseeded
100g (3½oz) raspberries
8 cherries, pitted
1 peach, quartered and diced
100g (3½oz) blackberries
2 passion fruit, halved and flesh
  scooped out
1 tbsp lemon juice

2 cloves, crushed in a mortar
¼ tsp each of cinnamon and ground
  coriander
1 tbsp almond butter
1 banana, peeled
25g (1oz) dark chocolate, grated
  (optional)
2 tbsp pistachio nuts, chopped

Scoop out the melon flesh with a melon baller. Layer the fruit (except for the banana) and berries in two tall parfait glasses. Blend the lemon juice and spices with the almond butter, banana and enough water to make a thick cream. Spoon the cream over the fruit and berries and allow it to run down through the layers. Garnish with chocolate (if using) and nuts, and serve immediately with a scoop of ice cream or soya ice cream.

HONEY FRUIT SALAD

⭐💚💧🫒

CALORIES	482
CHOLESTEROL	0
VEGAN CALORIES	482
POLYUNSATS	★☆☆
ANTIOXIDANTS	★★★
CALCIUM	★★☆
IRON	★★☆
B VITAMINS	★★☆

100g (3½oz) dried apricots, raisins and peaches
200ml (⅓pt) orange juice
1 tsp honey
1 honeydew melon, peeled, deseeded and cubed
1 banana, peeled and sliced
2 ripe peaches, halved and thinly sliced
8 strawberries, thinly sliced
1 apple, cored and diced
2 tbsp coconut, freshly grated or desiccated

Place the dried fruit in a small bowl, cover with the orange juice and honey and leave to marinate for 10 minutes. Mix the fresh fruit in a large bowl, add the marinated fruit and sprinkle with coconut. Serve with a sauce made of one banana and eight strawberries, blended with a little water.

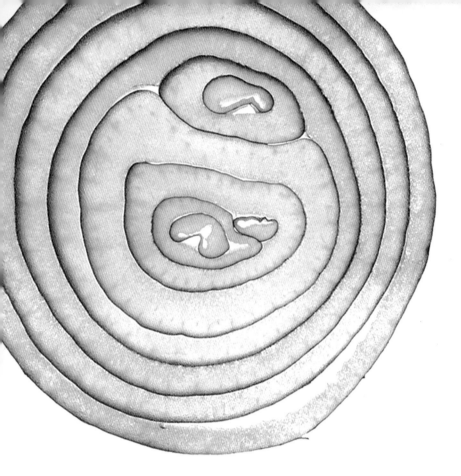

AUTUMN
RECIPES

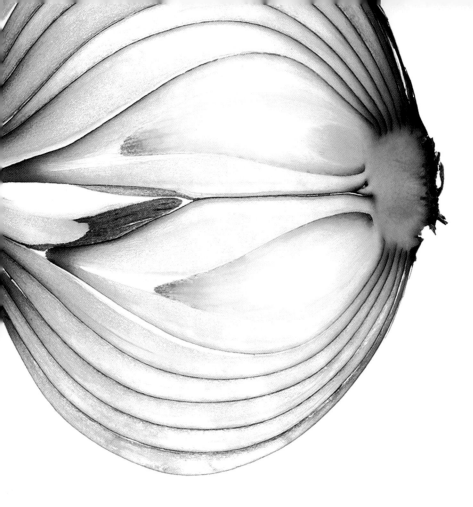

Autumn is the time when the explosive abundance of summer starts to withdraw down into the roots and the earth. As the colours of the fruits, vegetables and fields change from bright red to golden, it is time to collect some of the plenty, to share the summer's harvest.

In the forest, nuts ripen and game abounds, wild mushrooms appear and deep amber colours herald the parting of the sun. Cooking should reflect the season, with gently simmering stews taking over from hot summer grills. Root vegetables and potatoes, celery and salsify, pumpkin and corn become common ingredients, while sweet chestnuts and mushrooms, pears and apples, blueberries and grapes add colour and rich flavours to the autumn feast.

This is the season of equal night and day, and a good time to clear out the system. Cleansing autumn grape cures and fasts can help maximize our immunity. In naturopathic terms, autumn is connected with the stomach and the lungs – a chance to digest and store up reserves for the winter, and to take deep breaths of crisp fresh air to nourish and cleanse the body and mind.

183 AUTUMN VEGETABLE SOUP

CALORIES	318
CHOLESTEROL	0
VEGAN CALORIES	318
POLYUNSATS	★☆☆
ANTIOXIDANTS	★★★
CALCIUM	★★☆
IRON	★★☆
B VITAMINS	★★☆

1ltr (1¾pts) vegetable stock
1 leek, sliced
1 slice celeriac, diced
1 carrot, sliced
1 potato, diced
1 slice pumpkin, diced

3 tomatoes, blended
100g (3½oz) French beans, chopped
1 clove garlic, crushed
2 tbsp olive oil
sea salt and black pepper to taste
2 tbsp fresh parsley, chopped

Bring the stock to the boil in a large casserole dish with the leek, celeriac, carrot, potato and pumpkin and simmer for 5 minutes. Then add the tomatoes, together with the French beans, garlic and oil, and season. Cook for a further 5–10 minutes. Add the parsley, check the seasoning and serve with wholemeal bread.

184 MUSHROOM SOUP

CALORIES	292
CHOLESTEROL	0
VEGAN CALORIES	292
POLYUNSATS	★★☆
ANTIOXIDANTS	★★☆
CALCIUM	★☆☆
IRON	★★☆
B VITAMINS	★★☆

2 tbsp olive oil
1 shallot or small red onion, halved
    and sliced
1 clove garlic, crushed
250g (9oz) mushrooms, halved
    and sliced

1 tsp ground coriander
3 slices country bread, grated
1 tbsp tamari (soya sauce)
1ltr (1¾pts) vegetable stock
sea salt and plenty of black pepper
    to taste

Gently stir-fry the shallot or onion in a casserole dish with the oil for 2 minutes. Add the garlic, mushrooms and coriander and stir-fry for a further 5 minutes before adding the grated bread and the tamari. Continue to stir for 2 minutes, then add the stock. Bring to the boil and simmer for 10 minutes. Season and serve.

185 BEETROOT AND ORANGE SOUP

CALORIES	87
CHOLESTEROL	0
VEGAN CALORIES	87
POLYUNSATS	★☆☆
ANTIOXIDANTS	★★★
CALCIUM	★☆☆
IRON	★★☆
B VITAMINS	★☆☆

250g (9oz) raw beetroot, chopped
300ml (½pt) water
1 pinch salt

200ml (⅓pt) unsweetened
    orange juice
1 tbsp fresh mint, finely chopped

Place the beetroot and water in a saucepan, bring to the boil and simmer for 20 minutes. Remove from the heat and add the salt and orange juice. Blend to a smooth consistency. Serve hot or cold, garnished with mint.

SWEET CHESTNUT SOUP
★♥

186 ▼

CALORIES	481
CHOLESTEROL	23
VEGAN CALORIES	471
POLYUNSATS	★★☆
ANTIOXIDANTS	★★☆
CALCIUM	★★☆
IRON	★★☆
B VITAMINS	★★☆

300g (10½oz) sweet chestnuts, peeled
1ltr (1¾pts) water or stock
2 tbsp olive oil
1 shallot, finely chopped
1 slice celeriac, diced
2 tbsp vegetable margarine or butter, chopped
sea salt and black pepper to taste

Boil the sweet chestnuts in a saucepan with the water or stock for 5–10 minutes until they begin to disintegrate. Meanwhile, gently sauté the shallot and the celeriac with the oil in a frying pan over a medium heat until they begin to brown. Add the shallots and the celeriac to the pan with the chestnuts and cook for a further 10 minutes. Blend and season (adding a little more water or stock if necessary). Stir in the margarine or butter, check the seasoning and serve hot with garlic croutons.

187 SWEET POTATO AND PUMPKIN SOUP

⭐

CALORIES	444
CHOLESTEROL	0
VEGAN CALORIES	444
POLYUNSATS	★★☆
ANTIOXIDANTS	★★★
CALCIUM	★★☆
IRON	★★☆
B VITAMINS	★★☆

2 tbsp olive oil
½ red onion, chopped
300g (10½oz) pumpkin, peeled, deseeded and chopped
1 small sweet potato, peeled and chopped

850ml (1½pts) vegetable stock
200ml (⅓pt) coconut milk
sea salt and black pepper to taste
1 tbsp fresh coriander leaves, chopped

Heat the oil in a saucepan and gently stir-fry the onion, pumpkin and sweet potato for 3 minutes. Add the stock and the coconut milk, and season. Bring to the boil, cover and simmer for 15 minutes. Check the seasoning and garnish with fresh coriander. Serve with corn bread.

188 CURRIED CARROT SOUP

⭐❤💧✖🫘☕

CALORIES	319
CHOLESTEROL	0
VEGAN CALORIES	319
POLYUNSATS	★★☆
ANTIOXIDANTS	★★★
CALCIUM	★★☆
IRON	★☆☆
B VITAMINS	★★☆

2 tbsp olive oil
2 cloves garlic, crushed
1 tsp curry powder
½ small green chilli, deseeded and chopped
1 potato, chopped
450g (1lb) carrots, chopped

1 tsp fresh ginger, finely chopped
600ml (1pt) vegetable stock
1 orange, halved and squeezed
1 lemon, halved and squeezed
sea salt and black pepper to taste
sugar or maple syrup to taste (optional)

Gently heat the oil in a large casserole dish, add the garlic, curry powder and chilli and fry over a medium heat for 1 minute. Then add the chopped potato and the chopped carrots and stir-fry until they are well coated in the spices. Add the fresh ginger and stir-fry for a further minute before adding the stock. Bring to the boil, cover and simmer until the carrots are soft. Remove from the heat, add the juice from the orange and the lemon, and season. Blend and check the seasoning. (You may need to add a little sugar or maple syrup, depending on the sweetness of the carrots and the size of the lemon.) Serve hot or cold.

189 MEXICAN AVOCADO SOUP

⭐❤🌿☕

CALORIES	464
CHOLESTEROL	28
VEGAN CALORIES	399
POLYUNSATS	★★★
ANTIOXIDANTS	★★★
CALCIUM	★★☆
IRON	★☆☆
B VITAMINS	★☆☆

2 tbsp corn oil
1 onion, finely chopped
1 tbsp wheat flour
1ltr (1¾pts) vegetable stock
1 large avocado, peeled, pitted and mashed
1 pinch cayenne pepper

100ml (3½fl oz) almond milk/single cream
sea salt to taste
½ yellow pepper, finely chopped
½ red pepper, finely chopped
1 tsp paprika

Gently fry the onion in a casserole dish with the oil. Sprinkle with the flour and stir-fry until the onion is well coated. Continue to stir, and slowly add the stock. Bring to the boil, add the avocado and the cayenne pepper and gently simmer for 5 minutes. Stir in the almond milk or cream, season and serve garnished with red and yellow pepper and paprika.

190 QUICK TOMATO SOUP
⭐🫀💧❎⊘

CALORIES	46
CHOLESTEROL	0
VEGAN CALORIES	46
POLYUNSATS	★☆☆
ANTIOXIDANTS	★★★
CALCIUM	★☆☆
IRON	★☆☆
B VITAMINS	★☆☆

4 large tomatoes, stalks removed,
 quartered and blended
1 tsp tamari (soya sauce)
1 pinch ground coriander

1 tsp maple syrup
1 pinch Chinese Five-Spice
1 tbsp fresh oregano, chopped
sea salt and black pepper to taste

Place all of the ingredients in a saucepan. Gently heat through, stirring
often, and simmer for 5 minutes. Season and serve with croutons.

191 SOUPE AU PISTOU
⭐🫀💧🌾⊘

CALORIES	443
CHOLESTEROL	5
VEGAN CALORIES	431
POLYUNSATS	★★☆
ANTIOXIDANTS	★★★
CALCIUM	★★☆
IRON	★★★
B VITAMINS	★★☆

soup:
olive oil for frying
1 small leek, sliced
1 onion, halved and sliced
1 clove garlic, chopped
3 tomatoes, skinned and chopped
1ltr (1¾pts) vegetable stock
1 handful green beans, chopped
1 small stick celery, sliced
1 potato, diced
100g (3½oz) white beans, cooked or
 canned
2 tbsp small macaroni pasta
sea salt and black pepper to taste

pistou:
1 handful fresh basil leaves,
 chopped
3 cloves garlic
a little olive oil
Parmesan/brewer's yeast flakes
 to taste
a little sea salt

Heat a little oil in a casserole dish and gently fry the leek, onion and garlic
until soft. Add the tomatoes and cook for 5 minutes. Pour in the stock
and bring to the boil. Add the remaining soup ingredients (except for
the macaroni) and simmer until the vegetables are cooked. Add the
macaroni, bring to the boil and cook until the macaroni is soft, then
season. Meanwhile, prepare the pistou by placing the basil and the
garlic in a mortar with the oil, Parmesan or brewer's yeast flakes and
salt. Mash to a thick paste and add to the soup just before serving.

192 CHINESE CORN SOUP
🫀❎

CALORIES	162
CHOLESTEROL	98
VEGAN CALORIES	124
POLYUNSATS	★★☆
ANTIOXIDANTS	★★☆
CALCIUM	★☆☆
IRON	★★☆
B VITAMINS	★★☆

1 tsp fresh ginger, finely chopped
2 tsp tamari (soya sauce)
2 tsp dry sherry
750ml (1⅓pts) vegetable stock
150g (5½oz) sweetcorn
1 cinnamon stick
1 tsp cornflour dissolved in a little

cold water
1 tsp almond butter
1 egg, beaten (optional)
sea salt and black pepper to taste
1 small bunch chives, finely
 chopped

Marinade the ginger in the tamari and sherry in a bowl. Bring the stock
to the boil in a casserole dish, add the sweetcorn, cinnamon, marinated
ginger and a little salt. Simmer for 10 minutes. Slowly add the dissolved
cornflour and the almond butter while stirring continuously. Then add
the egg (if using), season, heat through and serve garnished with chives.

193 ◀ TOMATO SOUP WITH FRESH CORIANDER

⭐♥◊✖🌰

CALORIES	213
CHOLESTEROL	0
VEGAN CALORIES	213
POLYUNSATS	★★☆
ANTIOXIDANTS	★★★
CALCIUM	★☆☆
IRON	★★☆
B VITAMINS	★★☆

2 tbsp olive oil
500g (1lb 2oz) ripe tomatoes, quartered and stalks removed
1 red onion, chopped
1 clove garlic, chopped
250ml (9fl oz) vegetable stock

1 tsp raw cane sugar
1 handful fresh coriander leaves, chopped
sea salt and black pepper to taste
2 tbsp tamari (soya sauce)
1 tsp fresh ginger, finely chopped

Gently sauté the tomatoes, onion and garlic in a saucepan with the oil for approximately 10 minutes. Add the stock, sugar and half of the coriander leaves with a little salt and pepper. Bring to the boil, cover and gently simmer for 10 minutes. Remove from the heat and blend, then add the tamari and ginger and heat through. Check the seasoning and serve hot or cold, garnished with the remaining half of the coriander leaves.

194 HOT PEAR SOUP

♥◊✖🌰

CALORIES	241
CHOLESTEROL	0
VEGAN CALORIES	241
POLYUNSATS	★★★
ANTIOXIDANTS	★★☆
CALCIUM	★☆☆
IRON	★☆☆
B VITAMINS	★☆☆

2 tbsp grapeseed oil
500g (1lb 2oz) ripe pears, peeled, cored and chopped
1 tsp fresh ginger, grated

1 tbsp lemon juice
300ml (½pt) water
sea salt and black pepper to taste

Gently stir-fry the pears and the ginger in a saucepan with the oil for 1 minute. Add the lemon juice and stir for a further 30 seconds. Then add the water, bring to the boil, cover and simmer for 20 minutes. Blend and season. Serve hot or cold.

195 SPINACH AND CHICK PEA SOUP

⭐♥◊✖🌾🌰

CALORIES	389
CHOLESTEROL	0
VEGAN CALORIES	389
POLYUNSATS	★★☆
ANTIOXIDANTS	★★★
CALCIUM	★★★
IRON	★★★
B VITAMINS	★★☆

2 tbsp olive oil, plus some for frying
1 bay leaf
1 pinch cayenne pepper
1 tsp ground cumin
1 tsp turmeric
250g (9oz) chick peas, cooked or canned
250g (9oz) spinach or Swiss chard, finely chopped

750ml (1⅓pts) vegetable stock
1 head garlic
1 whole onion, peeled
1 slice country bread (a few days old, if possible), crumbled
2 tbsp fresh parsley, chopped
2 cloves garlic, crushed
sea salt to taste

Gently heat the oil in a saucepan and stir-fry the spices for 30 seconds. Add the chick peas and stir-fry for 5 minutes, then add the spinach or Swiss chard and fry for a further minute. Add the stock, together with the head of garlic, the whole onion and a little salt. Bring to the boil, cover and simmer for 15 minutes. Meanwhile, heat a little oil in a frying pan and gently fry the crumbled bread and the parsley for 2 minutes. Add the crushed garlic and blend with a little of the soup to make a thick paste. Add the paste to the soup and remove the head of garlic, whole onion and bay leaf. Heat through, season and serve.

196 WHITE CABBAGE, GRAPE AND WALNUT SALAD
★♥◐

CALORIES	407
CHOLESTEROL	0
VEGAN CALORIES	407
POLYUNSATS	★★★
ANTIOXIDANTS	★★☆
CALCIUM	★★☆
IRON	★★☆
B VITAMINS	★★☆

125g (4½oz) white cabbage, finely shredded
50g (1¾oz) raisins
1 red dessert apple, quartered, cored and finely chopped
50g (1¾oz) gherkins

150g (5½oz) grapes, halved
1 tbsp tarragon vinegar
sea salt and black pepper to taste
2 tbsp walnut oil
25g (1oz) walnuts, shelled
1 tbsp fresh parsley, finely chopped

Mix the cabbage, raisins, apple, gherkins and grapes in a salad bowl. Make the dressing by whisking the vinegar, salt, pepper and oil in a bowl. Then mix the dressing with the salad. Garnish with walnuts and fresh parsley, and serve with crusty bread.

197 CRUDITÉS WITH TAPENADE
★♥◐◐

CALORIES	652
CHOLESTEROL	0
VEGAN CALORIES	652
POLYUNSATS	★★★
ANTIOXIDANTS	★★★
CALCIUM	★★★
IRON	★★☆
B VITAMINS	★★☆

⅛ red cabbage, shredded
½ Florence fennel bulb, sliced
100g (3½oz) cep mushrooms, sliced and stir-fried in a little oil
2 potatoes, parboiled and sliced
2 carrots, cut into fine sticks
2 tomatoes, cut into boats

1 handful Brazil nuts
100g (3½oz) capers
100g (3½oz) black olives, pitted
2 cloves garlic, chopped
juice of 1 lemon
approximately 100ml (3½fl oz) olive oil

Make the tapenade by blending the capers, olives, garlic and lemon juice with enough oil to make a reasonably smooth paste. Divide the red cabbage between two large plates and place the remaining ingredients in groups on top of the cabbage. Finish with a spoonful of tapenade in the middle of the crudités. Serve with toasted bread.

198 AVOCADO AND MELON SALAD WITH CREAMY DRESSING
★◐

CALORIES	514
CHOLESTEROL	140
VEGAN CALORIES	748
POLYUNSATS	★★★
ANTIOXIDANTS	★★★
CALCIUM	★★★
IRON	★★★
B VITAMINS	★★☆

2 handfuls oakleaf lettuce
1 avocado, halved, pitted, peeled and sliced
½ small yellow melon, deseeded, peeled and sliced
8 sun-dried tomatoes, thinly sliced
100g (3½oz) prawns/cashew nuts (plus tamari [soya sauce])

100ml (3½fl oz) plain/soya yoghurt
1 tbsp olive oil
1 tbsp balsamic vinegar
1 tbsp tomato ketchup
½ tsp sea salt
plenty of black pepper
1 small bunch fresh dill

Arrange the lettuce leaves on two large plates. Add the avocado, followed by the melon, sun-dried tomatoes and prawns or cashews (if you are using cashews, dry-roast them first in a frying pan with a little tamari). To make the dressing, place the yoghurt in a bowl, add the oil, vinegar, ketchup, salt and pepper and mix well. Spoon the dressing onto the salads. Garnish with finely chopped dill and serve with fresh crusty bread.

199 CARROT SALAD WITH ALMOND DRESSING

⭐❤❌▱

CALORIES	394
CHOLESTEROL	25
VEGAN CALORIES	429
POLYUNSATS	★★★
ANTIOXIDANTS	★★★
CALCIUM	★★☆
IRON	★★☆
B VITAMINS	★★★

250g (9oz) carrots, grated
2 tbsp light almond butter
1 tsp red wine vinegar
1 tsp lemon juice
1 tsp Dijon mustard
sea salt and white pepper to taste

2 tbsp almonds, chopped
2 tbsp fresh parsley, finely chopped
oil for stir-frying (optional)
150g (5½oz) ham/tempeh, sliced
1 small lettuce, shredded

Place the grated carrots in a salad bowl. To make the dressing, whisk the the almond butter, vinegar, lemon juice, mustard, salt and pepper in a small bowl. Slowly add water until you have a smooth, even consistency. Add the dressing to the carrots, gently mix and top with almonds and parsley. If you are using tempeh, stir-fry the slices in a frying pan with a little oil until golden. Divide the shredded lettuce between two plates, add the slices of ham or fried tempeh, top with the dressed salad and serve.

200 TROPICAL SALAD

⭐❤💧▱

CALORIES	689
CHOLESTEROL	0
VEGAN CALORIES	689
POLYUNSATS	★★★
ANTIOXIDANTS	★★★
CALCIUM	★★☆
IRON	★★☆
B VITAMINS	★★☆

1 small butterhead lettuce,
   shredded
2 spring onions, thinly sliced
1 bunch watercress, chopped
1 papaya, halved, deseeded, peeled
   and diced
1 mango, peeled and diced

1 avocado, halved, pitted, peeled
   and sliced
10 Brazil nuts, chopped
juice of 1 lime
3 tbsp walnut oil
sea salt and black pepper to taste

Arrange the salad ingredients on two large plates, in the order given. Sprinkle with the lime juice and walnut oil, season and serve with corn bread or tortillas.

201 BALTIC SALAD

⭐❤🖊

CALORIES	434
CHOLESTEROL	39
VEGAN CALORIES	317
POLYUNSATS	★★★
ANTIOXIDANTS	★★★
CALCIUM	★★★
IRON	★★★
B VITAMINS	★★★

100g (3½oz) celeriac
2 carrots
1 medium turnip
2 potatoes
1 small beetroot
1 tbsp red wine vinegar
3 tbsp grapeseed oil

sea salt and black pepper to taste
2 gherkins, sliced
1 tbsp fresh parsley, chopped
3 herring fillets, cut into chunks/
   125g (4½oz) marinated tofu, cut
   into chunks
1 small onion, sliced

Cut the celeriac, carrots, turnip and potatoes into small cubes and boil them in a large saucepan until tender. Meanwhile, boil the beetroot in a separate pan until tender. Immediately cool the cooked vegetables under running water, drain and set aside. Make the dressing by whisking the vinegar, oil, salt and pepper in a bowl and set aside. Place the cooked vegetables in a salad bowl with the gherkins and the parsley. Gently toss with the dressing. Garnish with the herring fillets or tofu chunks and the onion slices. Serve with wholemeal rolls.

202 BULGUR AND BEETROOT SALAD

CALORIES	539
CHOLESTEROL	0
VEGAN CALORIES	539
POLYUNSATS	★★☆
ANTIOXIDANTS	★★☆
CALCIUM	★★☆
IRON	★★★
B VITAMINS	★★☆

100g (3½oz) bulgur wheat
250g (9oz) red kidney beans, cooked or canned and rinsed
100g (3½oz) green peas, fresh or defrosted
250g (9oz) raw beetroot, cut into small cubes
1 spring onion, finely chopped

1 tbsp fresh mint, finely chopped
1 tbsp fresh parsley, finely chopped
2 tbsp lemon juice
1 clove garlic, crushed
½ tsp Tabasco sauce
sea salt and black pepper to taste
2 tbsp olive oil, plus some for frying

Heat a little oil in a frying pan, add the bulgur and stir-fry for 2 minutes until it begins to brown. Then add twice the volume of water and a pinch of salt, lower the heat and very gently simmer for 10 minutes. Add the kidney beans and the peas for the last 2–3 minutes of the cooking time. Remove from the heat and place in a salad bowl. Add the beetroot, spring onion, mint and parsley to the bowl. Make the dressing by whisking the lemon juice, garlic, Tabasco sauce, salt and pepper, then add the oil. Pour the dressing over the bulgur salad and gently toss. Serve warm or cold.

203 LEBANESE BUTTER BEAN SALAD

CALORIES	350
CHOLESTEROL	0
VEGAN CALORIES	350
POLYUNSATS	★★★
ANTIOXIDANTS	★★★
CALCIUM	★★☆
IRON	★★★
B VITAMINS	★★☆

250g (9oz) butter beans, cooked or canned and blanched
1 spring onion, finely chopped
1 handful fresh parsley, chopped
3 thick slices lemon, peeled and chopped

3 tbsp walnut oil
1 clove garlic, crushed
sea salt and black pepper to taste
2 handfuls lettuce, shredded
12 grape tomatoes, halved

Drain and cool the butter beans and place them in a bowl. Add the onion, parsley and lemon. Make a marinade by mixing the oil, garlic, salt and pepper in a separate bowl. Then add the marinade to the butter beans and gently mix. Place the shredded lettuce on two large plates. Add the butter bean mixture, garnish with grape tomatoes and serve with fresh bread.

204 PASTA SALAD

CALORIES	422
CHOLESTEROL	0
VEGAN CALORIES	422
POLYUNSATS	★★★
ANTIOXIDANTS	★★★
CALCIUM	★☆☆
IRON	★★☆
B VITAMINS	★★☆

250g (9oz) cooked pasta of choice
1 green pepper, quartered and finely sliced
100g (3½oz) grape tomatoes, quartered
1 large handful rocket, sliced
50g (1¾oz) black olives, pitted

1 tbsp balsamic vinegar
1 clove garlic, crushed
sea salt and black pepper to taste
2 tbsp walnut oil
25g (1oz) almonds, chopped and toasted

Place the cooked pasta, green pepper, tomatoes, rocket and olives in a salad bowl. Make the dressing by whisking the vinegar, garlic, salt and pepper, then add the oil and whisk to a smooth consistency. Drizzle the dressing over the salad and gently toss. Garnish with almonds and serve.

205 ▲ CORN-ON-THE-COB SALAD
★♥◉✖∅

CALORIES	199
CHOLESTEROL	0
VEGAN CALORIES	199
POLYUNSATS	★★☆
ANTIOXIDANTS	★★★
CALCIUM	★☆☆
IRON	★★☆
B VITAMINS	★★☆

2 corn-on-the-cob, peeled and
   sliced into chunks
1 large handful lettuce
¼ cucumber, cut into sticks
2 tomatoes, cut into boats

1 small beetroot, cut into sticks
2 carrots, cut into sticks
12 black olives, pitted
sea salt and black pepper to taste

Plunge the corn chunks into a saucepan of boiling water and cook for
3–5 minutes. Meanwhile, arrange the salad ingredients on two plates,
in the order given. Top with the cooked corn, season and serve with
French dressing (see p.23) and vegetable margarine or butter.

206 KASHA, CORN AND BEAN SALAD

CALORIES	452
CHOLESTEROL	6
VEGAN CALORIES	449
POLYUNSATS	★★★
ANTIOXIDANTS	★★☆
CALCIUM	★★☆
IRON	★★☆
B VITAMINS	★★☆

100g (3½oz) kasha (roasted
  buckwheat)
200ml (⅓pt) water
2 cardamom pods
1 bay leaf
¼ tsp cinnamon
1 tsp cumin
2 tsp sunflower oil
100g (3½oz) sweetcorn kernels
150g (5½oz) flageolet beans,
  cooked or canned

1 small butterhead lettuce,
  shredded
1 tomato, sliced
¼ cucumber, sliced
1 small green pepper, sliced
1 shallot, finely chopped
100ml (3½oz) plain/soya yoghurt
1 tbsp lemon juice
2 tsp Dijon mustard
2 tsp tomato ketchup
sea salt and black pepper to taste

Boil the kasha in the water in a saucepan, together with the spices until nearly all the water is absorbed. Remove from the heat, add the sunflower oil and a pinch of salt. Stir, cover and set aside. Cook the sweetcorn and the beans in a saucepan of boiling water for 1 minute. Drain and set aside. To make the dressing, combine the yoghurt, lemon juice, mustard and tomato ketchup in a bowl. Set aside. Arrange the lettuce, tomato, cucumber, green pepper and shallot on a large serving plate. Spoon the kasha onto the centre of the plate and top with the sweetcorn and beans. Pour the dressing in a ring over the salad. Season and serve.

207 SALADE VERMEILLE

CALORIES	686
CHOLESTEROL	83
VEGAN CALORIES	577
POLYUNSATS	★★★
ANTIOXIDANTS	★★★
CALCIUM	★★☆
IRON	★★★
B VITAMINS	★★☆

4 tbsp olive oil
2 quails, cut into 4 pieces/175g
  (6oz) seitan
1 clove garlic, chopped
4 tbsp Vinaigre de Banyuls (or white
  wine vinegar or sherry vinegar)

2 handfuls fresh spinach, shredded
1 curly endive (frisée), shredded
sea salt and black pepper to taste
4 slices bread, fried in a little oil and
  rubbed with garlic
1 tbsp fresh parsley, finely chopped

Fry the quails or seitan in a frying pan with a little oil until golden or brown and set aside. Add the garlic and Vinaigre de Banyuls to the pan and simmer for 5 minutes. Meanwhile, divide the spinach and the curly endive between two large plates, sprinkle with oil and season. Place two slices of fried bread on either side of each plate and top with the fried quail or seitan. Add the simmered garlic and vinegar, garnish with fresh parsley and serve immediately.

208 CARROT SALAD WITH SUNFLOWER SEEDS AND PARSLEY

CALORIES	258
CHOLESTEROL	0
VEGAN CALORIES	258
POLYUNSATS	★★★
ANTIOXIDANTS	★★★
CALCIUM	★☆☆
IRON	★★☆
B VITAMINS	★☆☆

250g (9oz) carrots, grated
2 tbsp sunflower seeds
2 tbsp lemon juice

2 tbsp sunflower oil
sea salt and black pepper to taste
2 tbsp fresh parsley, finely chopped

Mix the grated carrots and sunflower seeds in a bowl with the lemon juice and oil. Season and garnish with fresh parsley. Serve with toast and pâté.

209 ▲ FETTUCCINE WITH WALNUT PESTO
⭐❤️🌾

CALORIES	637
CHOLESTEROL	0
VEGAN CALORIES	637
POLYUNSATS	★★★
ANTIOXIDANTS	★★☆
CALCIUM	★★☆
IRON	★★★
B VITAMINS	★★☆

200g (7oz) fettuccine pasta
50g (1¾oz) walnuts (shelled weight)
1 clove garlic, crushed
1 tbsp fresh flat-leaf parsley, chopped

1 thick slice bread, crumbled and soaked in milk/soya milk
1 tbsp olive oil
2 tbsp fresh basil, chopped
sea salt and black pepper to taste

Cook the pasta in plenty of boiling water with a little salt and oil. Meanwhile, pound the walnuts in a mortar (reserving a few to garnish), together with the garlic, parsley and a little salt, until you have a rough paste. Squeeze the milk from the crumbled bread, add the bread to the mortar and mix well. Then add the oil and the basil (and a little of the milk if necessary), and mix until you have a thick green sauce. Drain the cooked pasta and mix with the pesto sauce. Season, garnish with walnut halves and serve with Parmesan or brewer's yeast flakes.

210 GNOCCHI WITH SHIITAKE, LEMON AND THYME SAUCE
★♥🌿🥚🥛

CALORIES	581
CHOLESTEROL	30
VEGAN CALORIES	566
POLYUNSATS	★★☆
ANTIOXIDANTS	★★☆
CALCIUM	★★☆
IRON	★★☆
B VITAMINS	★★☆

1 tbsp olive oil
1 shallot, finely chopped
2 cloves garlic, crushed
1 knob vegetable margarine (or
   butter)
150g (5½oz) fresh shiitake
   mushrooms, thinly sliced

sea salt to taste
2 tsp fresh thyme leaves
250ml (9fl oz) plain/soya yoghurt
1 tbsp lemon juice
1 packet ready-made gnocchi pasta
paprika to garnish
black pepper to taste

Heat the oil in a frying pan over a low heat. Add the shallot and the garlic and very gently cook for 5 minutes. Then add the margarine and the shiitake and stir until the margarine is dissolved. Continue to cook over a low heat until the shiitake give off their liquid. Season, add the thyme and stir. Add the yoghurt and the lemon juice and stir until the sauce is heated through. Cook the gnocchi as indicated on the packet. Serve topped with the sauce and garnished with paprika and black pepper.

211 HOUMOUS AND CEP MACARONI
★♥🌿🥚🥛

CALORIES	616
CHOLESTEROL	0
VEGAN CALORIES	616
POLYUNSATS	★★☆
ANTIOXIDANTS	★★☆
CALCIUM	★★☆
IRON	★★★
B VITAMINS	★★☆

200g (7oz) chick peas, cooked or
   canned
1 clove garlic, crushed
2 tbsp lemon juice
4 tbsp cold water
½ tsp sea salt

1 tbsp tahini
200g (7oz) macaroni pasta
200g (7oz) fresh cep mushrooms
1 tbsp olive oil
1 tbsp fresh parsley, finely chopped
1 tsp paprika

Blend the chick peas with the garlic, lemon juice, water and salt in a bowl. Add the tahini and blend again to a smooth paste. Adjust the seasoning and set aside. Cook the macaroni in plenty of boiling water with salt and oil. Meanwhile, thinly slice the ceps and gently stir-fry them in a frying pan with the oil until they begin to brown. Drain the cooked macaroni and mix with the chick pea paste (houmous). Divide onto two plates and top with the fried ceps. Garnish with parsley and paprika, and serve immediately.

212 PASTA WITH PERSILLADE TOPPING
★♥💧🌿🥚

CALORIES	651
CHOLESTEROL	25
VEGAN CALORIES	686
POLYUNSATS	★★☆
ANTIOXIDANTS	★★★
CALCIUM	★★☆
IRON	★★★
B VITAMINS	★★★

150g (5½oz) lumache (pasta snails)
2 tbsp olive oil
1 red onion, halved and sliced
150g (5½oz) ham/smoked tempeh,
   cubed

1 red apple, quartered and cored
1 large tomato
1 handful parsley, finely chopped
2 cloves garlic, crushed
sea salt and black pepper to taste

Cook the pasta in plenty of boiling water with a little salt and oil. Gently stir-fry the onion in a casserole dish with the oil for 1 minute. Then add the ham or smoked tempeh and fry for a further 2 minutes. Chop the apple and the tomato and add them to the pan. Heat through. Add the parsley and the garlic, and season. Place the cooked and drained pasta on two large heated plates, top with the sauce and serve immediately.

213 SPAGHETTI WITH SAUCE TOMATE CONCASSÉ

★♥🌾🥚

CALORIES	498
CHOLESTEROL	0
VEGAN CALORIES	498
POLYUNSATS	★☆☆
ANTIOXIDANTS	★★★
CALCIUM	★☆☆
IRON	★★☆
B VITAMINS	★★☆

sauce tomate concassé:
2 tbsp olive oil
1 onion, finely chopped
1 clove garlic, finely chopped
½ tsp sugar
1 pinch thyme
1 bay leaf
4 ripe tomatoes, peeled and
    finely chopped

150g (5½oz) spaghetti pasta
sea salt and black pepper to taste

To make the sauce tomate concassé, heat the oil in a casserole dish and gently fry the onion until soft (don't let it brown). Add the garlic, sugar, thyme, bay leaf and chopped tomatoes. Bring to the boil, cover and gently simmer for 20 minutes. Meanwhile, cook the spaghetti in plenty of water with a little salt and oil. Season and drain the cooked spaghetti, and serve with the hot sauce tomate concassé.

214 PASTA ALLA PUTTANESCA

★♥🌾🥚

CALORIES	524
CHOLESTEROL	19
VEGAN CALORIES	615
POLYUNSATS	★★★
ANTIOXIDANTS	★★★
CALCIUM	★★☆
IRON	★★★
B VITAMINS	★★☆

150g (5½oz) spaghetti pasta
2–3 anchovy fillets/4–6 sun-dried
    tomatoes
1 tbsp olive oil
2 cloves garlic, crushed
2 large ripe tomatoes, chopped

12 black olives, pitted and chopped
1 tbsp capers
1 handful fresh flat-leaf parsley,
    chopped
1 pinch cayenne pepper
sea salt and black pepper to taste

Cook the spaghetti in plenty of boiling water with a little salt and oil. Meanwhile, chop the anchovies or sun-dried tomatoes. Heat the oil in a frying pan and add the garlic, then the chopped anchovies or sun-dried tomatoes. Stir-fry for 1 minute, add the chopped ripe tomatoes and cook for 5 minutes. Add the olives, capers, parsley and cayenne pepper. Season and gently simmer for a few minutes. Drain the cooked spaghetti, place in a large serving dish and top with the sauce. Serve immediately.

215 CEPS WITH NOODLES

★♥🌾

CALORIES	779
CHOLESTEROL	165
VEGAN CALORIES	439
POLYUNSATS	★★★
ANTIOXIDANTS	★★☆
CALCIUM	★☆☆
IRON	★★★
B VITAMINS	★★★

200g (7oz) fresh noodles
olive oil for cooking
300g (10½oz) fresh (firm) cep
    mushrooms, sliced
300g (10½oz) pork fillet/

150g (5½oz) seitan, sliced
1 small clove garlic, crushed
sea salt and black pepper to taste
1 tbsp fresh parsley, chopped

Cook the noodles in plenty of boiling water with a little salt and oil. Meanwhile, fry the ceps in oil in a non-stick frying pan until they give off their liquid. Remove from the pan and set aside. Fry the pork or seitan slices in the same pan with a little more oil. Add the ceps and garlic, and season. Mix in the cooked noodles and parsley. Serve on warmed plates.

PAPILLONS WITH CHANTERELLE AND THYME SAUCE

⭐ ❤️ 🌿

CALORIES	626
CHOLESTEROL	38
VEGAN CALORIES	560
POLYUNSATS	★★★
ANTIOXIDANTS	★★☆
CALCIUM	★★☆
IRON	★★☆
B VITAMINS	★★☆

200g (7oz) papillons (farfalle pasta)
2 tbsp olive oil
125g (4½oz) smoked ham/tofu, cubed
125g (4½oz) fresh chanterelle mushrooms, quartered

1 small red onion, finely chopped
1 clove garlic, crushed
2 tbsp crème fraîche/soya cream
1 tsp thyme
sea salt and black pepper to taste

Cook the pasta in plenty of boiling water with a little salt and oil. Meanwhile, heat the oil in a casserole dish and stir-fry the ham or tofu, chanterelles, onion and garlic over a medium heat for 5 minutes. Add the cream and the thyme, season and simmer for a further 5 minutes. Check the seasoning. Place the cooked pasta in a heated serving dish, top with the sauce and serve immediately.

217 RIGATONI WITH CREAM CHEESE AND HERB PANGRATTATO

CALORIES	996
CHOLESTEROL	104
VEGAN CALORIES	679
POLYUNSATS	★★★
ANTIOXIDANTS	★★☆
CALCIUM	★★★
IRON	★★★
B VITAMINS	★★★

200g (7oz) mascarpone/soya cream cheese
3–4 tbsp olive oil
4 cloves garlic, crushed
2 tbsp Parmesan/1tbsp brewer's yeast flakes
sea salt and black pepper to taste

200g (7oz) rigatoni pasta (or use macaroni pasta)
2 thick slices ciabatta bread, coarsely crumbled
1 tsp thyme
1 tsp oregano

Mix the cream cheese with 1 tablespoon of the oil in a bowl. Add 2 cloves of garlic and the Parmesan or brewer's yeast flakes, and season. Set aside. Cook the pasta in plenty of boiling water with a little salt and oil. To make the pangrattato, heat 2–3 tablespoons of oil in a small saucepan, add the remaining 2 cloves of garlic and the breadcrumbs and stir-fry until golden. Add the herbs at the last minute and remove from the heat. Drain the cooked pasta and mix with the cream cheese sauce. Garnish with the herb pangrattato and serve immediately.

218 BUCATINI WITH SEAFOOD

CALORIES	523
CHOLESTEROL	29
VEGAN CALORIES	561
POLYUNSATS	★★☆
ANTIOXIDANTS	★★★
CALCIUM	★★☆
IRON	★★★
B VITAMINS	★★★

1 tbsp olive oil
1 clove garlic, chopped
1 pinch cayenne pepper
1 tbsp fresh oregano, chopped
3 tbsp dry sherry/muscat
1 tsp paprika
2 large ripe tomatoes, chopped
200ml (⅓pt) mussel/soya-seaweed cooking/soaking liquid

1kg (2lb 4oz) mussels, cooked in shells, then shelled and chopped/50g (1¾oz) soya chunks, soaked with 3 tbsp dried seaweed
1 tbsp fresh flat-leaf parsley, chopped
sea salt and black pepper to taste
200g (7oz) bucatini pasta (or use pasta of choice)

Gently heat the oil in a saucepan, add the garlic, cayenne pepper and oregano and stir-fry for 30 seconds. Then add the sherry or muscat and the paprika and cook for a further 30 seconds. Add the chopped tomatoes, together with the cooking or soaking liquid, and the soaked soya chunks and seaweed (if using). Cook for 10 minutes, stirring regularly. Add the parsley, and the mussels (if using). Season and heat through. Cook the pasta in plenty of boiling water with a little salt and oil. Drain and add to the sauce. Serve immediately.

219 SPAGHETTI WITH BROCCOLI IN YOGHURT AND BASIL SAUCE ♥🌾

CALORIES	504
CHOLESTEROL	22
VEGAN CALORIES	494
POLYUNSATS	★★☆
ANTIOXIDANTS	★★☆
CALCIUM	★★★
IRON	★★★
B VITAMINS	★★☆

200g (7oz) spaghetti pasta
1 head broccoli, cut into florets
1 tbsp Dijon mustard
100ml (3½oz) plain/soya yoghurt

1 knob vegetable margarine or butter
½ small red onion, finely chopped
1 clove garlic, crushed
1 handful fresh basil, finely chopped

Cook the spaghetti in plenty of boiling water with a little salt and olive oil. Add the broccoli to the pan for the last 4–5 minutes of the cooking time. Mix the mustard, yoghurt and margarine or butter in a bowl. Add the onion, garlic and basil, season well and set aside. Drain the spaghetti and broccoli in a colander. Put the sauce mixture into the pan and gently heat. Add the drained spaghetti and broccoli and mix. Serve with a side salad.

220 CORN PASTA AND SPINACH WITH OLIVE PASTE ★♥💧

CALORIES	632
CHOLESTEROL	36
VEGAN CALORIES	559
POLYUNSATS	★★★
ANTIOXIDANTS	★★★
CALCIUM	★★★
IRON	★★★
B VITAMINS	★★☆

250g (9oz) fresh spinach, chopped
100ml (3½fl oz) milk/soya milk
1 pinch nutmeg
sea salt and black pepper to taste
200g (7oz) corn pasta

125g (4½oz) black Niçoise olives
2 cloves garlic, chopped
2 tbsp fresh basil, chopped
2 tbsp fresh parsley, chopped
100g (3½oz) ricotta/soya cheese

Gently cook the spinach in a saucepan with a little water until soft. Add the milk and nutmeg and heat through. Season and set aside. Cook the pasta in plenty of boiling water with a little salt and oil. Pit and finely chop the olives and mix with the garlic and herbs. Drain the cooked pasta and mix with the spinach. Then place in a serving bowl and top with the olive paste. Crumble the cheese and sprinkle over the pasta. Serve immediately.

221 PASTA FORESTIÈRE 💧🌾

CALORIES	823
CHOLESTEROL	125
VEGAN CALORIES	597
POLYUNSATS	★★☆
ANTIOXIDANTS	★★☆
CALCIUM	★☆☆
IRON	★★☆
B VITAMINS	★★☆

200g (7oz) fresh pasta of choice
oil for frying
300g (10½oz) venison medallions/
    150g (5½oz) seitan pieces
1 shallot, chopped
100ml (3½fl oz) red wine

10 juniper berries
100ml (3½fl oz) stock
25g (1oz) dried cep mushrooms,
    soaked in a bowl of warm water
1 tbsp crème fraîche/soya cream

Cook the pasta in plenty of boiling water with a little salt and oil. Heat some oil in a frying pan and fry the venison or seitan until lightly browned. Set aside (keep warm). Add a little more oil to the pan and fry the shallot until soft, then add the wine and the juniper berries. Cook until the liquid is reduced to half the volume. Add the stock. Drain and rinse the ceps and add to the sauce. Cook until the liquid is reduced by half again. Add the cream, heat through, season and cook until the sauce thickens. Serve the pasta and the venison or seitan on warmed plates, topped with the sauce.

222 ▲ PERUVIAN POLENTA CAKES

CALORIES	389
CHOLESTEROL	0
VEGAN CALORIES	389
POLYUNSATS	★★★
ANTIOXIDANTS	★★★
CALCIUM	★☆☆
IRON	★★☆
B VITAMINS	★★☆

300g (10½oz) precooked polenta
1 fresh red chilli, finely chopped
2 tbsp fresh coriander, finely
   chopped
½ tsp sea salt
approximately 250ml (9fl oz)
   boiling water

corn oil for frying
1 large tomato, diced
1 cucumber, grated
1 red pepper, quartered and sliced
2 tbsp lemon juice
1 tsp raw cane sugar
sea salt to taste

Place the polenta in a bowl, add the chilli, coriander and salt and mix well.
Gradually pour in the boiling water and stir to a thick consistency. Leave
to stand for 5 minutes, then mould the mixture with wet hands to make
twelve 5cm (2in) x 1cm (½in) round cakes. Fry the cakes in a frying pan
over a medium heat with a little oil until golden, turning them frequently
to prevent sticking. Make the relish by mixing the tomato, cucumber, red
pepper, lemon juice, sugar and salt. Serve the cakes hot with the relish.

223 EGYPTIAN CASSEROLE

CALORIES	348
CHOLESTEROL	0
VEGAN CALORIES	348
POLYUNSATS	★★☆
ANTIOXIDANTS	★★☆
CALCIUM	★☆☆
IRON	★★☆
B VITAMINS	★★☆

2 tbsp olive oil
1 leek, sliced
1 potato, diced
1 medium beetroot, diced
1 tsp ground cumin

100g (3½oz) red lentils
200ml (⅓pt) vegetable stock
2 tbsp lemon juice
sea salt and black pepper to taste
2 tbsp fresh parsley, chopped

Heat the oil in a casserole dish and gently stir-fry the leek, potato and beetroot with the cumin for 5 minutes. Add the lentils and stir for a further 30 seconds, then add the stock. Bring to the boil, cover and gently simmer until the lentils are soft (approximately 15 minutes). Stir from time to time (adding a little water if necessary). Add the lemon juice, season, garnish with parsley and serve with couscous, bulgur wheat or rice.

224 JAPANESE GOHAN

CALORIES	149
CHOLESTEROL	0
VEGAN CALORIES	149
POLYUNSATS	★★☆
ANTIOXIDANTS	★★☆
CALCIUM	★★★
IRON	★★☆
B VITAMINS	★★☆

100g (3½oz) tofu, cubed
1 tbsp tamari (soya sauce)
1 tbsp mirin or dry sherry
2 tsp sesame oil
1 pinch raw cane sugar
100g (3½oz) shiitake mushrooms, sliced

½ltr (18fl oz) vegetable stock
100g (3½oz) fresh spinach, cut into strips
½ tsp ginger, finely grated
1 spring onion, finely sliced
sea salt to taste
4 thin slices lemon

Place the tofu cubes in a casserole dish, add the tamari, mirin or sherry, sesame oil and sugar and mix well. Add the shiitake, mix again and bring to a simmer. Cover and cook for 1 minute. Add the stock and spinach and very gently simmer for 3–4 minutes. Add the ginger and spring onion and heat through. Season, garnish with lemon slices and serve with rice.

225 BRAZILIAN FEIJOADA

CALORIES	537
CHOLESTEROL	33
VEGAN CALORIES	447
POLYUNSATS	★★☆
ANTIOXIDANTS	★★★
CALCIUM	★★☆
IRON	★★★
B VITAMINS	★★★

2 cloves garlic, crushed
1 bay leaf
1 tsp paprika
1 tsp thyme
1 tsp cumin
1 leek, sliced
1 sweet potato, cubed
approximately 200ml (⅓pt) vegetable stock
oil for frying

125g (4½oz) bacon/smoked tofu
400g (14oz) black beans, cooked or canned
1 red pepper, deseeded and sliced
250g (9oz) tomatoes, crushed
1 small bunch parsley and chives, finely chopped
sea salt and black pepper to taste
1 orange, thinly sliced

Place the garlic, spices, leek and sweet potato in a medium casserole dish. Cover with the stock, bring to the boil and simmer over a medium heat for 10 minutes. Meanwhile, heat a little oil in a frying pan and stir-fry the bacon or smoked tofu and the beans for 2 minutes. Then add the red pepper, tomatoes, parsley and chives and stir-fry over a medium heat for a further 5 minutes. Add the bean mixture to the vegetables and heat through. Season, garnish with orange slices and serve with rice.

226 LOUISIANA GUMBO

CALORIES	355
CHOLESTEROL	25
VEGAN CALORIES	287
POLYUNSATS	★★★
ANTIOXIDANTS	★★★
CALCIUM	★★☆
IRON	★★☆
B VITAMINS	★★☆

1 tbsp corn oil
1 small red onion, halved and sliced
1 bay leaf
1 pinch cayenne pepper
1 tsp paprika
½ green pepper, sliced
½ red pepper, sliced
1 stick celery, sliced

200g (7oz) (hokaido) pumpkin,
  peeled, deseeded and chopped
1 tbsp wheat flour
250g (9oz) tomatoes, chopped
200ml (⅓pt) vegetable stock
100g (3½oz) smoked sausage
  (meat/soya), sliced
sea salt and plenty of black pepper

Heat the oil in a heavy-based casserole dish and gently sweat the onion
with the spices. Add the pepper slices, followed by the celery and the
pumpkin. Gently stir-fry for 3–5 minutes. Sprinkle with flour and stir
for 1 minute to coat the vegetables. Add the tomatoes, stir, then
add the stock. Bring to the boil, cover and simmer for 10 minutes.
Add the sausage and heat through. Season and serve with rice.

227 FLORENTINE SPINACH BAKE

CALORIES	763
CHOLESTEROL	74
VEGAN CALORIES	595
POLYUNSATS	★★★
ANTIOXIDANTS	★★★
CALCIUM	★★★
IRON	★★☆
B VITAMINS	★★☆

400g (14oz) cooked rice
2 tbsp olive oil
1 small leek, sliced
250g (9oz) fresh spinach, chopped
100ml (3½fl oz) crème fraîche/soya
  cream

1 pinch nutmeg
sea salt and black pepper to taste
½ green pepper, sliced
2 ripe tomatoes, cut into boats
50g (1¾oz) Emmental/soya cheese,
  grated

Preheat the oven to 220°C/425°F/gas mark 7. Press the cooked rice into
the bottom of a large, flat, greased ovenproof dish. Heat the oil in a
casserole dish and gently stir-fry the leek for 4–5 minutes. Add the spinach
and cook until it is wilted. Then add the cream and heat through (don't let
it boil). Add the nutmeg and season. Spoon the spinach mixture over the
rice and garnish with green pepper and tomato. Sprinkle with grated
cheese and bake in a hot oven until golden. Serve immediately.

228 AFRICAN CURRY

CALORIES	983
CHOLESTEROL	220
VEGAN CALORIES	743
POLYUNSATS	★★☆
ANTIOXIDANTS	★★☆
CALCIUM	★★☆
IRON	★★★
B VITAMINS	★★★

2 tbsp olive oil
400g (14oz) pork fillet/tempeh, cut
  into chunks
1 tbsp curry powder
1 onion, halved and sliced
½ red pepper, sliced

1 clove garlic, crushed
200ml (⅓pt) coconut milk
1 apple, peeled, cored and diced
sea salt and cayenne pepper
  to taste

Heat the oil in a casserole dish. Add the pork or tempeh chunks and
half of the curry powder. Stir-fry over a medium–high heat until the pork
or tempeh chunks begin to brown. Remove from the pan and set aside.
Stir-fry the onion, red pepper and garlic in the same pan with the
remaining curry powder (and a little more oil if necessary). Add the
coconut milk, apple and cooked pork or tempeh. Bring to the boil
and simmer for 5 minutes. Season and serve with rice.

229 ◄ KERALA CURRY WITH MANGO AND COCONUT
✱♥◩

CALORIES	644
CHOLESTEROL	123
VEGAN CALORIES	608
POLYUNSATS	★★☆
ANTIOXIDANTS	★★★
CALCIUM	★★☆
IRON	★★★
B VITAMINS	★★★

2 tbsp olive oil
1 small onion, halved and sliced
1 clove garlic, crushed
1 tsp fresh ginger, chopped
350g (12oz) chicken breast/175g (6oz) tempeh, diced
1–2 tsp curry powder to taste
1 ripe mango, halved, pitted, peeled and diced
200ml (⅓pt) coconut milk
1–2 tsp lemon juice (to taste)
sea salt and plenty of black pepper
water (optional)
1 handful fresh coriander leaves, chopped

Heat the oil in a heavy-based pan or wok and gently stir-fry the onion and garlic until they begin to soften. Add the ginger and the chicken or tempeh and fry until the chicken or tempeh begins to brown. Add the curry powder and mix well before adding the mango and the coconut milk. Season and very gently simmer for 5–7 minutes. (You may need to add a little water to prevent the curry from drying.) Garnish with fresh coriander leaves and serve with rice and/or chapati bread.

230 BOLIVIAN PALTA RELLENOS
✱✖◪◩

CALORIES	369
CHOLESTEROL	140
VEGAN CALORIES	490
POLYUNSATS	★★★
ANTIOXIDANTS	★★★
CALCIUM	★★☆
IRON	★★☆
B VITAMINS	★★☆

2 avocados, halved and pitted
½ banana, peeled and diced
2 tbsp lemon juice
¼ small onion, finely chopped
½ green chilli pepper, finely chopped
1 tomato, finely chopped
½ tsp paprika
sea salt and cayenne pepper to taste
100g (3½oz) shrimps, peeled and cooked/50g (1¾oz) Brazil nuts, chopped

Scoop out the avocado flesh and place it in a bowl. Add the banana, lemon juice, onion, chilli, tomato and paprika. Gently mix and season. Spoon the mixture back into the avocado shells, garnish with shrimps or Brazil nuts and serve immediately.

231 LEBANESE GREEN BEANS WITH POMEGRANATE
♥◖✖

CALORIES	226
CHOLESTEROL	0
VEGAN CALORIES	226
POLYUNSATS	★☆☆
ANTIOXIDANTS	★★☆
CALCIUM	★☆☆
IRON	★★☆
B VITAMINS	★☆☆

250g (9oz) green beans, topped and tailed
2 pomegranates, peeled and white skin removed
2 tbsp olive oil
1 clove garlic, crushed
1 tbsp fresh flat-leaf parsley, chopped
sea salt to taste

Place the beans in a saucepan with as little boiling, salted water as possible and cook over a low heat until tender. Drain and place in a serving bowl. Top with the pomegranate. Mix the oil and garlic with the chopped parsley in a small bowl, then pour the mixture over the beans and pomegranate. Gently mix and serve with rice or flat Arabic bread.

232 CARIBBEAN CASSEROLE
★♥

CALORIES	530
CHOLESTEROL	37
VEGAN CALORIES	513
POLYUNSATS	★★☆
ANTIOXIDANTS	★★★
CALCIUM	★★★
IRON	★★★
B VITAMINS	★★☆

2 tbsp olive oil
1 medium sweet potato, peeled and diced
100g (3½oz) Savoy cabbage, chopped
200g (7oz) (hokaido) pumpkin, peeled, deseeded and diced
100g (3½oz) fresh spinach, chopped
1 strip kombu seaweed, soaked in

100ml (3½fl oz) water for 10 minutes and chopped
1 tsp turmeric dissolved in 200ml (⅓pt) coconut milk
1 tsp thyme
1 tbsp fresh parsley, chopped
sea salt and black pepper to taste
150g (1¼oz) cod fillet/tofu, cut into chunks

Gently heat the oil in a heavy-based casserole dish and stir-fry the sweet potato, Savoy cabbage and pumpkin for 3 minutes until the cabbage begins to soften. Add the fresh spinach, together with the seaweed and its soaking water, followed by the tumeric and coconut milk. Sprinkle with the thyme and fresh parsley, and season. Bring to the boil, cover with a tight-fitting lid and simmer for 10 minutes. Add the cod or tofu chunks and sprinkle with a little more salt. Cover and simmer for a further 5 minutes, then remove the lid, turn up the heat a little and let the liquid reduce for 1 minute. Serve with rice.

233 KUWAITI OKRA
★♥◉✖◍◐

CALORIES	208
CHOLESTEROL	0
VEGAN CALORIES	208
POLYUNSATS	★☆☆
ANTIOXIDANTS	★★☆
CALCIUM	★★☆
IRON	★★☆
B VITAMINS	★★☆

2 tbsp olive oil
2 cloves garlic, crushed
300g (10½oz) fresh okra (lady's fingers), trimmed
2 tomatoes, chopped

50ml (2fl oz) water
1 pinch ground coriander
sea salt and cayenne pepper to taste
1 squeeze lemon juice

Heat the oil in a heavy-based casserole dish and gently stir-fry the garlic for 30 seconds, then add the okra and stir-fry for 1 minute. Add the tomatoes and heat through. Add the water and coriander, and season. Bring to the boil and simmer until the okra is cooked (approximately 15 minutes). Add the lemon juice and serve with rice or bread.

234 CHUNKY NORTH-INDIAN CURRY
★♥✖◉

CALORIES	365
CHOLESTEROL	55
VEGAN CALORIES	292
POLYUNSATS	★★☆
ANTIOXIDANTS	★★☆
CALCIUM	★☆☆
IRON	★★☆
B VITAMINS	★★☆

½ tsp cayenne pepper
1 tsp turmeric
1 tsp cumin
1 tsp coriander
2 tbsp olive oil
100g (3½oz) lamb fillet chunks/

25g (1oz) soya chunks (dry weight), soaked and drained
250g (9oz) aubergine, diced
2 potatoes (250g [9oz]), diced
1 tsp fresh ginger, finely chopped
3 tomatoes, blended

Place a dry casserole dish or a wok over a medium heat, add the spices and stir for 10 seconds. Then add the oil and the lamb or soya chunks and stir for 1 minute before adding the aubergine and the potatoes. (If you are using soya chunks, you may need to add more oil at this point.) Stir-fry for a further 2 minutes, then add the ginger and the blended tomatoes. Heat through, cover and simmer for 15 minutes. Serve with rice.

EGGLESS SEAFOOD OMELETTE

CALORIES	491
CHOLESTEROL	0
VEGAN CALORIES	491
POLYUNSATS	★★★
ANTIOXIDANTS	★★★
CALCIUM	★★☆
IRON	★★☆
B VITAMINS	★★☆

batter:
100g (3½oz) wheat flour
1 tbsp brewer's yeast flakes
1 tsp baking powder
1 phial saffron
¼ tsp sea salt
200ml (⅓pt) soya/rice milk
1 tsp olive oil, plus some for frying

filling:
1 sweet potato, chopped into
   thin sticks
100g (3½oz) fresh shiitake
   mushrooms, sliced
1 tbsp hiziki seaweed, soaked in hot
   water
1 tbsp tahini
sea salt and black pepper to taste
toasted ground salted sesame
   seeds (gomasio)

Mix the flour, brewer's yeast flakes, baking powder, saffron and salt
in a bowl. Add the milk and the oil and whisk to make a smooth batter.
Set aside. To prepare the filling, stir-fry the sweet potato and the shiitake
in a frying pan with a little hot oil. Add the seaweed with a little of its
soaking water and cook for 5 minutes, then add the tahini, season and
garnish with toasted sesame seeds. Set aside (keep warm). Add the
batter to a clean, oiled frying pan and cook over a medium heat until
the top is dry. Turn and cook the other side. Remove from the heat,
top with the filling, roll and serve.

236 AUTUMN MUSHROOM OMELETTE
★ ✕ 🌿

CALORIES	313
CHOLESTEROL	391
VEGAN CALORIES	322
POLYUNSATS	★★☆
ANTIOXIDANTS	★★☆
CALCIUM	★☆☆
IRON	★★☆
B VITAMINS	★★★

omelette:
4 eggs, beaten
sea salt and black pepper to taste
or 1 portion basic eggless omelette
    batter (see p.41)
olive oil for frying

topping:
1 small leek, sliced
200g (7oz) cep mushrooms, sliced
1 tsp thyme

Mix your chosen batter ingredients and set aside. Gently stir-fry the leek in a frying pan with a little oil until it begins to soften. Add the ceps and the thyme and stir-fry for 3–5 minutes. Set aside. Pour the batter into an oiled frying pan over a medium heat and cook until the top is dry. Turn and cook the other side. Remove from the heat, add the topping and serve.

237 OMELETTE SANDWICH
★ 🌿 🥜

CALORIES	366
CHOLESTEROL	418
VEGAN CALORIES	351
POLYUNSATS	★★★
ANTIOXIDANTS	★★★
CALCIUM	★★☆
IRON	★★☆
B VITAMINS	★★★

omelette:
4 eggs
a little milk/water
sea salt and black pepper to taste
or 1 portion basic eggless omelette
    batter (see p.41)
oil for frying

filling:
1 small red onion, finely chopped
1 small red pepper, finely chopped
100g (3½oz) bacon/
    smoked tempeh, diced and fried
1 tbsp hazelnut butter
2 tbsp fresh parsley, chopped
1 clove garlic, crushed

Mix your chosen batter ingredients in a bowl and add the red onion and red pepper to the batter. Make two thin omelettes out of the one mixture and cook them in a clean, oiled frying pan over a medium heat. Place the first omelette on a warmed serving plate, top with the hot, fried bacon or tempeh cubes and cover with the second omelette. Spread the hazelnut butter on top, then mix the chopped parsley and garlic and sprinkle over. Serve hot with tomato sauce.

238 OMELETTE WITH PINE KERNELS AND PARSLEY
★ 🌿

CALORIES	401
CHOLESTEROL	391
VEGAN CALORIES	410
POLYUNSATS	★★★
ANTIOXIDANTS	★★☆
CALCIUM	★★☆
IRON	★★☆
B VITAMINS	★★☆

omelette:
4 eggs
a little milk/water
sea salt and black pepper to taste
or 1 portion basic eggless omelette
    batter (see p.41)
oil for frying

filling:
2 tbsp pine kernels
1 shallot, finely chopped
2 tbsp fresh parsley

Mix your chosen batter ingredients in a bowl. Add the pine kernels, chopped shallot and fresh parsley to the batter and stir. Heat 1 tablespoon of oil in a frying pan and pour in the omelette mixture. Reduce the heat and cook until the underside is firm and slightly brown. Turn and cook the other side. Serve hot with a tomato salad.

239 SPINACH PANCAKES WITH HOUMOUS AND MUSHROOMS
■▨◧

CALORIES	594
CHOLESTEROL	112
VEGAN CALORIES	524
POLYUNSATS	★★☆
ANTIOXIDANTS	★★☆
CALCIUM	★★☆
IRON	★★☆
B VITAMINS	★★★

pancakes:
1 portion basic pancake batter
   (see p.42)
200g (7oz) fresh spinach, chopped,
   cooked and drained
olive oil for frying

filling:
300g (10½oz) cep (or other wild)
   mushrooms, chopped
2 cloves garlic, crushed
100g (3½oz) houmous
sea salt and black pepper to taste

Mix the batter. Add the spinach and mix well. Heat a little oil in a frying pan and cook the pancakes over a medium–low heat. Add more oil to a separate pan and stir-fry the ceps with the garlic. Spread a spoonful of houmous over each pancake, add the seasoned ceps, fold and serve hot.

240 CHICK PEA AND LEEK PANCAKES
■♥▨◧

CALORIES	664
CHOLESTEROL	112
VEGAN CALORIES	594
POLYUNSATS	★★★
ANTIOXIDANTS	★★★
CALCIUM	★★☆
IRON	★★★
B VITAMINS	★★★

pancakes:
150g (5½oz) wheat flour
1 egg/1 tbsp baking powder
1 pinch salt
200ml (⅓pt) milk/soya milk
200ml (⅓pt) water
1 tbsp grapeseed oil, plus some
   for frying

filling:
1 leek, finely chopped
250g (9oz) chick peas, cooked or
   canned
1 bay leaf
1 tsp turmeric and 1 pinch cinnamon
1 green pepper, finely chopped
100ml (3½fl oz) vegetable stock

Place the flour, baking powder or egg and salt in a bowl and mix well. Add the milk, water and oil and whisk until smooth. Set aside. Stir-fry the leek in a casserole dish with a little oil until soft. Add the chick peas and spices and stir-fry for 2 minutes. Add the pepper and heat through, then add the stock. Bring to the boil and gently simmer while you fry six–eight pancakes in a frying pan with a little oil. Fill the pancakes, roll and serve hot.

241 BUCKWHEAT PANCAKES
■♥◊◧

CALORIES	622
CHOLESTEROL	119
VEGAN CALORIES	529
POLYUNSATS	★★★
ANTIOXIDANTS	★★★
CALCIUM	★★☆
IRON	★★☆
B VITAMINS	★★☆

pancakes:
125g (4½oz) buckwheat flour
1 pinch sea salt
1 egg/2 tsp baking powder
300ml (½pt) milk/soya milk
grapeseed oil for frying

filling:
1 small onion, finely chopped
1 tsp cinnamon
2 tbsp pine kernels
2 carrots and 1 courgette, grated
1 clove garlic, chopped
1 tbsp fresh parsley, chopped
2 slices lemon, peeled and chopped

Mix the flour, salt and baking powder or egg in a bowl. Add the milk little by little until you have a thick batter. Heat a little oil in a frying pan and fry six–eight pancakes over a medium–high heat. Gently heat a little oil in a casserole dish and stir-fry the onion, cinnamon and pine kernels for 3 minutes. Add the courgette and carrot and stir-fry for a further 3 minutes. Add the garlic, parsley and lemon, and season. Serve with the pancakes.

242 CORN PANCAKES WITH KIDNEY BEAN FILLING

CALORIES	822
CHOLESTEROL	13
VEGAN CALORIES	798
POLYUNSATS	★★★
ANTIOXIDANTS	★★☆
CALCIUM	★★☆
IRON	★★☆
B VITAMINS	★★☆

pancakes:
125g (4½oz) cornflour
125g (4½oz) wheat flour
1 tbsp baking powder
½ tsp sea salt
2 tbsp corn oil
300ml (½pt) water

filling:
1 shallot, finely chopped
1 tsp each of cumin and coriander
250g (9oz) red kidney beans, cooked or canned
1 small sweet potato, diced
100ml (3½fl oz) water
sea salt and black pepper to taste
3 tbsp cheese/soya cheese, grated
corn oil for frying

Mix the two flours with the baking powder, salt, corn oil and water in a bowl and whisk to a smooth consistency. Set aside. Gently stir-fry the shallot in a casserole dish with a little oil until soft. Add the spices, kidney beans and sweet potato. Stir-fry over a medium heat for 5 minutes, then add the water and season. Leave to simmer while you heat a little more oil in a frying pan and fry approximately six pancakes. Gently mash the sweet potato and some of the beans with a potato masher. Divide the filling between the pancakes. Sprinkle with grated cheese and serve hot.

243 TOMATO AND GARLIC PIZZA

CALORIES	556
CHOLESTEROL	29
VEGAN CALORIES	503
POLYUNSATS	★★☆
ANTIOXIDANTS	★★☆
CALCIUM	★★☆
IRON	★★☆
B VITAMINS	★★☆

1 pizza base
100g (3½oz) mozzarella/soya cheese
4 fresh ripe tomatoes, chopped
4 cloves garlic, sliced and mixed

with 1 tbsp olive oil
10 black olives
sea salt and black pepper to taste
2 tbsp fresh basil, chopped

Preheat the oven to 240°C/475°F/gas mark 9 and warm up the pizza tray. Cut the cheese into cubes. Set aside. Spread the tomatoes over the prepared base and add a pinch of salt. Top with the garlic, cheese cubes and olives. Season and bake in a hot oven for approximately 15 minutes. Garnish with basil and more black pepper. Serve hot.

244 ◄ PIZZA GRILL

CALORIES	462
CHOLESTEROL	29
VEGAN CALORIES	409
POLYUNSATS	★★☆
ANTIOXIDANTS	★★☆
CALCIUM	★★☆
IRON	★★☆
B VITAMINS	★★☆

French baguette (halved lengthways) or 2 bagels (split) or 2 pitta bread
2 tbsp tomato sauce (passata) or sauce tomate concassé (see p.115)
100g (3½oz) mozzarella/soya

cheese, grated
1 tomato, sliced
1 small red onion, sliced
½ red pepper, sliced
1 small fresh hot chilli, sliced
2 cloves garlic, crushed
1 tbsp fresh basil, chopped

Preheat the grill and toast the underside of the bread. Turn and spread the tomato sauce over the untoasted side. Cover with the grated cheese and the remaining topping ingredients, and season. Grill for 4–5 minutes, or until the cheese has melted. Garnish with fresh basil and serve.

245 PIZZA A LA PIZZAIOLA

CALORIES	511
CHOLESTEROL	37
VEGAN CALORIES	447
POLYUNSATS	★★☆
ANTIOXIDANTS	★★★
CALCIUM	★★★
IRON	★★☆
B VITAMINS	★★☆

1 pizza base
3 tbsp tomato sauce (passata) or
  sauce tomate concassé
  (see p.115)
1 tsp thyme
1 tsp marjoram
1 bay leaf, crushed
1 clove garlic, crushed

¼ green pepper, finely sliced
¼ red pepper, finely sliced
¼ yellow pepper, finely sliced
50g (1¾oz) smoked ham/smoked
  tofu, thinly sliced
sea salt and black pepper to taste
100g (3½oz) mozzarella/soya
  cheese, grated

Preheat the oven to 240°C/475°F/gas mark 9 and warm up the pizza tray.
Spread the tomato sauce over the prepared base. Sprinkle with the
thyme, marjoram, bay leaf and garlic. Arrange the pepper slices and the
smoked ham or smoked tofu on top. Season, sprinkle with the grated
cheese and bake in a hot oven for approximately 15 minutes. Serve hot
with a side salad.

246 AUTUMN SPECIAL

CALORIES	618
CHOLESTEROL	62
VEGAN CALORIES	518
POLYUNSATS	★★☆
ANTIOXIDANTS	★★☆
CALCIUM	★★★
IRON	★★★
B VITAMINS	★★★

1 pizza base
2–3 tbsp tomato sauce (passata) or
  sauce tomate concassé
  (see p.115)
100g (3½oz) fresh spinach, sautéed
150g (5½oz) wild mushrooms
  (as available), chopped
2 cloves garlic, crushed

1 shallot, chopped
4 slices pancetta or bacon/smoked
  tempeh, fried
sea salt and black pepper to taste
100g (3½oz) mozzarella/soya
  cheese, grated
1 tbsp grated Parmesan/brewer's
  yeast flakes

Preheat the oven to 220°C/425°F/gas mark 7 and warm up the pizza tray.
Spread the tomato sauce over the prepared base. Cover with the sautéed
spinach, wild mushrooms, garlic, shallot and pancetta or bacon or smoked
tempeh. Season, sprinkle with the grated cheese or brewer's yeast flakes
and bake in a hot oven for approximately 20 minutes. Serve hot with a
side salad.

247 PIZZA AL FUNGHI

CALORIES	518
CHOLESTEROL	46
VEGAN CALORIES	488
POLYUNSATS	★★☆
ANTIOXIDANTS	★★☆
CALCIUM	★★☆
IRON	★★☆
B VITAMINS	★★★

1 pizza base
2–3 tbsp tomato sauce (passata) or
  sauce tomate concassé
  (see p.115)
½ small hot chilli, finely chopped
4 mushrooms, sliced

100g (3½oz) ham/tempeh, diced
1 spring onion, sliced
a little oregano
sea salt and black pepper to taste
100g (3½oz) mozzarella/soya
  cheese, grated

Preheat the oven to 240°C/475°F/gas mark 9 and warm up the pizza tray.
Spread the tomato sauce over the prepared base and top with the hot
chilli, mushroom slices, ham or tempeh cubes and spring onion slices,
then add a sprinkling of oregano. Season, sprinkle with the grated cheese
and bake in a hot oven for approximately 15 minutes. Serve hot with a
side salad.

248 RICH CEP CASSEROLE

★ ✕ ◉

CALORIES	315
CHOLESTEROL	42
VEGAN CALORIES	298
POLYUNSATS	★★☆
ANTIOXIDANTS	★★☆
CALCIUM	★★☆
IRON	★★☆
B VITAMINS	★★☆

2 tbsp olive oil
1 small red onion, halved and sliced
100g (3½oz) venison steak, sliced into chunks/50g (1¾oz) soya chunks (dry weight), rehydrated
250g (9oz) fresh cep mushrooms, sliced into chunks
1 slice celeriac, chopped

75ml (2½fl oz) red wine
300ml (½pt) vegetable stock
1 tbsp tomato paste (purée)
5 black olives, pitted and chopped
1 tbsp red wine vinegar
1 tbsp tamari (soya sauce)
1 tsp thyme
sea salt and black pepper to taste

Heat the oil in a heavy-based casserole dish and sweat the onion over a medium heat for 1 minute. Add the venison chunks or soya chunks, turn up the heat and fry until they begin to brown, then add the ceps and fry for a further 2–3 minutes over a medium heat. Add the celeriac, red wine and stock and heat through before adding the tomato paste, olives, vinegar, tamari and thyme. Stir, bring to the boil and gently simmer for 15 minutes. Season and serve with rice.

249 SPICY RAGOUT

★ 🌾 ◉

CALORIES	483
CHOLESTEROL	83
VEGAN CALORIES	357
POLYUNSATS	★★☆
ANTIOXIDANTS	★★★
CALCIUM	★★☆
IRON	★★☆
B VITAMINS	★★★

olive oil for sautéing
150g (5½oz) pork/seitan, sliced
1 red onion, halved and sliced
150g (5½oz) oyster mushrooms, sliced
1 sweet potato, cut into sticks
1 small courgette, cut into sticks

1 small aubergine, cut into sticks
1 large tomato, finely chopped
½ tsp cinnamon
1 bay leaf
1 pinch turmeric
1 pinch cayenne pepper
100ml (3½fl oz) vegetable stock

Heat some oil in a casserole dish and sauté the pork or seitan until brown. Add the onion and the mushrooms and stir for 3 minutes, then add the sweet potato, courgette and aubergine and stir for a further 2 minutes. Add the tomato and the spices and heat through. Heat the stock and add it to the pan. Season, bring to the boil, cover and simmer for 10–15 minutes. Check the seasoning and serve with boiled or baked potatoes.

250 AUTUMN GRILL

★ ◉ ◔

CALORIES	587
CHOLESTEROL	168
VEGAN CALORIES	629
POLYUNSATS	★★★
ANTIOXIDANTS	★★★
CALCIUM	★★☆
IRON	★★☆
B VITAMINS	★★★

2 corn-on-the-cobs, peeled and sliced into chunks
1 yellow pepper, quartered
4 cep (or other) mushrooms, sliced
4 small tomatoes
1 sweet potato, cut into thick sticks
12 scampi/sweet chestnuts

olive oil for brushing
sea salt and black pepper to taste
150ml (¼pt) tomato ketchup
2 tbsp lemon juice
75ml (2½fl oz) red wine vinegar
1 tbsp raw cane sugar
1 tbsp mustard

Brush the corn-on-the-cobs, yellow pepper, mushrooms, tomatoes, sweet potato and scampi (if using) with the oil and cook them on a hot barbecue with the shelled and peeled chestnuts (if using), then season. Meanwhile, make the barbecue sauce by mixing the tomato ketchup, lemon juice, vinegar, sugar and mustard. Serve the vegetables hot with the sauce.

251 ▼ BULGUR PILAF

CALORIES	440
CHOLESTEROL	17
VEGAN CALORIES	441
POLYUNSATS	★★★
ANTIOXIDANTS	★★★
CALCIUM	★★☆
IRON	★★☆
B VITAMINS	★★☆

2 tbsp grapeseed oil
100g (3½oz) smoked ham/
    chick peas, cooked or canned
1 tbsp tamari (soya sauce)
    (optional)
100g (3½oz) bulgur wheat
200ml (⅓pt) hot water

100g (3½oz) green peas
sea salt and black pepper to taste
½ small red onion, finely chopped
½ lemon, peeled and chopped
10–12 small grape tomatoes,
    quartered
2–3 tbsp fresh mint, finely chopped

Gently sweat the ham or chick peas in a frying pan with 1 tablespoon of oil until they begin to brown. Add the tamari (if using), then the bulgur wheat and stir-fry for 2–3 minutes. Pour in the water and simmer at the lowest possible heat for 10–12 minutes, adding the peas after 5 minutes. Stir from time to time (adding a little more water if necessary). Remove from the heat and season. Add the onion, lemon, tomatoes and mint, and sprinkle with the remaining tablespoon of oil. Serve immediately.

252 TARTLETS PROVENÇALE
★🌿⌀

CALORIES	772
CHOLESTEROL	525
VEGAN CALORIES	663
POLYUNSATS	★★★
ANTIOXIDANTS	★★★
CALCIUM	★★☆
IRON	★★★
B VITAMINS	★★★

100g (3½oz) ready-made shortcrust pastry, rolled out
300g (10½oz) chicken liver, cut into strips/175g (6oz) tempeh, cut into chunks
1 sweet potato, cut into thin sticks
2 tbsp plain flour

sea salt and black pepper to taste
olive oil for frying
1 small clove garlic, chopped
2 tbsp tomato paste (purée)
10 black olives, halved and pitted
100ml (3½fl oz) vegetable stock
1 tbsp parsley, chopped

Place the rolled-out pastry into two individual 10cm (4in) round pastry dishes. Spread a handful of dried beans or lentils over each one and bake at 220°C/425°F/gas mark 7 until firm (10–15 minutes). Allow to cool and remove the beans. Meanwhile, flour the liver or tempeh and the sweet potato, season and fry in a frying pan with a little oil for 5 minutes. Add the garlic and stir for 30 seconds before adding the tomato paste and the olives. Then add the stock, heat up the sauce and let it thicken. Fill the tartlets with the sauce and heat in the oven for 2 minutes. Garnish with parsley and serve with a seasonal salad (such as lamb's lettuce or rocket) and vinaigrette dressing.

253 AUTUMN CASSEROLE
★◊🥔⌀🥕

CALORIES	559
CHOLESTEROL	88
VEGAN CALORIES	524
POLYUNSATS	★★☆
ANTIOXIDANTS	★★★
CALCIUM	★★☆
IRON	★★☆
B VITAMINS	★★☆

250g (9oz) chicken breast, sliced/60g (2¼oz) soya chunks (dry weight), soaked and drained
1 tbsp maple syrup
1 tbsp tomato paste (purée)
1 tsp paprika
1 tsp ground cumin
seeds from 2 cardamom pods
1 tbsp tamari (soya sauce)
1 tbsp red wine vinegar

1 dash Tabasco sauce
2 tbsp olive oil
2 shallots, quartered
4 cloves garlic, quartered
½ lemon, cut into wedges
350g (12oz) sweet potato, sliced
sea salt and black pepper to taste
1 handful fresh parsley, chopped
1 tsp maple syrup or raw cane sugar (optional)

In a bowl, marinate the chicken or soya chunks in the maple syrup, tomato paste, paprika, cumin, cardamom seeds, tamari, vinegar, Tabasco sauce and 1 tablespoon of oil. Set aside. Gently heat the remaining tablespoon of oil in a casserole dish and stir-fry the shallots for 3 minutes. Add the marinated chicken or soya chunks (with their marinade) and cook over a medium heat for 5 minutes. Then add the garlic, lemon and sweet potato and heat through. Cover and simmer for 15 minutes, or until the chicken is tender. (Adding a little water if necessary.) Season and garnish with fresh parsley and maple syrup or sugar (if using). Serve with rice.

NORMANDIE SUPRÊME

⭐🌿

CALORIES	581
CHOLESTEROL	292
VEGAN CALORIES	368
POLYUNSATS	★★★
ANTIOXIDANTS	★★☆
CALCIUM	★☆☆
IRON	★★☆
B VITAMINS	★★☆

vegetable oil for frying
2 pheasant breasts/175g (6oz)
  seitan, cut into strips
2 dessert apples
1 pinch sugar
sea salt and black pepper to taste

50ml (2fl oz) apple cider
100ml (3½fl oz) stock
50ml (2fl oz) crème fraîche/soya
  cream
20ml (⅔fl oz) calvados

Fry the pheasant breasts or seitan strips in a frying pan with a little oil. Remove from the pan and set aside (keep hot). Core and quarter the apples, then sauté them in the same pan with a little more oil and the sugar and seasoning until they begin to brown. Remove from the pan. Set aside. Add the cider and the stock to the pan and leave to reduce to half the volume. Add the cream and the calvados. Leave to reduce again, until the sauce thickens. Check the seasoning. Place the pheasant breast or seitan strips on a heated serving plate with the apples next to them, pour over the sauce and serve with steamed potatoes and sautéed mushrooms.

SUSIE'S LENTILS

⭐❤💧✖🌾

CALORIES	322
CHOLESTEROL	0
VEGAN CALORIES	322
POLYUNSATS	★★☆
ANTIOXIDANTS	★★★
CALCIUM	★☆☆
IRON	★★☆
B VITAMINS	★★☆

100g (3½oz) Puy lentils
olive oil for stir-frying
1 onion, finely chopped
2 carrots, finely chopped
2 cloves garlic, finely chopped

1 small courgette, finely chopped
2 tomatoes, finely chopped
1 tbsp tamari (soya sauce)
1 bay leaf
1 tsp thyme

Bring the lentils to the boil in a saucepan with twice their volume of water and gently simmer while you prepare the other ingredients. Heat a little oil in a separate pan and stir-fry the onion, carrots, garlic, courgette and tomatoes (adding them one at a time). Then add the tamari, bay leaf and thyme, together with the partially-cooked lentils and enough water to cover. Heat through and simmer until the lentils are soft (10–15 minutes). Season and serve with bread and slices of ham or fried tempeh.

CHESTNUT CASSEROLE

⭐❤✖🌾🌿

CALORIES	327
CHOLESTEROL	0
VEGAN CALORIES	327
POLYUNSATS	★★☆
ANTIOXIDANTS	★★☆
CALCIUM	★★☆
IRON	★★☆
B VITAMINS	★★☆

oil for sautéing
1 shallot, sliced
1 clove garlic, sliced
250g (9oz) button mushrooms
300g (10½oz) sweet chestnuts, fresh,
  peeled and soaked or canned
1 tbsp wheat flour

2cm (¾in) cube fresh ginger, sliced
1 tsp curry powder
300ml (½pt) vegetable stock
1 sprinkle Tabasco sauce
1 tbsp horseradish root, freshly
  grated
2 tbsp fresh parsley, finely chopped

Sweat the shallot, garlic and mushrooms in a casserole dish with a little oil for 3–4 minutes, stirring occasionally. Stir in the chestnuts and sauté for 3 minutes. Add the flour, ginger and curry powder and cook for 1–2 minutes. Then add the stock, Tabasco sauce and horseradish. Season and bring to the boil. Cover and gently simmer until the chestnuts are tender. Garnish with parsley and serve with green beans, carrots and (mashed) potato.

257 WILD MUSHROOM PIE

CALORIES	475
CHOLESTEROL	203
VEGAN CALORIES	450
POLYUNSATS	★★★
ANTIOXIDANTS	★★★
CALCIUM	★★☆
IRON	★★☆
B VITAMINS	★★☆

200g (7oz) puff pastry, rolled out
2 tbsp olive oil
3 small shallots, halved and sliced
250g (9oz) wild mushrooms

1 tsp thyme
100ml (3½fl oz) milk/soya milk
2 eggs/125g (4½oz) tofu, crumbled
1 pinch nutmeg

Place the rolled-out pastry on greaseproof paper in a 23cm (9in) round baking tin. Scatter with baking beans and bake blind in a preheated oven at 220°C/425°F/gas mark 7 for 10–15 minutes. Allow to cool and remove the beans. Gently sweat the shallots in a heavy-based frying pan with the oil for 5 minutes. Add the mushrooms and the thyme and stir-fry for 10 minutes. Blend the milk, eggs or tofu and nutmeg to a smooth consistency, and season. Place the mushrooms on the pastry, pour the blended mixture over, return to the oven and bake for 15–20 minutes until firm, and serve.

258 SPICY CHICK PEAS WITH AUBERGINE

CALORIES	466
CHOLESTEROL	0
VEGAN CALORIES	466
POLYUNSATS	★☆☆
ANTIOXIDANTS	★★★
CALCIUM	★★☆
IRON	★★☆
B VITAMINS	★★☆

2 tbsp olive oil
1 leek, sliced
400g (14oz) chick peas, cooked or
   canned
1 aubergine, diced

1 clove garlic, crushed
½ tsp ground cumin
½ tsp ground coriander
500g (1lb 2oz) tomatoes, chopped
sea salt and black pepper to taste

Heat the oil in a casserole dish and gently sweat the leek for 5 minutes. Turn up the heat a little and add the chick peas, aubergine, garlic, cumin and coriander. Stir-fry for 5 minutes. Add the tomatoes and bring to the boil. Cover and simmer for 15 minutes (adding a little water if necessary). Season and serve with rice.

259 TURKISH BOREG

CALORIES	658
CHOLESTEROL	55
VEGAN CALORIES	598
POLYUNSATS	★★★
ANTIOXIDANTS	★★★
CALCIUM	★★☆
IRON	★★★
B VITAMINS	★★★

2 tbsp olive oil
1 shallot, chopped
100g (3½oz) minced pork/tempeh,
   grated
4 mushrooms, chopped
1 carrot, grated
25g (1oz) couscous, covered with
   boiling water and soaked for

10 minutes
2 tbsp fresh parsley, chopped
1 tsp thyme
zest of ½ lemon
sea salt and black pepper to taste
1 packet ready-made shortcrust
   pastry, rolled out thinly

Preheat the oven to 220°C/425°F/gas mark 7. Soften the onion in a saucepan or a wok with the oil. Add the minced pork or grated tempeh and the mushrooms and stir-fry for 5 minutes, then add the carrot, soaked couscous, parsley, thyme and lemon zest, and season. Pile the filling onto the centre of the rolled-out pastry and fold in the edges to form a parcel. Turn upside down onto a greased baking tray. Glaze with cold water and bake for 15–20 minutes. Serve with steamed vegetables and plain or soya yoghurt mixed with fresh mint, cayenne pepper and celery salt.

260 ▼ BLENDED PUMPKIN HOTPOT WITH GRILLED AUTUMN VEGETABLES

★♥◊🌿◉

CALORIES	580
CHOLESTEROL	70
VEGAN CALORIES	592
POLYUNSATS	★★★
ANTIOXIDANTS	★★★
CALCIUM	★★☆
IRON	★★☆
B VITAMINS	★★★

200g (7oz) chicken breast/seitan,
  cut into chunks
1 parsnip, cut into chunks
1 small beetroot, quartered
4 potatoes, quartered
1 tbsp paprika
olive oil for stir-frying
300g (10½oz) pumpkin

1 red onion, halved and sliced
1 clove garlic, crushed
1 tbsp fresh marjoram
200ml (⅓pt) vegetable stock,
  heated
1–2 tbsp white almond butter
sea salt and black pepper to taste

Preheat the oven to 220°C/425°F/gas mark 7. Scatter the chicken
or seitan, parsnip, beetroot and potatoes on an oiled baking tray and
sprinkle with paprika and a little salt and pepper. Grill in a hot oven
until they begin to turn brown and soft. Check and turn from time to time.
Meanwhile, peel, deseed and chop the pumpkin, then gently stir-fry the
pieces with the onion and garlic in a casserole dish with a little oil for 5
minutes. Add the marjoram and the stock and bring to the boil.
Cover and gently simmer for 10 minutes. Blend the
pumpkin mixture and add the almond butter.
Season and serve with the grilled seitan
or chicken and the grilled vegetables.

261 ▼ BAKED FRUIT KEBABS
♥✕▣

CALORIES	287
CHOLESTEROL	0
VEGAN CALORIES	287
POLYUNSATS	★☆☆
ANTIOXIDANTS	★★☆
CALCIUM	★☆☆
IRON	★☆☆
B VITAMINS	★☆☆

1 orange, peeled and cut into chunks
1 pear, cored and cut into chunks
1 apple, cored and cut into chunks
1 banana, peeled and cut into chunks
8 sweet chestnuts, shelled and peeled
150ml (¼pt) grape juice
2 tsp Grand Marnier
2 tsp maple syrup
oil for brushing

Preheat the oven to 240°C/475°F/gas mark 9. Thread the fruit chunks and the sweet chestnuts onto barbecue skewers. Make a marinade of the grape juice, Grand Marnier and maple syrup and brush over the fruit. Place the skewers on greaseproof paper brushed with oil. Roll each skewer in the paper and bake in a hot oven for 15 minutes.
Serve with the remaining marinade as a dip.

262 MELLOW MELON

CALORIES	306
CHOLESTEROL	0
VEGAN CALORIES	306
POLYUNSATS	★☆☆
ANTIOXIDANTS	★★☆
CALCIUM	★★☆
IRON	★☆☆
B VITAMINS	★☆☆

½ cantaloupe melon, peeled,
   deseeded and diced
1 bunch green grapes, halved
1 orange, peeled, halved and sliced

2 ripe green figs, quartered
1 banana, peeled and sliced
1 large fresh date, pitted
1 tsp maple syrup

Mix the melon, grapes, orange and figs in a bowl. Blend the banana with the date, maple syrup and enough water to make a thick, smooth sauce. Pour the sauce over the fruit and serve.

263 BLUEBERRY SALAD

CALORIES	220
CHOLESTEROL	0
VEGAN CALORIES	220
POLYUNSATS	★☆☆
ANTIOXIDANTS	★★★
CALCIUM	★★☆
IRON	★★☆
B VITAMINS	★☆☆

100g (3½oz) fresh blueberries
200g (7oz) red grapes, halved
1 banana, peeled and sliced

1 sharon fruit, halved and sliced
1 papaya, peeled and deseeded
4 fresh dark figs, chopped

Mix the blueberries, grapes, banana and sharon fruit in a glass bowl. Chop the papaya and blend it with the figs and a little water to make a thick sauce. Pour the sauce over the berries and fruit, and serve.

264 SHARON FRUIT WITH JUICY PEARS

CALORIES	269
CHOLESTEROL	0
VEGAN CALORIES	269
POLYUNSATS	★☆☆
ANTIOXIDANTS	★★★
CALCIUM	★☆☆
IRON	★☆☆
B VITAMINS	★☆☆

1 sharon fruit, sliced
1 large ripe pear, halved, cored and
   sliced
1 small bunch red grapes, halved

4 fresh dates, pitted and chopped
100ml (3½fl oz) apple juice
1 pinch cinnamon
juice of 1 mandarin

Place the sharon fruit, pear and grapes in a glass bowl. Blend the dates, apple juice, cinnamon and mandarin juice. Pour the mixture over the fresh fruit and leave to marinate until serving.

265 PINEAPPLE BOATS

CALORIES	255
CHOLESTEROL	0
VEGAN CALORIES	255
POLYUNSATS	★☆☆
ANTIOXIDANTS	★★★
CALCIUM	★★☆
IRON	★☆☆
B VITAMINS	★☆☆

1 small pineapple, halved
   lengthways
1 small bunch red grapes, halved
1 kiwi, peeled and diced
1 banana, peeled and sliced

zest and juice of ½ lime
1 tbsp maple syrup
juice of 1 orange
1 tbsp Grand Marnier (optional)
1 tsp fresh ginger, finely chopped

Scoop out the pineapple flesh to make two boats and set the boats aside. Cut the pineapple flesh into chunks and place them in a bowl with the remaining ingredients. Gently toss, then spoon into the pineapple boats and serve with plain or soya yoghurt or custard (see p.140).

266 AUTUMN COLOURS

CALORIES	196
CHOLESTEROL	0
VEGAN CALORIES	196
POLYUNSATS	★☆☆
ANTIOXIDANTS	★★★
CALCIUM	★☆☆
IRON	★☆☆
B VITAMINS	★☆☆

1 red apple, cored and sliced
1 small bunch red grapes, halved
1 mango, peeled and sliced
1 pomelo, peeled and sliced

100ml (3½fl oz) orange juice
1 tbsp lemon juice
2 tsp honey
fresh coriander leaves, chopped

Mix the fruit in a glass bowl. Heat the orange juice in a small casserole dish, add the lemon juice and the honey and simmer until the honey is dissolved. Remove from the heat, allow to cool a little and pour over the fruit. Gently toss, garnish with fresh coriander and serve.

267 PLUM TART

CALORIES	312
CHOLESTEROL	0
VEGAN CALORIES	312
POLYUNSATS	★★☆
ANTIOXIDANTS	★★☆
CALCIUM	★★☆
IRON	★☆☆
B VITAMINS	★☆☆

1 packet ready-made puff pastry,
   rolled out
300g (10½oz) ripe plums, quartered

and pitted
1 tbsp liquid honey
1 pinch cinnamon

Preheat the oven to 220°C/425°F/gas mark 7. Place the rolled-out pastry in a 20cm (8in) round baking tray. Line with the plums and brush with the honey. Sprinkle with the cinnamon and bake in a hot oven for 15 minutes. Serve with crème fraîche or soya cream.

268 APPLE SALAD, WALDORF-STYLE

CALORIES	478
CHOLESTEROL	0
VEGAN CALORIES	478
POLYUNSATS	★★★
ANTIOXIDANTS	★★★
CALCIUM	★☆☆
IRON	★★☆
B VITAMINS	★★☆

2 large lettuce leaves
2 red apples, cored and sliced
2 sticks celery, sliced
100g (3½oz) grapes, halved
100g (3½oz) raisins

100ml (3½fl oz) apple juice
½ avocado, halved, pitted, peeled
   and chopped
2 tbsp pecan nuts

Place the lettuce leaves on two plates. Arrange the apples, celery, grapes and raisins on top of the leaves. Blend the apple juice with the avocado and pour over the salads. Garnish with pecan nuts and serve.

269 FRESH AND FRUITY SALAD

CALORIES	137
CHOLESTEROL	0
VEGAN CALORIES	137
POLYUNSATS	★☆☆
ANTIOXIDANTS	★★★
CALCIUM	★★☆
IRON	★☆☆
B VITAMINS	★★☆

1 handful Iceberg lettuce leaves,
   shredded
1 orange, peeled and sliced
1 carrot, grated

100g (3½oz) blackberries
1 apple, cored and sliced
100ml (3½fl oz) grape juice
½ lime, sliced

Place the lettuce on two plates. Top with the orange, carrot, blackberries and apple. Sprinkle with grape juice, garnish with slices of lime and serve.

270 SILKY FRUIT SALAD
🟦🟦🟦🟦

CALORIES	356
CHOLESTEROL	0
VEGAN CALORIES	356
POLYUNSATS	★★★
ANTIOXIDANTS	★★☆
CALCIUM	★☆☆
IRON	★★☆
B VITAMINS	★★☆

2 tbsp dried apricots, sliced
100ml (3½fl oz) grape juice
1 banana, peeled and sliced
1 sharon fruit, halved and sliced

1 large ripe pear, cored and sliced
2 blue plums, pitted and sliced
1 pomegranate, peeled and chopped
2 tbsp pine kernels, chopped

Soak the dried apricots in the grape juice while you prepare the other fruit. Then place all the fresh fruit in a glass bowl, add the soaked apricots together with the grape juice and gently toss. Garnish with chopped pine kernels and serve.

271 ORCHARD HARVEST WITH CUSTARD
🟦🟦

CALORIES	370
CHOLESTEROL	18
VEGAN CALORIES	320
POLYUNSATS	★☆☆
ANTIOXIDANTS	★★☆
CALCIUM	★☆☆
IRON	★☆☆
B VITAMINS	★★☆

2 ripe pears, cored and sliced
1 red apple, cored and sliced
1 sharon fruit, sliced
2 fresh figs, quartered
2 plums, pitted and quartered

custard:
1 tbsp cornflour
1 tbsp raw cane sugar
1 tsp vanilla essence
1 pinch salt
250ml (9fl oz) milk/soya milk

Arrange the fruit on two plates. To make the custard, put the cornflour into a bowl with the sugar, vanilla essence, salt and enough milk to make a smooth paste. Heat the remaining milk in a saucepan (don't let it boil), then slowly add it to the cornflour mixture, stirring continuously.
Pour the custard back into the saucepan, stir and bring to the boil.
Remove from the heat and serve with the fruit.

272 APPLE CRUMBLE
🟦🟦

CALORIES	534
CHOLESTEROL	0
VEGAN CALORIES	534
POLYUNSATS	★★★
ANTIOXIDANTS	★★☆
CALCIUM	★☆☆
IRON	★★☆
B VITAMINS	★★☆

20g (¾oz) raisins
1 tbsp rum (optional)
2 (reinette) apples, thinly sliced
1 tbsp grapeseed oil

125g (4½oz) rolled oats
25g (1oz) chopped walnuts
2 tbsp maple syrup

Preheat the oven to 230°C/450°F/gas mark 8. Soak the raisins in a bowl with the rum (if using) and enough cold water to cover. Place the sliced apples in an oiled, ovenproof dish. Cover with the soaked raisins and their liquid. Heat the oil in a small frying pan and stir in the oats and the walnuts. Add the maple syrup and gently heat through for 1 minute, stirring continuously. Evenly spoon the crumble mixture over the apples and bake in a hot oven for approximately 15 minutes until the topping is golden brown. Serve with ice cream or soya ice cream.

LAYERED FRUIT SALAD

⭐ ♡ 💧

CALORIES	402
CHOLESTEROL	6
VEGAN CALORIES	399
POLYUNSATS	★★☆
ANTIOXIDANTS	★★★
CALCIUM	★★☆
IRON	★★☆
B VITAMINS	★★☆

1 mango, peeled and sliced
1 banana, peeled and sliced
    lengthways
4 plums, pitted and sliced
100g (3½oz) raspberries

1 papaya, peeled, deseeded
    and diced
2 tbsp cashew nuts
1 tbsp maple syrup
100ml (3½oz) plain/soya yoghurt

Arrange the mango, banana, plums and raspberries in layers in a dish.
Blend the papaya with the cashew nuts, maple syrup and yoghurt.
Pour the sauce over the fruit layers and serve.

WINTER
RECIPES

Winter is the lean season. The energy is resting deep in the ground and, in Chinese philosophy, it is thought of as the season of most yin, when the energy is inward-looking. Nature sleeps and prepares, and it is time to let go of the old and to favour peace. Outside, all is barren and still, but inside there is warmth, an opportunity to study and learn, time for leisure, culture and rest.

Winter is also the festive season, where we gather to enjoy each other's company in coziness indoors. It is the inner light that shines while we wait for the sun to return and, from a nutritional viewpoint, winter is the time to use the reserves that have been built up in the autumn. We need more calorie-rich meals to keep us warm, and the most favoured ingredients are pulses, rice and grain, cabbage, leeks and root vegetables. Fish and fatty foods help keep us warm, and dried fruits provide energy. The element of this season is water, which corresponds to the kidneys and the bladder, and special attention should be paid to the basic life energies. Keep warm and well nourished, stay quiet and peaceful, and enjoy this season of still life.

274 WALNUT AND CELERY SOUP
♡◦◯

CALORIES	579
CHOLESTEROL	18
VEGAN CALORIES	529
POLYUNSATS	★★★
ANTIOXIDANTS	★★☆
CALCIUM	★★☆
IRON	★★☆
B VITAMINS	★★☆

15 walnuts (30 halves), shelled
2 tbsp olive oil
1 shallot, sliced
2 cloves garlic, chopped
2 sticks celery, chopped
250ml (9fl oz) water

1 pinch ground mace
2 tbsp tamari (soya sauce)
1 tbsp lemon juice
250ml (9fl oz) milk/soya milk
sea salt and black pepper to taste

Place the shelled walnuts in a saucepan of boiling water for 2 minutes. Drain and set aside. Heat the oil in a saucepan and gently fry the shallots until soft. Add the garlic and celery and fry for a further minute. Pour in the water and bring to the boil. Simmer for 5 minutes. Remove from the heat. Add the cooked walnuts, mace, tamari, lemon juice and milk. Gently heat through, stirring continuously. Season and serve with crusty bread rolls.

275 CALDO VERDE
★✕◎

CALORIES	302
CHOLESTEROL	25
VEGAN CALORIES	235
POLYUNSATS	★★☆
ANTIOXIDANTS	★★★
CALCIUM	★☆☆
IRON	★★☆
B VITAMINS	★★☆

850ml (1½pts) water or vegetable
    stock
50g (1¾oz) curly kale leaves,
    chopped
2 potatoes, diced
1 shallot, chopped

4 cloves garlic, chopped
100g (3½oz) spicy sausage
    (pork/soya), sliced
1 tbsp olive oil, plus some for frying
sea salt and black pepper to taste

Bring the water or stock to the boil in a saucepan with the curly kale, potatoes, shallot, garlic and a little salt. Heat through and simmer for 20 minutes. Meanwhile, fry the sausage slices in a frying pan with a little oil. Set aside. Blend the soup, check the seasoning and add the oil. Garnish with pepper and spicy sausage, and serve hot with corn bread.

276 UKRAINIAN BORSCH
★♡◦✕✿◎

CALORIES	294
CHOLESTEROL	0
VEGAN CALORIES	294
POLYUNSATS	★☆☆
ANTIOXIDANTS	★★★
CALCIUM	★★☆
IRON	★★☆
B VITAMINS	★★☆

2 tbsp olive oil
1 onion, chopped
100g (3½oz) raw beetroot, diced
100g (3½oz) white cabbage,
    shredded
1 carrot, diced
1 potato, diced
100g (3½oz) mushrooms, chopped

1 stick celery, finely chopped
1 tbsp wheat flour
2 ripe tomatoes, blended
1ltr (1¾pts) vegetable stock
1 handful fresh parsley, finely
    chopped
sea salt and black pepper to taste

Gently stir-fry the onion, beetroot, cabbage, carrot and potato in a saucepan with the oil for 5 minutes. Add the mushrooms and the celery and stir-fry for a further 3 minutes. Sprinkle the flour into the pan and mix with the vegetables for 1 minute. Continue to stir while adding the blended tomatoes, followed by the stock. Bring to the boil, add the fresh parsley and simmer for 20 minutes. Season and serve with garlic croutons.

277 CHINESE SOUP WITH SHIITAKE AND NOODLES
⭐❤️❌🌿

CALORIES	344
CHOLESTEROL	0
VEGAN CALORIES	344
POLYUNSATS	★★☆
ANTIOXIDANTS	★★★
CALCIUM	★★★
IRON	★★☆
B VITAMINS	★★☆

2 tbsp olive oil
1 spring onion, chopped
125g (4½oz) tofu
100g (3½oz) shiitake mushrooms, sliced
5 pieces bamboo shoots, cut into squares
1 small carrot, sliced into sticks

1ltr (1¾pts) vegetable stock
2 tbsp tamari (soya sauce)
2 tbsp dry sherry
1 pinch Chinese Five-Spice
1 small bunch watercress, chopped
1 tsp sesame oil
1 handful noodles

Gently heat the oil in a casserole dish and stir-fry the spring onion for 30 seconds. Add the tofu, shiitake, bamboo shoots and carrot and stir-fry for 2 minutes before adding the stock, tamari, sherry, Five-Spice and watercress. Bring to the boil. Add the oil and noodles. Cover, remove from the heat and leave for 2 minutes until the noodles are cooked, and serve.

278 LEEK AND POTATO SOUP
❤️❌🌾

CALORIES	223
CHOLESTEROL	0
VEGAN CALORIES	223
POLYUNSATS	★★☆
ANTIOXIDANTS	★★☆
CALCIUM	★☆☆
IRON	★★☆
B VITAMINS	★★☆

2 tbsp olive oil
2 leeks, sliced
2 potatoes, diced

1ltr (1¾pts) vegetable stock
sea salt and black pepper to taste

Gently heat the oil in a saucepan, add the leeks and the potatoes and sauté for 3 minutes, then add the stock. Heat through and simmer for 15 minutes. Season and serve with croutons.

279 BEANY SOUP
⭐❤️🌾

CALORIES	429
CHOLESTEROL	0
VEGAN CALORIES	429
POLYUNSATS	★☆☆
ANTIOXIDANTS	★★★
CALCIUM	★★☆
IRON	★★☆
B VITAMINS	★★☆

100g (3½oz) green lentils
3 tbsp olive oil
1 small leek, sliced
1 thin slice celeriac, diced
1 small carrot, sliced
1 tsp paprika
1ltr (1¾pts) vegetable stock
100g (3½oz) red kidney beans, cooked or canned

100g (3½oz) broad beans, fresh or frozen
50g (1¾oz) French beans, chopped
1 bay leaf
1 tbsp tomato paste (purée)
1 tsp thyme
1 tsp sage
sea salt and black pepper to taste
fresh parsley to garnish (optional)

Boil the lentils in a saucepan with plenty of water. Meanwhile, gently heat the oil in a large casserole dish and stir fry the leek for 1 minute. Add the celeriac, carrot and paprika and stir-fry for a further minute, then add the stock. Bring to boil, add the remaining ingredients (except for the parsley) and heat through. Add the partially-cooked lentils with a little of their cooking water. Bring to the boil again, and simmer for 10 minutes until the lentils are cooked. Remove the bay leaf, check the seasoning and serve garnished with fresh parsley (if using).

JAPANESE SPINACH SOUP

★♥◊✕🌿◻

CALORIES	207
CHOLESTEROL	0
VEGAN CALORIES	207
POLYUNSATS	★★★
ANTIOXIDANTS	★★★
CALCIUM	★★★
IRON	★★☆
B VITAMINS	★★☆

1 tbsp grapeseed oil
1 shallot, sliced
1 small carrot, finely chopped
125g (4½oz) tofu, diced
4 medium mushrooms, sliced
100g (3½oz) spinach, chopped
   into strips
2 tsp tamari (soya sauce)
10cm (4in) strip kombu seaweed

¼ tsp raw cane sugar
1 tsp mirin (Japanese rice wine) or
   dry sherry (optional)
1ltr (1¾pts) water
sea salt and black pepper to taste
½ tsp sesame oil
1 tsp lemon juice
lemon peel, cut into strips
   to garnish

Heat the grapeseed oil in a saucepan, add the shallot, carrot and tofu
cubes and stir-fry for 1 minute. Add the mushrooms and stir for a further
minute, then add the spinach and continue to stir over a medium heat
until the spinach is wilted. Add the remaining ingredients (except for the
sesame oil, lemon juice and lemon peel). Bring to the boil and simmer for
10 minutes. Then add the sesame oil and lemon juice. Check the seasoning
and serve garnished with strips of lemon peel.

281 CREAMY PARSNIP SOUP
♥

CALORIES	396
CHOLESTEROL	6
VEGAN CALORIES	393
POLYUNSATS	★★☆
ANTIOXIDANTS	★★☆
CALCIUM	★★☆
IRON	★★☆
B VITAMINS	★★☆

2 tbsp olive oil
2 tsp mustard powder
500g (1lb 2oz) parsnips,
   chopped
1 cooking apple, peeled, cored
   and chopped

1ltr (1¾pts) vegetable stock
1 tbsp tamari (soya sauce)
1 tsp thyme
sea salt and black pepper to taste
100ml (3½fl oz) plain/soya yoghurt

Gently heat the oil in a large saucepan. Stir in the mustard powder and let it dissolve. Add the parsnips and the apple and stir-fry for a few minutes, then add the stock and bring to the boil. Cover and simmer for 10 minutes. Add the tamari and the thyme, and season. Blend to a rich, creamy texture, check the seasoning and serve with a spoonful of plain or soya yoghurt in each bowl.

282 MONKFISH AND FENNEL SOUP

CALORIES	317
CHOLESTEROL	26
VEGAN CALORIES	281
POLYUNSATS	★★☆
ANTIOXIDANTS	★★★
CALCIUM	★★☆
IRON	★★☆
B VITAMINS	★★☆

2 tbsp olive oil
1 small red onion, sliced
1 Florence fennel bulb, halved
   and sliced
2 potatoes, diced
½ltr (18fl oz) vegetable (/fish) stock
100ml (3½fl oz) dry white wine
½ lemon (unpeeled), quartered and
   sliced

1 tsp raw cane sugar
2 tbsp tomato paste (purée)
250g (9oz) monkfish, skinned,
   boned and diced/125g (4½oz)
   tofu, diced and fried with a little
   tamari (soya sauce)
2 tbsp fresh dill, finely chopped
sea salt and black pepper to taste

Heat the oil in a saucepan and sweat the onion over a low heat for 2–3 minutes. Add the fennel and the potatoes, turn the heat to medium and sauté for 2 minutes. Then add the stock, wine, lemon, sugar and tomato paste. Bring to the boil, add the monkfish or tofu and gently simmer for 5–7 minutes. Garnish with dill and season. Serve with crusty bread rolls.

283 CAULIFLOWER SOUP

CALORIES	281
CHOLESTEROL	7
VEGAN CALORIES	261
POLYUNSATS	★★☆
ANTIOXIDANTS	★★★
CALCIUM	★★☆
IRON	★★☆
B VITAMINS	★★☆

850ml (1½pts) vegetable stock
1 small cauliflower, cut into
   small florets
1 small onion, finely chopped
1 small carrot, finely chopped
2 medium potatoes, finely chopped

2 tbsp olive oil
1 pinch asafoetida
1 pinch saffron
sea salt and black pepper to taste
100ml (3½fl oz) milk/soya milk
1 handful fresh parsley, chopped

Bring the stock to the boil in a casserole dish with the cauliflower florets and the chopped onion, carrot and potatoes. Add the oil, asafoetida, saffron and a little seasoning. Simmer for 10–15 minutes. Turn off the heat and add the milk. Blend if you prefer. Adjust the seasoning, garnish with fresh parsley and serve with fresh country bread and goat's cheese or soya cheese.

284 ► WINTER VEGETABLE SOUP

★ ♥ ∅

CALORIES	524
CHOLESTEROL	20
VEGAN CALORIES	444
POLYUNSATS	★★☆
ANTIOXIDANTS	★★★
CALCIUM	★★☆
IRON	★★★
B VITAMINS	★★★

75g (2³⁄₄oz) Puy lentils, rinsed
3 tbsp olive oil
1 small leek, sliced
75g (2³⁄₄oz) bacon/smoked tempeh, diced
1 carrot, sliced
1 thin slice celeriac, diced

12 shiitake mushrooms, sliced
100g (3½oz) cabbage, finely sliced
1ltr (1³⁄₄pts) vegetable stock
1 bay leaf
1 tsp thyme
1 tbsp tomato paste (purée)
sea salt and black pepper to taste

Boil the lentils in a saucepan with twice their volume of water. Meanwhile, gently heat the oil in a saucepan, add the leek and the smoked bacon or tempeh and stir-fry for 2 minutes. Add the carrot, celeriac, shiitake and cabbage and continue to stir-fry for a further 5 minutes. Stir in the stock, bay leaf, thyme and tomato paste and bring to the boil. Drain the partially-cooked lentils and add them to the saucepan. Bring the soup to the boil again, and simmer for 10 minutes, or until the lentils are soft. Remove the bay leaf, season and serve with warm, crusty bread rolls.

285 CURLY KALE SOUP

★ ♥ ◍ ☒ ✿ ∅

CALORIES	315
CHOLESTEROL	0
VEGAN CALORIES	315
POLYUNSATS	★★☆
ANTIOXIDANTS	★★★
CALCIUM	★★☆
IRON	★★☆
B VITAMINS	★★☆

2 tbsp olive oil
1 tsp turmeric
1 small leek, sliced
1 small carrot, sliced
1 small parsley root, quartered and sliced

1 potato, quartered and sliced
1 bay leaf
1 tbsp wheat flour
1ltr (1³⁄₄pts) vegetable stock
200g (7oz) curly kale, chopped
sea salt and black pepper to taste

Gently heat the oil in a saucepan. Add the turmeric and the leek, followed by the carrot, parsley root, potato and bay leaf. Stir-fry for 2 minutes over a medium heat. Sprinkle the flour into the pan and stir until the vegetables are coated in flour. Continue to stir while you add the stock and bring to the boil. Simmer for 10 minutes. Add the curly kale and boil for a further 5 minutes. Season and serve with croutons.

286 SMOKY BUTTER BEAN SOUP

★ ♥

CALORIES	493
CHOLESTEROL	47
VEGAN CALORIES	475
POLYUNSATS	★☆☆
ANTIOXIDANTS	★★☆
CALCIUM	★★☆
IRON	★★☆
B VITAMINS	★★★

2 tbsp olive oil
1 leek, sliced
450g (1lb) butter beans, cooked or canned
1ltr (1³⁄₄pts) vegetable stock

200g (7oz) smoked haddock, skinned, boned and cubed/100g (3½oz) smoked tempeh, cubed
sea salt and black pepper to taste
1 tbsp fresh dill, finely chopped

Gently stir-fry the leek in a saucepan with the oil until soft. Add the butter beans. Then mash the beans a little and stir-fry for a further 3–5 minutes. Pour in the stock and bring to the boil. Cover and simmer for 5 minutes. Add the smoked haddock or smoked tempeh cubes and simmer for a further 10 minutes. Season, garnish with chopped fresh dill and serve with soft bread.

287 WINTER CRUDITÉS WITH AVOCADO DRESSING

★ ♥ ◔ ◎ ◉

CALORIES	570
CHOLESTEROL	0
VEGAN CALORIES	570
POLYUNSATS	★★★
ANTIOXIDANTS	★★★
CALCIUM	★★☆
IRON	★★☆
B VITAMINS	★★★

2 potatoes, parboiled and sliced
⅛ white cabbage, shredded
¼ celeriac, cut into thin sticks
8 brown mushrooms, sliced
1 black radish, sliced
2 avocados, halved, pitted and flesh scooped out
juice of ½ lemon

sea salt to taste
½ small red chilli, deseeded and finely chopped
½ small onion, finely chopped
2–4 curly kale leaves, finely chopped
1 handful walnuts, shelled

Arrange the potatoes, cabbage, celeriac, mushrooms and radish on two large plates. Blend the avocado flesh with lemon juice and salt. Add the chilli and onion to the dressing, mix and spoon onto the middle of each plate. Garnish with curly kale and walnuts, and serve with wholemeal rolls.

288 SPANISH POTATO SALAD

★ ♥ ◎

CALORIES	628
CHOLESTEROL	70
VEGAN CALORIES	502
POLYUNSATS	★★★
ANTIOXIDANTS	★★★
CALCIUM	★★★
IRON	★★★
B VITAMINS	★★☆

2 tbsp olive oil
1 tsp paprika
300g (10½oz) potatoes, sliced
½ Spanish onion, finely chopped
2 cloves garlic, chopped
sea salt and black pepper to taste
75ml (2½fl oz) water

2 chicory (Belgian endive), sliced lengthways
1 tbsp walnut oil
1 tbsp red wine vinegar
1 handful fresh parsley, chopped
150g (5½oz) goat's/soya cheese, sliced

Heat the oil in a frying pan, add the paprika and stir in the potatoes, onion and garlic. Season and stir-fry for 5 minutes. Add the water and bring to the boil. Cover and gently simmer for 10 minutes until the potatoes are tender. Arrange the chicory on two plates, top with the potato slices and drizzle with the walnut oil and the vinegar. Check the seasoning, sprinkle with parsley and cheese, and serve.

289 WARM PASTA SALAD

★ ♥ ◌ ◉

CALORIES	444
CHOLESTEROL	26
VEGAN CALORIES	392
POLYUNSATS	★★☆
ANTIOXIDANTS	★★★
CALCIUM	★★☆
IRON	★★★
B VITAMINS	★★★

160g (5¾oz) tricolor pasta
1 thick slice celeriac, chopped into matchsticks
1 leek, chopped into matchsticks
1 carrot, chopped into matchsticks
2 tbsp olive oil
juice of ½ lemon

sea salt and black pepper to taste
1 pinch ground coriander
150g (5½oz) smoked salmon/tofu, cut into strips
4 mushrooms, sliced and sprinkled with lemon juice
2 tsp fresh parsley, finely chopped

Cook the pasta in boiling water with a little salt and oil. Drain and set aside. Blanch the celeriac, leek and carrot in a saucepan of boiling water for 1 minute. Drain and set aside. Make the dressing by whisking the oil, lemon juice, salt, pepper and coriander in a bowl. Mix the cooked pasta, blanched vegetables, smoked salmon or tofu and mushrooms in a salad bowl. Add the dressing and gently toss. Garnish with parsley and serve.

290 CARROT, DATE AND PECAN SALAD WITH GINGER DRESSING AND PAN BREAD

⭐❤🌾⬛

CALORIES	824
CHOLESTEROL	0
VEGAN CALORIES	824
POLYUNSATS	★★★
ANTIOXIDANTS	★★★
CALCIUM	★★☆
IRON	★★☆
B VITAMINS	★★☆

250g (9oz) carrots, grated
75g (2¾oz) dates, pitted
   and chopped
75g (2¾oz) pecans, chopped
3 tbsp lemon juice
2 tsp fresh ginger, finely chopped
1 tsp liquid honey

pan bread:
200g (7oz) wheat flour
1 tsp baking powder
1 pinch salt
vegetable oil for frying

Mix the carrots, dates and pecans in a salad bowl. To make the dressing, pour the lemon juice into a small bowl and mix in the ginger and honey. Set aside. Place the wheat flour in a bowl, mix in the baking powder and salt, and add enough water to form a soft dough. Break the dough into small balls, then flatten into thick pancakes and fry in a frying pan with a little oil over a medium–high heat. Mix the dressing with the salad and serve with the hot pan bread and cream cheese or soya cheese mixed with basil. Alternatively, you can serve the dressed salad with pitta bread.

291 RED CABBAGE SALAD

⭐❤💧🌿

CALORIES	698
CHOLESTEROL	94
VEGAN CALORIES	385
POLYUNSATS	★★★
ANTIOXIDANTS	★★☆
CALCIUM	★☆☆
IRON	★★☆
B VITAMINS	★★☆

1 duck breast/150g (5½oz) seitan,
   cut into chunks
oil for frying (optional)
½ small red cabbage, finely sliced
1 dessert apple, cored and cubed

1 stick celery, sliced
1 tbsp cider vinegar
2 tbsp walnut oil
sea salt and black pepper to taste
8 walnut halves

Fry the duck breast in a frying pan (without oil, beginning with the skin-side facing downward) and set aside. Alternatively, fry the seitan pieces in a frying pan with a little oil, slice and set aside. To make the vinaigrette, mix the vinegar, oil, salt and pepper in a small bowl. Place the red cabbage, apple and celery in a large bowl, add the vinaigrette and mix well. Place on a serving dish and top with the fried duck or seitan and the walnut halves. Serve with French baguette.

292 FRUITY AVOCADO SALAD

⭐❤💧⬛

CALORIES	642
CHOLESTEROL	0
VEGAN CALORIES	642
POLYUNSATS	★★★
ANTIOXIDANTS	★★★
CALCIUM	★★☆
IRON	★★☆
B VITAMINS	★★☆

1 handful rocket or curly kale,
   chopped
2 avocados, quartered, pitted,
   peeled and sliced
1 small pink grapefruit, quartered,
   peeled and diced

1 large ripe pear or apple,
   quartered and sliced
12 Brazil nuts, chopped
3 tbsp walnut oil
1 tbsp balsamic vinegar
sea salt and black pepper to taste

Place the rocket or curly kale, avocados, grapefruit, pear or apple and Brazil nuts in a salad bowl. Add the walnut oil and the vinegar, and season. Gently toss and serve with bread and cheese or soya cheese.

293 ▲ WILD RICE SALAD
★♥◍▢

CALORIES	483
CHOLESTEROL	0
VEGAN CALORIES	483
POLYUNSATS	★★☆
ANTIOXIDANTS	★★☆
CALCIUM	★★☆
IRON	★★☆
B VITAMINS	★★☆

200g (7oz) wild rice, cooked (100g
  [3½oz] uncooked)
100g (3½oz) fresh raw baby leaf
  spinach, chopped
½ red onion, finely chopped
100g (3½oz) Florence fennel bulb,
  halved and sliced
1 thick slice pineapple, chopped

1 tbsp lemon juice
1 tsp Dijon mustard
1 tsp maple syrup
sea salt and black pepper to taste
3 tbsp hazelnut oil
1 handful bean sprouts
25g (1oz) hazelnuts, chopped

Place the cooked rice in a salad bowl with the spinach, onion, fennel
and pineapple and mix well. To make the dressing, whisk the lemon juice,
mustard, maple syrup, salt and pepper in a small bowl, slowly adding
the oil. Pour the dressing over the rice salad, garnish with bean sprouts
and hazelnuts, and serve.

294 ROCKET AND TROUT SALAD
★♥✖🍃

CALORIES	370
CHOLESTEROL	56
VEGAN CALORIES	392
POLYUNSATS	★★★
ANTIOXIDANTS	★★★
CALCIUM	★★★
IRON	★★☆
B VITAMINS	★★★

1 large bunch rocket (or curly kale),
  chopped
1 handful radicchio leaves
1 pear, cored and sliced
1 handful chopped walnuts
150g (5½oz) smoked trout/tempeh

3 tbsp plain/soya yoghurt
1 tbsp lemon juice
1 tsp grated horseradish
2 tsp tamari (soya sauce)
sea salt and black pepper to taste

Place the salad leaves in a large bowl. Add the pear and the walnuts.
Cut the tempeh or trout into chunks. Fry or grill the tempeh until golden
(if using) and add to the salad, or add the trout. Make the dressing
by mixing the yoghurt, lemon juice, horseradish and tamari in a bowl.
Pour over the salad and gently toss. Season and serve with fresh bread.

295 DRESSED WINTER SALAD
★♥💧🍃

CALORIES	521
CHOLESTEROL	6
VEGAN CALORIES	518
POLYUNSATS	★★★
ANTIOXIDANTS	★★★
CALCIUM	★★★
IRON	★★★
B VITAMINS	★★☆

250g (9oz) red kidney beans,
  cooked or canned
250g (9oz) butter beans, cooked or
  canned
100g (3½oz) button mushrooms,
  sliced
100g (3½oz) artichoke hearts, sliced
1 small shallot, finely chopped

2 chicory (Belgian endive), sliced
  lengthways
100g (3½oz) plain/soya yoghurt
1 tsp Dijon mustard
1 tbsp lemon juice
1 tbsp fresh tarragon, chopped
sea salt and black pepper to taste
50g (1¾oz) Brazil nuts, chopped

Rinse the beans and blanch them in a saucepan of boiling water for
1 minute. Drain, cool under running water and set aside to dry. Mix the
mushrooms, artichoke hearts and shallot in a bowl. To make the dressing,
pour the yoghurt into a bowl, add the mustard, lemon juice, tarragon, salt
and pepper. Mix well and spoon over the vegetables. Add the beans and
gently toss. Arrange the chicory on a large serving plate, top with the
dressed beans and vegetables, garnish with Brazil nuts and serve.

296 RED CABBAGE AND POTATO SALAD
★♥💧🍃

CALORIES	796
CHOLESTEROL	0
VEGAN CALORIES	796
POLYUNSATS	★★★
ANTIOXIDANTS	★★★
CALCIUM	★★☆
IRON	★★☆
B VITAMINS	★★★

¼ fresh red cabbage, finely
  shredded
4 tbsp red wine vinegar, boiling
1 tsp raw cane sugar
400g (14oz) potatoes, washed
2 tbsp grapeseed oil
1 small raw beetroot, grated
100g (3½oz) cauliflower florets

1 small shallot, finely chopped
½ red pepper, grated (optional)
1 stick celery, finely chopped
1 handful raisins
1 handful walnuts
2 tbsp walnut oil
celery salt and black pepper to taste

Place the red cabbage in a heatproof bowl. Pour the boiling vinegar over
and add the sugar. Mix well and set aside. Slice and season the potatoes
and sauté them in a frying pan with the grapeseed oil until golden brown.
Set aside. Add the beetroot, cauliflower, shallot, red pepper (if using),
celery, raisins and walnuts to the bowl of red cabbage. Drizzle with walnut
oil, and season. Gently toss and serve with the sautéed potatoes.

297 ROYAL COUSCOUS

CALORIES	983
CHOLESTEROL	47
VEGAN CALORIES	983
POLYUNSATS	★★★
ANTIOXIDANTS	★★☆
CALCIUM	★★☆
IRON	★★★
B VITAMINS	★★☆

150g (5½oz) couscous
50g (1¾oz) coconut, freshly grated
 or desiccated
½ tsp sea salt
200ml (⅓pt) boiling water
1 tbsp olive oil

75g (2¾oz) pine kernels
1 tbsp tamari (soya sauce)
1 Little Gem lettuce, shredded
10 dried apricots, chopped
10 sun-dried tomatoes, chopped
French dressing (see p.23)

Place the couscous in a medium bowl. Mix in the coconut and salt. Pour the boiling water over the couscous and leave to stand for a few minutes. When the water is absorbed, add the oil and mix well. Dry-roast the pine kernels in a frying pan. When they start to brown, add the tamari, remove from the heat and stir until the kernels are well coated. Divide the lettuce between two plates. Add the couscous, then the apricots, sun-dried tomatoes and roasted pine kernels. Top with French dressing and serve.

298 SMOKY WINTER SALAD

CALORIES	277
CHOLESTEROL	18
VEGAN CALORIES	243
POLYUNSATS	★★★
ANTIOXIDANTS	★★☆
CALCIUM	★★☆
IRON	★★☆
B VITAMINS	★★☆

2 chicory (Belgian endive),
 diagonally sliced
1 radicchio, shredded
1 handful lamb's lettuce
100g (3½oz) mushrooms, sliced
100g (3½oz) smoked fish (salmon,

 trout or eel), sliced/100g (3½oz)
 smoked tofu, cut into cubes
juice of 1 lemon
3 tbsp grapeseed oil
sea salt and black pepper to taste

Make a vinaigrette by whisking the lemon juice, oil, salt and pepper in a small bowl. Place the chicory, radicchio, lamb's lettuce and mushrooms in a salad bowl. Add the vinaigrette and gently toss. Top with the smoked fish or tofu and serve with thick slices of country bread.

299 BEETROOT SALAD WITH BAKED POTATOES

CALORIES	414
CHOLESTEROL	52
VEGAN CALORIES	360
POLYUNSATS	★★★
ANTIOXIDANTS	★★★
CALCIUM	★★☆
IRON	★★☆
B VITAMINS	★★★

4 potatoes, halved and slices
 made nearly all the way through
 each half
grapeseed oil for brushing
 and stir-frying
125g (4½oz) turkey breast/tofu,
 diced
a little tamari (soya sauce)

250g (9oz) raw beetroot, grated
1 stick celery, finely chopped
½ apple, cored and chopped
100ml (3½fl oz) plain/soya yoghurt
1 tbsp lemon juice
2 tsp Dijon mustard
sea salt and black pepper to taste

Place the potato halves on an oiled baking tray, brush with oil, sprinkle with salt and bake at 200°C/400°F/gas mark 6 for 30 minutes, or until golden. Meanwhile, gently stir-fry the turkey or tofu in a frying pan with a little oil until golden, sprinkling with a little tamari as you remove from the heat. Mix the beetroot, celery and apple in a salad bowl. Make a dressing of the yoghurt, lemon juice, mustard, salt and pepper in a bowl, and mix with the beetroot salad. Serve with the baked potatoes.

300 ▲ LEBANESE MACARONI

⭐ ♥ 🌾

CALORIES	718
CHOLESTEROL	6
VEGAN CALORIES	715
POLYUNSATS	★★★
ANTIOXIDANTS	★★☆
CALCIUM	★★☆
IRON	★★☆
B VITAMINS	★★☆

225g (8oz) macaroni pasta
100g (3½oz) plain/soya yoghurt
2 cloves garlic, crushed
1 tbsp fresh mint leaves, chopped

sea salt and black pepper to taste
75g (2¾oz) pine kernels
1 tbsp olive oil
2 tsp tamari (soya sauce)

Boil the macaroni in plenty of water with a little salt and oil until just
tender. Meanwhile, mix the yoghurt, garlic and mint in a bowl, and season.
Roast the pine kernels in a frying pan with the oil until they begin to
brown. Remove from the heat, quickly add the tamari and stir well.
Set aside. Drain the cooked macaroni, run it under cold water for a
few seconds, and drain again. Place in a serving bowl and gently mix
in the yoghurt mixture. Garnish with roasted pine kernels and serve.

301 SPINACH AND ARTICHOKE TAGLIATELLE
★♥◊🌿🥥

CALORIES	568
CHOLESTEROL	0
VEGAN CALORIES	568
POLYUNSATS	★★☆
ANTIOXIDANTS	★★★
CALCIUM	★★★
IRON	★★★
B VITAMINS	★★☆

200g (7oz) tagliatelle pasta
2 tbsp olive oil
1 small onion, chopped
1 clove garlic, chopped
250g (9oz) fresh spinach, chopped
100g (3½oz) flageolet beans, cooked or canned

250g (9oz) artichoke hearts, cooked or canned
1 tbsp tomato paste (purée)
1 tsp herbes de Provence
a little grated Parmesan/brewer's yeast flakes (optional)

Cook the pasta in plenty of boiling water with a little salt and oil. Heat the oil in a frying pan or a wok and gently stir-fry the onion for 1 minute. Add the garlic and the spinach and cook until the spinach is soft. Add the beans, artichoke hearts and tomato paste. Heat through. Add the herbs and season. Serve on top of the cooked and drained pasta, sprinkled with Parmesan or brewer's yeast flakes (if using).

302 PASTA TRICOLOR IN WALNUT SAUCE
★♥◊🌿

CALORIES	893
CHOLESTEROL	0
VEGAN CALORIES	893
POLYUNSATS	★★★
ANTIOXIDANTS	★★★
CALCIUM	★★☆
IRON	★★★
B VITAMINS	★★☆

200g (7oz) tricolor fusilli pasta
100g (3½oz) walnuts, shelled and crushed in a mortar
2 cloves garlic, crushed
2 tbsp olive oil
1 tbsp balsamic vinegar

1 handful fresh parsley or basil
1 small beetroot, finely chopped
⅛ celeriac, finely chopped
1 medium carrot, finely chopped
¼ Florence fennel bulb, chopped
sea salt and black pepper to taste

Boil the pasta in plenty of water with a little salt and oil. Mix the walnuts, garlic, oil, vinegar and herbs with 1 tablespoon of salt in a bowl to make a sauce. Set aside. Heat a little oil in the pan, add the vegetables and stir-fry for a couple of minutes over a medium heat. Add the cooked and drained pasta and the sauce, and gently mix. Heat through, season and serve.

303 CONCHIGLIE WITH CHUNKY SAUCE
★♥🌿🥥

CALORIES	664
CHOLESTEROL	38
VEGAN CALORIES	563
POLYUNSATS	★★☆
ANTIOXIDANTS	★★☆
CALCIUM	★★☆
IRON	★★★
B VITAMINS	★★☆

200g (7oz) conchiglie pasta
olive oil for stir-frying
1 small red onion, halved and sliced
150g (5½oz) spicy sausage (pork/soya), sliced
75g (2¾oz) shiitake mushrooms, sliced

1 clove garlic, chopped
200ml (⅓pt) vegetable stock
75g (2¾oz) green peas
2 tbsp tomato paste (purée)
1 tsp maple syrup
2 tsp dried oregano
sea salt and black pepper to taste

Boil the pasta in plenty of water with a little salt and oil. Gently stir-fry the onion in a frying pan or a wok with a little oil until soft. Add the sausage, turn up the heat and sauté for 1 minute, then add the shiitake and continue to stir-fry until the sausage and mushrooms begin to brown. Add the garlic, stock and peas and heat through. Then add the tomato paste, maple syrup and oregano. Season and leave to simmer until the pasta is cooked. Drain the pasta and serve immediately, topped with the sauce.

304 PASTA WITH VEGETABLES AND CREAMY MUSTARD SAUCE

★♥🌾

CALORIES	631
CHOLESTEROL	0
VEGAN CALORIES	631
POLYUNSATS	★★☆
ANTIOXIDANTS	★★★
CALCIUM	★★☆
IRON	★★★
B VITAMINS	★★☆

200g (7oz) pasta shapes of choice
1 small leek, finely sliced
½ small hokaido pumpkin, deseeded, peeled and diced
1 small head broccoli, cut into small florets
1 handful fresh parsley, finely chopped, plus some to garnish
1 tbsp fresh tarragon (or 1 tsp dried), finely chopped
2 tbsp Dijon mustard
1 clove garlic, crushed
3 tbsp olive oil
sea salt and black pepper to taste

Boil the pasta in plenty of water with a little salt and oil. After 4 minutes, add the vegetables and continue to boil until the pasta is just cooked. Mix the herbs with the mustard, garlic, oil, salt and pepper in a bowl. Drain the cooked pasta and vegetables in a colander. Gently heat the mustard sauce in the pasta pan. Return the pasta and vegetables to the pan and gently mix. Check the seasoning and serve garnished with parsley.

305 PENNE WITH SMOKY PESTO SAUCE

★♥🌾

CALORIES	859
CHOLESTEROL	41
VEGAN CALORIES	807
POLYUNSATS	★★★
ANTIOXIDANTS	★★☆
CALCIUM	★★☆
IRON	★★★
B VITAMINS	★★★

2 tbsp pine kernels
3 tbsp fresh basil, finely chopped
3 tbsp olive oil, plus some for frying
1–2 cloves garlic, crushed (optional)
200g (7oz) penne pasta
175g (6oz) green beans, chopped
100g (3½oz) smoked bacon/tempeh
100ml (3½fl oz) plain/soya yoghurt
1 tbsp grated Parmesan/brewer's yeast flakes

Crush the pine kernels in a mortar and mix in the basil, oil, garlic (if using) and a little salt to make the pesto. Boil the pasta in plenty of water with a little salt and oil. After 4 minutes, add the beans. Cut the bacon or tempeh into cubes and sauté them in a frying pan with oil until they begin to brown. Remove from the heat, add the pesto and the yoghurt and mix well. Return the drained pasta and beans to the pan, add the pesto sauce and gently mix. Sprinkle with Parmesan or brewer's yeast, and serve.

306 PASTA WITH SAUCE PROVENÇALE

★♥🌾🥚

CALORIES	674
CHOLESTEROL	32
VEGAN CALORIES	658
POLYUNSATS	★★☆
ANTIOXIDANTS	★★★
CALCIUM	★★☆
IRON	★★★
B VITAMINS	★★★

olive oil for (stir-)frying
1 onion, chopped
450g (1lb) tomatoes, chopped
1 clove garlic, crushed
50ml (2fl oz) vegetable stock
50ml (2fl oz) dry white wine
1 tbsp herbes de Provence
125g (4½oz) tuna in oil/smoked tofu, cubed
200g (7oz) macaroni pasta
1 handful black olives, pitted
goat's/soya cheese (optional)

Gently fry the onion in a saucepan with the oil until soft. Add the tomatoes and simmer for 10 minutes, then add the garlic, stock, wine and herbs. Season and continue to simmer. Stir-fry the tuna or tofu in a separate pan with a little oil until golden. Set aside. Boil the pasta in plenty of water with a little salt and oil. Drain and place in a large serving dish. Pour the sauce over and top with the fried tuna or tofu and the olives. Sprinkle with a little grated cheese (if using), and serve.

307 LINGUINE MUSCOLI
★ ♥ 🌿 ▱

CALORIES	518
CHOLESTEROL	23
VEGAN CALORIES	575
POLYUNSATS	★☆☆
ANTIOXIDANTS	★★☆
CALCIUM	★★☆
IRON	★★★
B VITAMINS	★★☆

1 tbsp olive oil
2 shallots, finely chopped
100ml (3½fl oz) dry white wine
750g (1lb 10 oz) mussels (with shells)/60g (2¼oz) soya chunks, soaked in water with mixed seaweed

100g (3½oz) mushrooms, sliced
juice of ½ lemon
160g (5¾oz) linguine pasta
1 tsp cornflour dissolved in a little cold water
sea salt and black pepper to taste
1 tbsp fresh parsley, finely chopped

Gently fry the shallots in a large casserole dish with the oil until soft. Add the wine and the mussels or soya chunks (with their soaking water) and boil for 5 minutes, or until the mussels have opened (shake from time to time to ensure they cook evenly). Drain and set aside, reserving the cooking liquid. (If you are using mussels, shell them, sieve their liquid and add it to the reserved cooking liquid.) Bring the cooking liquid to the boil, add the mushrooms and lemon juice and let the sauce reduce for 5 minutes. Meanwhile, cook the pasta in plenty of boiling water with a little salt and oil. Thicken the sauce with the dissolved cornflour. Season and add the parsley and the mussels or soya chunks. Divide the cooked and drained pasta between two plates, top with the sauce and serve.

308 BUCKWHEAT PASTA WITH SWEET AND SOUR SAUCE
♥ 💧 🌿 ◉

CALORIES	558
CHOLESTEROL	61
VEGAN CALORIES	569
POLYUNSATS	★☆☆
ANTIOXIDANTS	★★☆
CALCIUM	★☆☆
IRON	★★☆
B VITAMINS	★★☆

olive oil for stir-frying
2 shallots, sliced
1 tsp ground coriander
175g (6oz) chicken breast/seitan, cut into chunks
1 red dessert apple, cored and sliced
225g (8oz) courgettes, sliced
2 cloves garlic, crushed

1 tbsp cider vinegar
1 tsp maple syrup
1 tsp Tabasco sauce
1 tbsp tamari (soya sauce)
200ml (⅓pt) vegetable stock
200g (7oz) buckwheat pasta
1 tsp cornflour diluted in a little cold water
sea salt and black pepper to taste

Heat a little oil in a casserole dish and stir-fry the shallots, coriander and chicken or seitan chunks over a medium heat until golden. Add the apple, courgettes and garlic, turn up the heat a little and stir-fry for a further minute. Turn down the heat, add the vinegar, maple syrup, Tabasco sauce, tamari and stock. Bring to the boil and simmer for 5–10 minutes, or until the chicken is tender. Meanwhile, boil the pasta in plenty of water with a little salt and oil. Add the diluted cornflour to the sauce and heat through, stirring continuously, until the sauce thickens. Season and serve with the cooked and drained pasta.

309 ▼ SPAGHETTI BOLOGNESE

★♥🌾🥜🍫

CALORIES	728
CHOLESTEROL	47
VEGAN CALORIES	758
POLYUNSATS	★★☆
ANTIOXIDANTS	★★★
CALCIUM	★★☆
IRON	★★★
B VITAMINS	★★★

3 tbsp olive oil
1 onion, chopped
150g (5½oz) minced pork/75g
    (2¾oz) burgamix (dry weight)
2 cloves garlic, crushed
1 carrot, diced
1 stick celery (with leaves), chopped
2 tsp thyme
1 sprig each of rosemary and sage

1 tbsp fresh basil (or 1 tsp dried)
1 tbsp tamari (soya sauce)
450g (1lb) tomatoes, blended
1 tsp raw cane sugar
2 tbsp tomato paste (purée)
sea salt
200g (7oz) spaghetti pasta
fresh parsley and black pepper
    to garnish

Gently fry the onion in the oil until soft. Add the minced pork or burgamix,
together with the garlic and stir-fry until it browns. (If you are using
burgamix, you may need to add more oil.) Add the carrot, celery, herbs and
tamari. Heat through, then add the blended tomatoes, sugar and tomato
paste. Bring to the boil and simmer for 10 minutes, stirring occasionally.
Meanwhile, boil the spaghetti in plenty of water with a little salt and oil.
Season the sauce. Divide the cooked spaghetti between two large plates.
Top with the bolognese sauce, garnish with plenty of fresh parsley and
black pepper and serve immediately.

310 TAGLIATELLE WITH A-PLUS SAUCE

■★■

CALORIES	817
CHOLESTEROL	219
VEGAN CALORIES	785
POLYUNSATS	★★☆
ANTIOXIDANTS	★★★
CALCIUM	★★☆
IRON	★★★
B VITAMINS	★★★

200g (7oz) tagliatelle pasta
olive oil for stir-frying
1 small leek, sliced
2 cloves garlic, chopped
125g (4½oz) chicken livers/seitan,
  sliced
2 carrots, diced

225g (8oz) spinach or Swiss chard,
  chopped
2 tsp paprika
1 small bunch parsley, chopped
1 sprig sage, chopped
100ml (3½fl oz) port
sea salt and black pepper to taste

Boil the pasta in plenty of water with a little salt and oil. Gently stir-fry the leek and garlic in a frying pan with a little oil. Add the chicken or seitan slices, turn up the heat and stir-fry until they begin to brown. Add the carrots, spinach or Swiss chard and herbs. Heat through, add the port and season. Continue to stir the ingredients until blended. Place the cooked and drained pasta in a serving dish, add the sauce, gently mix and serve.

311 SPAGHETTI WITH CREOLE SAUCE

■♥■

CALORIES	693
CHOLESTEROL	31
VEGAN CALORIES	679
POLYUNSATS	★★☆
ANTIOXIDANTS	★★★
CALCIUM	★★★
IRON	★★★
B VITAMINS	★★★

2 tbsp olive oil
100g (3½oz) mushrooms, sliced
125g (4½oz) cod fillet/tofu, cut
  into chunks
2 tbsp parsley, chopped
1 tsp each of thyme and turmeric
1 tsp black pepper

175g (6oz) yellow pumpkin, diced
200g (7oz) spinach, chopped
3 tbsp dried mixed seaweed flakes,
  soaked in water for 10 minutes
100ml (3½fl oz) coconut milk
200g (7oz) spaghetti pasta
sea salt to taste

Sauté the mushrooms and the cod or tofu in a wok or a frying pan with the oil for 3 minutes. Add the herbs and spices, followed by the pumpkin and spinach, then add the seaweed (with its soaking water). Heat through, add the coconut milk, partially cover and gently simmer for 10 minutes. Boil the pasta in plenty of water with a little salt and oil. Check the seasoning of the sauce and serve with the cooked and drained pasta.

312 PASTA WITH GOUJONS IN A SPINACH SAUCE

■■★

CALORIES	922
CHOLESTEROL	177
VEGAN CALORIES	694
POLYUNSATS	★★★
ANTIOXIDANTS	★★★
CALCIUM	★★☆
IRON	★★★
B VITAMINS	★★★

150ml (¼pt) crème fraîche/soya
  cream
1 pinch freshly grated nutmeg
250g (9oz) fresh spinach, cooked in
  boiling water, drained, rinsed and
  water pressed out

sea salt and black pepper to taste
160g (5¾oz) penne pasta
olive oil for frying
250g (9oz) turkey breast/seitan,
  sliced
1 tomato, grilled whole

Heat the cream in a casserole dish with the nutmeg. When it boils, add the spinach. Mix well, season and set aside. Cook the pasta in plenty of boiling water with a little salt and oil. Heat a little oil in a frying pan and sauté the turkey or seitan slices over a medium heat for 5 minutes. Reheat the sauce. Place the pasta on a large plate with the turkey or seitan slices, pour the sauce over the middle, garnish with the grilled tomato and serve.

313 MOROCCAN TAJINE
★♥◐

CALORIES	515
CHOLESTEROL	0
VEGAN CALORIES	515
POLYUNSATS	★☆☆
ANTIOXIDANTS	★★★
CALCIUM	★★☆
IRON	★★☆
B VITAMINS	★★☆

2 tbsp olive oil
1 shallot, sliced
1 cinnamon stick (2cm [¾in] long)
½ tsp ground cumin
½ tsp ground coriander
2 cloves garlic, crushed
200g (7oz) (hokaido) pumpkin, peeled, deseeded and cubed
200g (7oz) sweet potatoes, peeled and cubed

200g (7oz) chick peas, cooked or canned
1 tbsp tomato paste (purée)
100ml (3½fl oz) red wine
250ml (9fl oz) vegetable stock
1 handful dried (unsulphured) apricots or raisins
sea salt, saffron and cayenne pepper to taste

Heat the oil in a heavy-based casserole dish (or a tajine dish), add the shallot and gently sweat for 2 minutes. Then add the spices and the garlic and fry for 30 seconds before adding the pumpkin, sweet potatoes and chick peas. Stir-fry for 3 minutes, then add the tomato paste, red wine, stock and apricots or raisins. Season, bring to the boil and simmer until the vegetables are soft. Serve with steamed couscous.

314 ARABIAN HALF-MOON PASTRIES
★♥🌿◐🍃

CALORIES	425
CHOLESTEROL	0
VEGAN CALORIES	425
POLYUNSATS	★★★
ANTIOXIDANTS	★★★
CALCIUM	★★★
IRON	★★★
B VITAMINS	★★☆

1 packet ready-made shortcrust pastry, rolled out thinly
500g (1lb 2oz) fresh spinach, curly kale or Swiss chard, chopped

2 tbsp lemon juice
2 tbsp olive oil
½ tsp allspice and 1 pinch salt
1 tsp sumac (optional)

Preheat the oven to 200°C/400°F/gas mark 6. Cut the rolled-out pastry into approximately 10cm (4in) rounds with a biscuit cutter. Place the spinach, curly kale or Swiss chard in a bowl and mix in the remaining ingredients. Place a large spoonful of filling on each pastry round and fold each one into a half-moon shape. Firmly pinch together the edges of each pastry and place them on a greased baking tray. Bake in the middle of a hot oven until they brown (approximately 15 minutes). Serve with a salad.

315 INDIAN KORMA
★🌿◐

CALORIES	587
CHOLESTEROL	125
VEGAN CALORIES	465
POLYUNSATS	★★★
ANTIOXIDANTS	★★☆
CALCIUM	★★☆
IRON	★★☆
B VITAMINS	★★☆

2 tbsp olive oil
1 small onion, chopped
1 clove garlic, chopped
350g (12oz) chicken breast/ 175g (6oz) tofu, diced
2 tbsp wheat flour
1 tbsp mild curry powder

1 tbsp raisins
200ml (⅓pt) chicken/vegetable stock
2 tsp lemon juice
1 tbsp plain/soya yoghurt
1 tbsp almond butter
sea salt and black pepper to taste
1 tbsp flaked almonds, toasted

Heat the oil in a heavy-based saucepan and gently stir-fry the onion and garlic until they begin to soften. Coat the chicken or tofu cubes with a mixture of flour and curry powder, add to the pan and fry until they begin to brown. Add the raisins and stock, bring to the boil and simmer for 10 minutes. Remove from the heat, add the lemon juice, yoghurt and almond butter. Season, garnish with toasted almond flakes and serve with rice.

316 ◄ CUBAN COD
★ ♥ ▱

CALORIES	522
CHOLESTEROL	98
VEGAN CALORIES	405
POLYUNSATS	★★★
ANTIOXIDANTS	★★★
CALCIUM	★★☆
IRON	★★☆
B VITAMINS	★★☆

300g (10½oz) potatoes, finely sliced
corn oil for drizzling and frying
1 onion, chopped
1 clove garlic, chopped
1 tsp tomato paste (purée)
200ml (⅓pt) fish/vegetable stock

1 phial saffron
2 dried hot chillies
400g (14oz) fresh cod fillet,
   halved/200g (7oz) marinated
   tofu, sliced
sea salt and cayenne pepper

Preheat the oven to 220°C/425°F/gas mark 7. Place the potato slices
in a baking dish and drizzle with oil. Bake in a hot oven for 10 minutes.
Meanwhile, fry the onion and the garlic in a frying pan with a little oil,
add the tomato paste, stock, saffron and chillies and bring to the boil.
Season to taste and set aside. Place the cod fillet or tofu slices on top
of the partially-cooked potato slices. Pour the sauce over and bake for a
further 10 minutes (until the fish is tender). Serve with wedges of lemon.

317 TURKISH PILAF
★ ♥ 🌿

CALORIES	549
CHOLESTEROL	52
VEGAN CALORIES	558
POLYUNSATS	★★☆
ANTIOXIDANTS	★★★
CALCIUM	★★☆
IRON	★★★
B VITAMINS	★★☆

75g (2¾oz) Puy lentils
150g (5½oz) chicken breast/seitan
2 tbsp olive oil
½ tsp ground cinnamon
½ tsp ground coriander
1 tsp turmeric
1 leek, sliced

1 carrot, sliced
75g (2¾oz) bulgur wheat
1 tbsp raisins
150ml (¼pt) vegetable stock
sea salt and black pepper to taste
1 handful fresh coriander leaves

Boil the lentils in a saucepan with three times their volume of water. Cut
the chicken or seitan into cubes. Heat the oil in a heavy-based pan and
add the spices, then the leek. Add the chicken or seitan cubes and stir-fry
for 5 minutes until they begin to brown. Add the carrot, bulgur wheat and
raisins. Stir-fry for a further minute before adding the stock. Bring to the
boil. Add the partially-cooked lentils (with their cooking water), cover and
very gently simmer for 10–15 minutes until the water is absorbed. Season,
garnish with coriander leaves and serve hot with plain or soya yoghurt.

318 SRI LANKAN MALLUNG
★ ♥ ▱ ◐

CALORIES	495
CHOLESTEROL	0
VEGAN CALORIES	495
POLYUNSATS	★★★
ANTIOXIDANTS	★★★
CALCIUM	★★☆
IRON	★★☆
B VITAMINS	★★☆

2 tbsp grapeseed oil
1 leek, sliced
1 clove garlic, crushed
1 tsp black mustard seeds
1 pinch cayenne pepper
½ tsp each of turmeric and cumin

300g (10½oz) broccoli florets
300g (10½oz) pumpkin, peeled,
   deseeded and cubed
200ml (⅓pt) coconut milk
1 tbsp lime juice
2 tbsp shredded coconut

Gently heat the oil in a large casserole dish or a wok and sweat the leek
for 2 minutes, then add the garlic and the spices. When the mustard seeds
start to pop, add the broccoli and pumpkin and stir-fry for 3–5 minutes.
Add the coconut milk and bring to the boil. Gently simmer until the
broccoli is tender. Spoon in the lime juice and season with salt to taste.
Remove from the heat, garnish with shredded coconut and serve with rice.

319 RUSSIAN PARCELS
★♥🌿🍃🍳

CALORIES	569
CHOLESTEROL	35
VEGAN CALORIES	577
POLYUNSATS	★★★
ANTIOXIDANTS	★★★
CALCIUM	★★★
IRON	★★☆
B VITAMINS	★★☆

olive oil for frying and brushing
150g (5½oz) smoked salmon/
  tempeh, coarsely chopped
250g (9oz) fresh curly kale, chopped
1 small black radish, finely chopped

1 tbsp capers
10 black olives, pitted and chopped
1 pinch cayenne pepper
sea salt to taste
1 packet filo pastry sheets

Preheat the oven to 220°C/425°F/gas mark 7. Heat a little oil in a large casserole dish and fry the tempeh (if using) for 2 minutes until golden. Add the curly kale and gently stir-fry until it begins to soften. Then add the black radish, capers and olives, stir-fry for a further minute and season. Lay a pastry sheet on top of another sheet and brush with oil. Place a generous portion of filling (including the smoked salmon, if using) in the middle. Fold into a parcel and firmly press together the edges. Repeat to make as many parcels as you have filling or pastry for. Brush each parcel with a little more oil and place on a greased baking tray. Bake in a hot oven until golden (approximately 10 minutes) and serve.

320 SWEDISH PYTTIPANNA
★♥🍳

CALORIES	635
CHOLESTEROL	25
VEGAN CALORIES	568
POLYUNSATS	★★☆
ANTIOXIDANTS	★★☆
CALCIUM	★★☆
IRON	★★☆
B VITAMINS	★★☆

oil for stir-frying
1 onion, halved and sliced
2 spicy sausages (pork/soya), sliced
8–10 mushrooms, sliced
500g (1lb 2oz) potatoes, diced

2 sticks celery, sliced
250g (9oz) kidney beans, cooked or
  canned
100g (3½oz) green beans
sea salt and black pepper to taste

Heat a little oil in a large frying pan and stir-fry the onion over a medium heat for 2 minutes. Add the sausages and the mushrooms, followed by the potatoes, and gently stir-fry for several more minutes until the potatoes begin to brown. Add the celery and beans. Heat through, season and serve hot, accompanied by tomato ketchup and mustard.

321 CHINESE SWEET AND SOUR VEGETABLES
★♥🍳

CALORIES	574
CHOLESTEROL	0
VEGAN CALORIES	574
POLYUNSATS	★★★
ANTIOXIDANTS	★★☆
CALCIUM	★★☆
IRON	★★☆
B VITAMINS	★★☆

2 tbsp grapeseed oil
1 tbsp honey
1 tsp fresh ginger, chopped
1 pinch cayenne pepper
1 leek, diagonally sliced
200g (7oz) celeriac, cut into sticks

2 tbsp white wine vinegar
3 tbsp miso or vegetable stock
¼ small white cabbage, finely sliced
100g (3½oz) rice noodles
30 almonds, chopped and toasted

Heat the oil in a wok or a heavy-based pan over a medium heat and add the honey, ginger and cayenne pepper. Add the leek and celeriac and stir-fry for 30 seconds. Turn down the heat, cover and simmer for 5 minutes. Add the vinegar and the miso or stock. Continue to simmer for a further 5 minutes. Add the cabbage and the noodles and stir and simmer until the noodles are cooked. (You may need to add a little more stock or a little water.) Garnish with toasted almonds and serve immediately.

322 ▼ SCANDINAVIAN BEETROOT BURGERS

⭐❤🌾

CALORIES	485
CHOLESTEROL	0
VEGAN CALORIES	485
POLYUNSATS	★★★
ANTIOXIDANTS	★★☆
CALCIUM	★★★
IRON	★★☆
B VITAMINS	★★☆

200g (7oz) well-cooked rice
100g (3½oz) tofu, grated
1 medium beetroot, grated
50g (1¾oz) breadcrumbs
1 tbsp red wine vinegar

1 tbsp olive oil, plus some for frying
1 tsp dried basil
sea salt and black pepper to taste
plain flour for dipping

Mix the cooked rice, tofu, beetroot, breadcrumbs, vinegar, oil and basil in a bowl. Season and shape into six 70g (2½oz) flat cakes. Dip the flat cakes in the flour and fry in a frying pan with a little oil over a high temperature for 2 minutes on each side. Turn down the heat and continue to fry for approximately 5 minutes on each side. Serve each burger in a bun with mustard, tomato ketchup, red onion, lettuce, tomato and pickled cucumber.

323 MUMBAI CAULIFLOWER CURRY
★♥∅◐

CALORIES	579
CHOLESTEROL	0
VEGAN CALORIES	579
POLYUNSATS	★★☆
ANTIOXIDANTS	★★★
CALCIUM	★★☆
IRON	★★★
B VITAMINS	★★☆

vegetable oil for stir-frying
1 small red onion, chopped
1 small red pepper, quartered,
    deseeded and chopped
1 small aubergine, chopped
1 small cauliflower, cut into florets
100g (3½oz) flageolet beans,
    cooked or canned

1 tsp curry powder
½ tsp ground coriander
400ml (14fl oz) coconut milk
1 clove garlic, crushed
½ lime, peeled and chopped
1 tsp maple syrup
1 pinch cayenne pepper
1 tbsp almonds, chopped and toasted

Stir-fry the vegetables and the beans in a heavy-based pan with a little oil, adding them in the order given. Add the curry powder and coriander and stir for 30 seconds, then add the coconut milk, garlic, lime, maple syrup, cayenne pepper and a little salt. Bring to the boil and simmer until the cauliflower is tender. Garnish with toasted almonds and serve with rice.

324 TROPICAL FILLETS
★♥∅◐

CALORIES	413
CHOLESTEROL	91
VEGAN CALORIES	390
POLYUNSATS	★★☆
ANTIOXIDANTS	★★☆
CALCIUM	★★☆
IRON	★★★
B VITAMINS	★★☆

250g (9oz) sole fillets/tofu strips
sea salt for rubbing
juice of 1 lemon
100ml (3½fl oz) cold water
2 tsp ginger, finely chopped
1 tsp black pepper
1 tsp ground cinnamon

1 tbsp olive oil
2 cloves garlic, crushed
1 small green chilli, finely sliced
1 onion, sliced
1 pinch saffron
200ml (⅓pt) coconut milk
1 lime, cut into wedges

Rub the sole or tofu with salt. Mix the lemon juice, water, ginger, black pepper and cinnamon in a bowl and marinate the sole or tofu for 15 minutes. Meanwhile, heat the oil in a large frying pan or a wok and gently stir-fry the garlic, chilli and onion for 2 minutes. Stir in the saffron and coconut milk and very gently simmer for 2 minutes. Add the sole or tofu (with the marinade) and gently simmer for a further 7–10 minutes (or until the fish is tender). Garnish with wedges of lime and serve with wild rice.

325 CHINESE CAULIFLOWER AND OYSTER MUSHROOMS
♥✕

CALORIES	195
CHOLESTEROL	0
VEGAN CALORIES	195
POLYUNSATS	★★★
ANTIOXIDANTS	★★☆
CALCIUM	★☆☆
IRON	★☆☆
B VITAMINS	★★☆

2 tbsp vegetable oil
1 shallot, finely chopped
100g (3½oz) oyster mushrooms,
    sliced
1 small cauliflower, cut into florets
2 tsp tamari (soya sauce)

1 clove garlic, finely chopped
½ tsp Chinese Five-Spice
200ml (⅓pt) vegetable stock
1 tsp cornflour dissolved in a little
    cold water
sea salt and black pepper to taste

Heat the oil in a frying pan or a wok and stir-fry the shallot for 30 seconds. Add the mushrooms and cauliflower and stir-fry for 2–3 minutes, then add the tamari, garlic, Five-Spice and stock. Bring to the boil and simmer until the cauliflower is tender. Add the dissolved cornflour and heat through until the sauce thickens. Season and serve with rice or noodles.

326 ITALIAN OMELETTE

CALORIES	400
CHOLESTEROL	391
VEGAN CALORIES	409
POLYUNSATS	★★★
ANTIOXIDANTS	★★★
CALCIUM	★★☆
IRON	★★☆
B VITAMINS	★★☆

omelette:
4 eggs
a little milk/cold water
sea salt and black pepper to taste
or 1 portion basic eggless omelette
    batter (see p.41)

filling:
oil for frying
100g (3½oz) mushrooms, chopped
4 sun-dried tomatoes, chopped
2 artichoke hearts, chopped
sea salt and black pepper to taste
a little vegetable margarine or butter
1 tbsp fresh parsley mixed with 1
    crushed clove garlic

Sauté the mushrooms in a frying pan with a little oil for 2 minutes. Add the tomatoes and the artichoke hearts and heat through. Season and set aside. Beat the eggs in a bowl, add the milk or water and season. Alternatively, prepare the eggless omelette batter. Add the filling to your batter and pour into an oiled frying pan. Reduce the heat and cook each side until firm. Fold and remove from the heat. Spread a little margarine or butter over the top, garnish with the mixed parsley and garlic, and serve.

327 SPICY CHICK PEA PANCAKE

CALORIES	316
CHOLESTEROL	0
VEGAN CALORIES	316
POLYUNSATS	★★☆
ANTIOXIDANTS	★★★
CALCIUM	★★☆
IRON	★★☆
B VITAMINS	★★☆

batter:
100g (3½oz) chick pea flour
1 tsp fresh ginger, finely chopped
1 pinch sea salt
1 tsp baking powder
200ml (⅓pt) water
olive oil for frying

filling:
1 small red onion
2 medium potatoes, finely diced
200g (7oz) fresh curly kale (or
    spinach), chopped
¼ tsp ground cardamom seeds
¼ tsp hot chilli paste

Mix the batter ingredients in a bowl and pour into an oiled frying pan. Turn down the heat and gently fry each side until golden brown. Meanwhile, stir-fry the onion and potatoes in a separate pan with a little oil until they begin to soften. Add the curly kale, the cardamom seeds and a little water. Season and simmer until the potatoes are soft. Place the filling on one half of the omelette, spread the chilli paste on the other half, fold and serve.

328 BEIJING-STYLE OMELETTE

CALORIES	249
CHOLESTEROL	391
VEGAN CALORIES	258
POLYUNSATS	★★☆
ANTIOXIDANTS	★★☆
CALCIUM	★★☆
IRON	★★☆
B VITAMINS	★★☆

batter:
4 eggs
a little milk/water
sea salt and black pepper to taste
or 1 portion basic eggless omelette
    batter (see p.41)

filling:
1 pinch ground Chinese Five-Spice
2 spring onions or 1 small leek
oil for frying
oyster mushrooms, sliced and fried,
    and bean sprouts to garnish

Beat the eggs in a bowl, add the milk or water and season. Alternatively, prepare the eggless omelette batter. Chop the spring onions or leek and add to your chosen batter, together with the Five-Spice. Pour the batter into an oiled frying pan. Reduce the heat and fry each side until firm. Serve garnished with oyster mushrooms and bean sprouts.

329 SPICY WINTER OMELETTE

CALORIES	351
CHOLESTEROL	417
VEGAN CALORIES	389
POLYUNSATS	★★☆
ANTIOXIDANTS	★★★
CALCIUM	★★☆
IRON	★★☆
B VITAMINS	★★★

omelette:
4 eggs, beaten and seasoned
1 tbsp milk
¼ tsp hot chilli paste
1 tsp fresh ginger, finely chopped
or 1 portion basic eggless omelette
    batter (see p.41)

filling:
olive oil for frying
1 shallot, finely sliced
150g (5½oz) ham/smoked tempeh,
    diced
1 carrot, grated
2 tbsp fresh parsley, finely chopped

Mix your chosen batter ingredients and set aside. Sweat the onion in a frying pan with a little oil until soft. Add the ham or tempeh and the carrot and fry for 5 minutes, then add the parsley, and season. Heat a little oil in a separate pan. Pour in the batter and stir with a fork. When the omelette is cooked, add the filling, fold and serve.

330 LEEK AND POTATO PANCAKES

CALORIES	605
CHOLESTEROL	112
VEGAN CALORIES	603
POLYUNSATS	★★★
ANTIOXIDANTS	★★★
CALCIUM	★★☆
IRON	★★☆
B VITAMINS	★★☆

pancakes:
1 portion basic pancake batter
    (see p.42)
grapeseed oil for frying

filling:
4 slim leeks, trimmed, kept whole
2 carrots and 2 potatoes, diced
½ tsp caraway seeds, crushed
1 handful fresh parsley, chopped
sea salt and black pepper to taste

Cook the leeks in a saucepan of boiling, salted water until tender, then halve them lengthways. Mix the pancake batter and set aside. Cook the carrots and potatoes in the leek pan with a little boiling, salted water until soft, then blend with the caraway seeds, parsley and a little cooking water. Fry the pancakes in a frying pan with a little oil. When they are cooked, place some of the purée and one leek on each one, fold and serve.

331 ENCHILADAS WITH BRAZIL NUTS AND POMEGRANATE

CALORIES	842
CHOLESTEROL	0
VEGAN CALORIES	842
POLYUNSATS	★★★
ANTIOXIDANTS	★★★
CALCIUM	★★☆
IRON	★★☆
B VITAMINS	★★☆

enchiladas:
1 packet ready-made corn tortillas

filling:
corn oil for frying
1 small leek, finely sliced
60g (2¼oz) Brazil nuts, chopped
1 stick celery (with leaves), chopped

100ml (3½fl oz) vegetable stock
1 tbsp tomato paste (purée)
1 tbsp raisins
1 clove garlic, crushed
1 dash Tabasco sauce
sea salt and black pepper to taste
1 pomegranate, quartered, peeled
    and seeds separated

Gently stir-fry the leek in a casserole dish with a little oil for 3 minutes. Add the Brazil nuts and celery and stir-fry for a further 3 minutes, then add the stock, tomato paste and raisins. Bring to the boil. Add the garlic and Tabasco sauce, and season. Leave to simmer while you prepare six ready-made tortillas as indicated on the packet. Add the pomegranate seeds to the filling, heat through, divide between the tortillas and serve.

332 ▲ INDIAN PANCAKES

CALORIES	386
CHOLESTEROL	6
VEGAN CALORIES	383
POLYUNSATS	★☆☆
ANTIOXIDANTS	★★☆
CALCIUM	★★☆
IRON	★★☆
B VITAMINS	★★☆

pancakes:
100g (3½oz) wheat flour
1 tbsp desiccated coconut
100ml (3½fl oz) plain/soya yoghurt
approximately 200ml (⅓pt) water
1 pinch cayenne pepper
1 pinch sea salt
oil for frying

filling:
1 black radish, chopped into thin
   sticks
1 handful bean sprouts
200g (7oz) green beans, topped,
   tailed and blanched
1 handful fresh coriander leaves
1 tsp tamari (soya sauce)

Mix the flour, coconut, yoghurt, water, cayenne pepper and salt to a
smooth batter in a bowl, then cook approximately four thin pancakes
in a frying pan with a little oil. Set aside (keep warm). Stir-fry the black
radish, bean sprouts and green beans in a separate pan with a little oil.
Add the tamari just before removing from the heat and garnish with fresh
coriander. Fill and fold the pancakes, and serve with mango chutney.

333 BUCKWHEAT GALETTES
⭐❤

CALORIES	548
CHOLESTEROL	98
VEGAN CALORIES	455
POLYUNSATS	★★★
ANTIOXIDANTS	★★☆
CALCIUM	★★☆
IRON	★★☆
B VITAMINS	★★★

galettes:
125g (4½oz) buckwheat flour
1 pinch salt
1 egg/2 tsp baking powder
2 tbsp grapeseed oil, plus some for frying
300ml (½pt) milk/soya milk

filling:
1 shallot, finely chopped

1 bay leaf
1 pinch mace
1 clove garlic, crushed
250g (9oz) mushrooms, chopped
200ml (½pt) vegetable stock
1 tsp cornflour dissolved in a little cold water
125g (4½oz) each of green beans (chopped into tiny pieces) and sweetcorn kernels, cooked

Mix the flour, salt and egg or baking powder in a bowl. Add the oil and the milk, little by little, until you have a smooth batter. Set aside. Gently fry the shallot in a casserole dish with a little oil for 3 minutes. Add the bay leaf, mace and garlic. Heat through and add the mushrooms. Stir-fry for 2 minutes, then add the stock. Leave to simmer while you fry the galettes in a frying pan with a little oil. Add the cornflour to the mushroom sauce and cook until it thickens. Fill the galettes with a spoonful each of the mushroom sauce and the cooked bean and sweetcorn mixture, and serve.

334 PIZZA NAPOLETANA
⭐❤🌾🥥

CALORIES	501
CHOLESTEROL	45
VEGAN CALORIES	426
POLYUNSATS	★★☆
ANTIOXIDANTS	★★☆
CALCIUM	★★☆
IRON	★★☆
B VITAMINS	★★☆

1 pizza base
3 tbsp tomato sauce (passata) or sauce tomate concassé (see p.115)
100g (3½oz) mozzarella/soya cheese, thinly sliced

50g (1¾oz) anchovy fillets/black olives, pitted
100g (3½oz) mushrooms, sliced
1 tbsp capers
1 pinch oregano
sea salt and black pepper to taste

Preheat the oven to 240°C/475°F/gas mark 9 and warm up the pizza tray. Cover the prepared base with the tomato sauce, followed by the cheese. Top with the anchovies or olives, mushrooms and capers. Season (remembering that anchovies and olives are both quite salty) and bake in a hot oven for approximately 20 minutes. Serve hot with a side salad.

335 WINTER SPECIAL
⭐❤🌾🥥

CALORIES	503
CHOLESTEROL	29
VEGAN CALORIES	450
POLYUNSATS	★★☆
ANTIOXIDANTS	★★☆
CALCIUM	★★☆
IRON	★★☆
B VITAMINS	★★☆

1 pizza base
2–3 tbsp tomato sauce (passata) or sauce tomate concassé (see p.115)
1 clove garlic, finely chopped
1 onion, finely chopped

50g (1¾oz) shiitake mushrooms
150g (5½oz) broccoli florets, blanched
oregano, sea salt and black pepper
100g (3½oz) mozzarella/soya cheese, grated

Preheat the oven to 240°C/475°F/gas mark 9 and warm up the pizza tray. Spread the tomato sauce over the prepared base and sprinkle with garlic and onion. Slice the shiitake and add them to the pizza, together with the broccoli. Season to taste, sprinkle with cheese and bake in a hot oven for approximately 15 minutes. Serve hot with a side salad.

336 PIZZA POSILLIPO

CALORIES	510
CHOLESTEROL	197
VEGAN CALORIES	750
POLYUNSATS	★★☆
ANTIOXIDANTS	★★★
CALCIUM	★★★
IRON	★★★
B VITAMINS	★★★

1 pizza base
2 tbsp tomato sauce (passata) or
sauce tomate concassé
(see p.115)
100g (3½oz) prawns and 8 prepared
calamares/100g (3½oz) shelled
walnuts and 1 sheet toasted

nori seaweed
½ small red chilli, finely chopped
100g (3½oz) fresh spinach, sautéed
juice of ½ lime
sea salt and black pepper to taste
100g (3½oz) mozzarella/soya
cheese, grated

Preheat the oven to 240°C/475°F/gas mark 9 and warm up the pizza tray.
Cover the prepared base with the tomato sauce. Top with the prawns and
calamares or walnuts and nori. Add the red chilli and the spinach. Sprinkle
with lime juice, season and sprinkle with cheese. Bake in a hot oven for
approximately 15 minutes. Serve hot with a side salad.

337 PIZZA MARIO

CALORIES	495
CHOLESTEROL	39
VEGAN CALORIES	462
POLYUNSATS	★★☆
ANTIOXIDANTS	★★☆
CALCIUM	★★☆
IRON	★★☆
B VITAMINS	★★★

1 pizza base
2–3 tbsp tomato sauce (passata) or
sauce tomate concassé
(see p.115)
8 cooked mussels/50g (1¾oz)
seitan, cut into chunks
1 shallot, finely chopped

6 anchovy fillets/12 black olives,
pitted and chopped, plus some
to garnish
sea salt and black pepper to taste
2 tbsp Parmesan/brewer's yeast
flakes
1 tbsp olive oil

Preheat the oven to 230°C/450°F/gas mark 8 and warm up the pizza tray.
Mix the tomato sauce with the mussels or seitan, shallot and anchovies
or olives in a bowl, and season. Place the prepared base on the preheated,
oiled tray and spread the topping over it. Garnish with anchovies or olives,
sprinkle with Parmesan or brewer's yeast flakes and drizzle with oil.
Bake in a hot oven for 12–15 minutes. Serve hot with a side salad.

338 PIZZA QUATTRO STAGIONI (FOUR SEASONS)

CALORIES	510
CHOLESTEROL	35
VEGAN CALORIES	450
POLYUNSATS	★★☆
ANTIOXIDANTS	★★☆
CALCIUM	★★☆
IRON	★★☆
B VITAMINS	★★☆

1 pizza base
2–3 tbsp tomato sauce (passata) or
sauce tomate concassé
(see p.115)
2 artichoke hearts (in oil), sliced
1 tomato and ½ green pepper, sliced
100g (3½oz) mushrooms, sliced and

sautéed
1 clove garlic, crushed
3 anchovy fillets/8 black olives,
pitted
oregano, sea salt and black pepper
100g (3½oz) mozzarella/soya
cheese, grated

Preheat the oven to 240°C/475°F/gas mark 9 and warm up the pizza tray.
Spread the tomato sauce over the prepared base and divide into quarters.
Top the first quarter with artichoke, the second with tomato and pepper,
the third with mushrooms and garlic, and the fourth with anchovies or
olives. Season to taste, sprinkle with cheese and bake in a hot oven
for approximately 20 minutes. Serve hot with a side salad.

339 ▾ PIZZA CALZONE
★◐🌾⊘

CALORIES	527
CHOLESTEROL	46
VEGAN CALORIES	497
POLYUNSATS	★★☆
ANTIOXIDANTS	★★☆
CALCIUM	★★☆
IRON	★★☆
B VITAMINS	★★★

1 dough pizza base
2–3 tbsp tomato sauce (passata) or
   sauce tomate concassé
   (see p.115)
100g (3½oz) cooked ham/tempeh,
   cubed

100g (3½oz) oyster mushrooms,
   sautéed
2 tbsp fresh pineapple chunks
oregano, sea salt and black pepper
100g (3½oz) mozzarella/soya
   cheese, grated

Preheat the oven to 220°C/425°F/gas mark 7 and warm up the pizza tray.
Spread the tomato sauce over half of the prepared and rolled-out dough
base. Top with the ham or tempeh, mushrooms and pineapple chunks.
Season to taste and sprinkle with grated cheese. Fold the base over the
filling, press the edges together to seal and cut a couple of slits over
the top. Bake in a hot oven for approximately 20 minutes, or until
the crust is beginning to brown. Serve hot with a side salad.

340 ▲ SPICED BEAN AND JUNIPER CASSEROLE

⭐♥◉∅

CALORIES	423
CHOLESTEROL	0
VEGAN CALORIES	423
POLYUNSATS	★☆☆
ANTIOXIDANTS	★★★
CALCIUM	★★☆
IRON	★★☆
B VITAMINS	★★☆

2 tbsp olive oil
1 red onion, chopped
1 clove garlic, crushed
1 potato, cut into chunks
1 carrot, sliced
1 stick celery, sliced
1 tsp ground cumin and coriander
sea salt and cayenne pepper
  to taste

400g (14oz) butter beans, cooked or
  canned and drained
250g (9oz) tomatoes, chopped
1 sprig each of fresh thyme and
  rosemary
300ml (½pt) vegetable stock, heated
4 juniper berries, lightly crushed
1 tbsp fresh parsley, finely chopped

Heat the oil in a casserole dish and gently sauté the onion, garlic, potato,
carrot and celery for 5 minutes. Add the cumin and coriander, and season.
Sauté for a couple more minutes, then add the beans, followed by the
tomatoes, thyme and rosemary. Sauté for a further 2 minutes, then add
the stock and the juniper berries. Bring to the boil, cover and gently
simmer until the vegetables are cooked. Garnish with parsley and serve
with rice or thick slices of wholemeal bread and cheese or soya cheese.

341 ESCALOPES IN MUSHROOM SAUCE

CALORIES	619
CHOLESTEROL	73
VEGAN CALORIES	611
POLYUNSATS	★★★
ANTIOXIDANTS	★★★
CALCIUM	★★☆
IRON	★★☆
B VITAMINS	★★★

2 turkey escalopes, flattened and seasoned/2 ready-made vegetarian escalopes
1 tsp paprika
olive oil for (stir-)frying
300g (10½oz) mushrooms, chopped
1 tbsp wheat flour
6 tbsp water
1 tbsp lemon juice
approximately 2 tbsp cream/ soya cream
sea salt to taste

Sprinkle the escalopes with paprika and fry them in a frying pan with a little oil until golden and cooked through. Set aside (keep warm). Heat a little more oil in a small casserole dish, add the mushrooms and stir-fry until they give off their juices. Sprinkle with the flour and stir for a further minute. Add the water and the lemon juice, and enough cream to make a thick sauce. Gently simmer for 5 minutes, then season. Place the fried escalopes on two plates, cover with the mushroom sauce and serve with boiled potatoes and just-cooked artichoke hearts and carrots.

342 SPICY PEAS AND POTATOES

CALORIES	408
CHOLESTEROL	0
VEGAN CALORIES	408
POLYUNSATS	★☆☆
ANTIOXIDANTS	★★☆
CALCIUM	★☆☆
IRON	★★☆
B VITAMINS	★★☆

2 tbsp olive oil
1 onion, chopped
250g (9oz) potatoes, chopped
150g (5½oz) chick peas, cooked or canned
150g (5½oz) green peas, fresh or frozen
1 tsp turmeric
1 pinch cayenne pepper
1 tsp ground cumin
200ml (⅓pt) water
1 tbsp tomato paste (purée)
1 pinch raw cane sugar and sea salt
½ tsp garam masala

Heat the oil in a casserole dish or a wok, add the onion, followed by the chopped potatoes and stir-fry for 2 minutes. Add the chick peas, green peas and spices. Stir-fry for a further 2 minutes, then pour in the water and bring to the boil. Add the tomato paste, sugar and salt, and simmer for 10–15 minutes until the potatoes are tender. Check the seasoning, garnish with garam masala and serve with rice.

343 BROCCOLI AND BRAZIL NUT STIR-FRY

CALORIES	568
CHOLESTEROL	0
VEGAN CALORIES	568
POLYUNSATS	★★★
ANTIOXIDANTS	★★★
CALCIUM	★★★
IRON	★★☆
B VITAMINS	★★☆

2 tbsp olive oil
1 clove garlic, chopped
75g (2¾oz) Brazil nuts, chopped
500g (1lb 2oz) broccoli
2 tbsp tamari (soya sauce)
100ml (3½fl oz) vegetable stock
2 tbsp lemon juice
1 tbsp toasted sesame oil
2 tsp cornflour dissolved in a little cold water
black pepper to taste

Heat the olive oil in a wok and add the garlic and Brazil nuts. Cut the broccoli into florets and add to the wok. Stir-fry for 1 minute, then add the tamari and the stock. Simmer for 5 minutes and add the lemon juice and sesame oil. Add the cornflour, stir and simmer for a few more minutes until the mixture thickens. Season and serve hot with rice noodles.

344 LEMON AND MUSHROOM RISOTTO
♥ ◐ ∅ ⬛

CALORIES	596
CHOLESTEROL	0
VEGAN CALORIES	596
POLYUNSATS	★★☆
ANTIOXIDANTS	★★☆
CALCIUM	★★☆
IRON	★★☆
B VITAMINS	★★☆

200g (7oz) wholegrain rice
3 tbsp olive oil
1 onion, thinly sliced
150g (5½oz) mushrooms, sliced
300ml (½pt) vegetable stock
sea salt to taste
1 tsp turmeric

4 cloves garlic, crushed
1 large handful fresh parsley, chopped
flesh of ½ lemon, chopped
1 tbsp fresh chervil, chopped
1 dash Tabasco sauce

Par-boil the rice in a saucepan for 10 minutes. Meanwhile, gently stir-fry the onion and the mushrooms in a casserole dish with 2 tablespoons of oil. Then add the par-boiled and drained rice and stir-fry for a few more minutes before adding the stock and a little salt. Bring to the boil and simmer for 15 minutes. Add the rest of the ingredients (except the oil). Heat through. Add the remaining tablespoon of oil and serve immediately.

345 CHICK PEAS AND POTATOES IN RICH TOMATO SAUCE
★ ∅

CALORIES	414
CHOLESTEROL	0
VEGAN CALORIES	414
POLYUNSATS	★★☆
ANTIOXIDANTS	★★☆
CALCIUM	★☆☆
IRON	★★☆
B VITAMINS	★★☆

3 tbsp olive oil
1 small onion, sliced
2 medium potatoes, sliced
250g (9oz) chick peas, cooked or canned

100ml (3½fl oz) water
1 tbsp tomato paste (purée)
2 cloves garlic, crushed
2 tsp maple syrup
sea salt and black pepper to taste

Gently stir-fry the onion in a casserole dish or a wok with the oil for 3 minutes. Add the potatoes and continue to stir-fry until they begin to brown. Add the chick peas, stir-fry for 3 minutes and pour in the water. Bring to the boil and simmer until the potatoes are tender (approximately 5–10 minutes). Add the tomato paste, garlic, maple syrup, and season. Heat through, adjust the seasoning and serve hot or cold on a bed of rice.

346 PICCATA IN GARLIC CREAM
★ 🌿

CALORIES	815
CHOLESTEROL	222
VEGAN CALORIES	510
POLYUNSATS	★★★
ANTIOXIDANTS	★★★
CALCIUM	★★☆
IRON	★★☆
B VITAMINS	★★☆

olive oil for frying
2 shallots, chopped
400g (14oz) carrots, sliced
4 cloves garlic
300g (10½oz) pork escalopes, flattened/2 ready-made

vegetarian escalopes
100ml (3½fl oz) white wine
100ml (3½fl oz) vegetable stock
100ml (3½fl oz) crème fraîche/soya cream
sea salt and black pepper to taste

Sweat the shallots in a casserole dish with a little oil. Add the carrots, cover with cold water, season, bring to the boil and slowly cook until tender. Meanwhile, blanch the garlic in a saucepan of boiling water for 2 minutes. Fry the escalopes in a frying pan with a little oil until golden brown. Set aside (keep warm). Pour the wine and stock into the frying pan, then add the blanched garlic and cream. Leave to reduce for 5 minutes. Blend and season. Place the escalopes on two plates, with the carrots on the side. Top with the sauce. Serve with boiled potatoes and green beans.

347 ▶ WINTER TAPAS TARTS
★♥🌾🥥

CALORIES	521
CHOLESTEROL	77
VEGAN CALORIES	483
POLYUNSATS	★★★
ANTIOXIDANTS	★★★
CALCIUM	★★★
IRON	★★★
B VITAMINS	★★★

½ shallot, chopped
1 tbsp tomato paste (purée)
1 tbsp fresh parsley, chopped
1 tsp paprika
1 pinch each of sugar and salt
1 dash Tabasco sauce
2 cloves garlic, chopped
oil for stir-frying
175g (6oz) tuna cut into chunks/
60g (2¼oz) soya chunks, soaked
in water with 2 tbsp seaweed for
5–10 minutes

1 packet ready-made puff pastry,
halved and rolled out
100g (3½oz) cauliflower florets,
blanched
8–10 brown mushrooms, thinly
sliced
sea salt and black pepper to taste
1 tbsp capers
25g (1oz) mozzarella/soya cheese,
grated
2 tbsp Parmesan/brewer's yeast
flakes

Preheat the oven to 220°C/425°F/gas mark 7. Blend the shallot, tomato paste, parsley, paprika, sugar, salt, Tabasco sauce and garlic in a bowl with a little water. Stir-fry the tuna or soya chunks in a frying pan with a little oil until golden. Line two 4 x 10cm (1½ x 4in) pie dishes with the pastry. Add the blended tomato mixture, followed by a layer of blanched cauliflower and mushroom slices. Season and sprinkle with capers and mozzarella or soya cheese. Sprinkle with Parmesan or brewer's yeast flakes, bake in the middle of a hot oven until the tarts begin to brown, and serve.

348 SWEET CHESTNUT CASSEROLE
★♥

CALORIES	467
CHOLESTEROL	0
VEGAN CALORIES	467
POLYUNSATS	★★☆
ANTIOXIDANTS	★★★
CALCIUM	★★☆
IRON	★★☆
B VITAMINS	★★☆

2 tbsp olive oil
100g (3½oz) shallots, kept whole
300g (10½oz) peeled sweet
chestnuts, fresh, canned or dried
and soaked

250ml (9fl oz) vegetable stock
300g (10½oz) Brussels sprouts,
trimmed
sea salt and black pepper to taste

Gently sauté the shallots in a casserole dish with the oil until they begin to brown. Add the chestnuts and stir-fry for 5 minutes, then add the stock. Bring to the boil and gently simmer for 15 minutes. Add the Brussels sprouts and simmer until they are tender. Season and serve with rice.

349 LIVER OR SEITAN WITH GARLIC AND RED WINE VINEGAR
★🌾

CALORIES	818
CHOLESTEROL	483
VEGAN CALORIES	601
POLYUNSATS	★★★
ANTIOXIDANTS	★★★
CALCIUM	★★☆
IRON	★★☆
B VITAMINS	★★★

300g (10½oz) lamb's liver,
sliced/175g (6oz) seitan, sliced
1 tbsp plain flour
sea salt and black pepper to taste

vegetable oil for frying
2 cloves garlic, chopped
200ml (⅓pt) red wine vinegar
1 tbsp fresh parsley, chopped

Flour the liver or seitan, season and fry on both sides in a frying pan with a little oil over a high heat. Set aside (keep hot). Fry the garlic in a separate pan with a little oil. Add the vinegar and leave to reduce to one-third of its volume. Season and add parsley. Cover the liver or seitan with the sauce and serve on warmed plates with steamed potatoes, carrots and broccoli.

350 SEAFOOD RISOTTO

CALORIES	594
CHOLESTEROL	72
VEGAN CALORIES	638
POLYUNSATS	★★★
ANTIOXIDANTS	★★★
CALCIUM	★★☆
IRON	★★☆
B VITAMINS	★★★

2 tbsp olive oil
1 small red onion, finely chopped
1 Florence fennel bulb, finely chopped
2 cloves garlic, crushed
½ tsp fennel seeds, crushed in a mortar
½ tsp cayenne pepper
1 phial saffron
150g (5½oz) risotto rice

1 cup dried hiziki (seaweed), soaked in cold water
1 tbsp tomato paste (purée)
50ml (2fl oz) dry white wine
750ml (1⅓pts) fish/vegetable stock, heated
200g (7oz) crab meat/50g (1¾oz) chopped walnuts
2 tbsp lemon juice
2 tbsp fresh parsley, finely chopped

Heat the oil in a large heavy-based casserole dish and gently stir-fry the onion and the chopped fennel until soft. Add the garlic, fennel seeds, cayenne pepper, saffron, rice and hiziki and stir-fry for 3 minutes. Add the tomato paste and stir for 1 minute until the rice is coated. Pour in the wine and continue to stir until it is absorbed, then slowly add the stock. Bring to the boil, cover and very gently simmer until the rice is cooked and all the liquid is absorbed. Stir in the crab meat or walnuts and the lemon juice. Heat through. Adjust the seasoning, garnish with parsley and serve.

351 TRANCHES LYONNAISES

CALORIES	711
CHOLESTEROL	483
VEGAN CALORIES	479
POLYUNSATS	★★☆
ANTIOXIDANTS	★★★
CALCIUM	★★☆
IRON	★★★
B VITAMINS	★★★

300g (10½oz) lamb's liver, sliced/150g (5½oz) seitan, sliced
2 tbsp plain flour
2 onions, halved and sliced
100ml (3½fl oz) white wine

100ml (3½fl oz) meat/vegetable stock
sea salt and black pepper to taste
1 tbsp fresh parsley, chopped

Flour the liver or seitan and fry in a frying pan with a little oil until just brown on both sides. Set aside (keep hot). Add a little more oil to the pan and sweat the onions (don't let them brown). Add the white wine and the stock. Leave to reduce to one-third of the volume, then season. Return the fried liver or seitan to the pan, sprinkle with parsley and serve with steamed potatoes and Brussels sprouts.

352 GRILLED WINTER KEBABS

CALORIES	517
CHOLESTEROL	56
VEGAN CALORIES	455
POLYUNSATS	★★★
ANTIOXIDANTS	★★★
CALCIUM	★★☆
IRON	★★☆
B VITAMINS	★★☆

150g (5½oz) turkey breast steaks/tofu, cut into chunks
1 sweet potato, cut into chunks
4 cloves garlic, kept whole
1 beetroot, cut into chunks
6 Brussels sprouts, blanched

6 button mushrooms, kept whole
2–3 tbsp olive oil
25g (1oz) finely chopped walnuts
1 tsp basil
sea salt to taste
1 tbsp tomato paste (purée)

Alternately thread the turkey or tofu chunks and the vegetables onto two skewers. Mix the oil with the chopped walnuts, basil, salt and tomato paste in a bowl, and brush the kebabs with the mixture. Place on a greased baking tray and grill for 5–6 minutes on each side, or until golden and cooked through. Serve on a bed of rice with a side salad.

353 TROPICAL FRUIT FLAMBÉ

CALORIES	508
CHOLESTEROL	0
VEGAN CALORIES	508
POLYUNSATS	★★★
ANTIOXIDANTS	★★★
CALCIUM	★★☆
IRON	★★☆
B VITAMINS	★☆☆

1 tbsp grapeseed oil
2 thick slices pineapple, peeled,
    cored and halved
2 bananas, peeled and halved
    lengthways
1 papaya, peeled, deseeded and
    sliced
¼ fresh coconut, peeled and thinly
    sliced
2 tbsp maple syrup
1 tbsp rum

Heat the oil in a frying pan and fry the fruit pieces for 1 minute. Turn,
sprinkle with the maple syrup and fry for a further 1–2 minutes until the
fruit is tender (but still firm). Add the rum, heat through and carefully
ignite the mixture with a match. Gently shake the pan while allowing the
rum to burn for a minute. When the rum has burned out, serve the sautéed
fruit with ice cream, soya cream, plain or soya yoghurt.

354 PINEAPPLE PIE

CALORIES	378
CHOLESTEROL	0
VEGAN CALORIES	378
POLYUNSATS	★★☆
ANTIOXIDANTS	★★☆
CALCIUM	★☆☆
IRON	★☆☆
B VITAMINS	★☆☆

½ pineapple, peeled, cored and
    chopped, plus 2 thin slices
    (halved) to garnish
1 tsp maple syrup
1 tbsp agar-agar

3 tbsp water
1 prebaked 20cm (8in) shortcrust
    pastry shell
2 tbsp fresh coconut, shredded

Blend the pineapple and maple syrup until smooth and set aside. Heat
the agar-agar with the water in a small casserole dish over a low heat,
stirring continuously until the mixture bubbles and becomes gelatinous
(3–4 minutes). Stir in the blended pineapple and pour into the prebaked
pastry shell. Allow to cool, then garnish with halved pineapple slices and
fresh coconut. Chill before serving.

355 BAKED CINNAMON APPLES

CALORIES	504
CHOLESTEROL	0
VEGAN CALORIES	504
POLYUNSATS	★★★
ANTIOXIDANTS	★★☆
CALCIUM	★★☆
IRON	★★☆
B VITAMINS	★★☆

2 dessert apples, cored
2 bananas, peeled and mashed
4–6 dates, pitted and chopped
1 tbsp flaked almonds

ground cinnamon to taste
2 tbsp tahini
1 tbsp lemon juice
3 tbsp maple syrup

Preheat the oven to 180°C/350°F/gas mark 4. Cut a horizontal line in the
skin of the apples around the middle and set aside. Mix one of the mashed
bananas with the dates in a bowl. Stuff the cored apples with the banana
and date mixture. Sprinkle the almonds and the cinnamon on top and bake
in a hot oven for approximately 20 minutes. Meanwhile, mix the tahini with
the remaining mashed banana, lemon juice and maple syrup in a bowl with
enough cold water to make a thick sauce. Place the baked apples on two
dessert plates, garnish with the sauce and serve.

356 CREAMY ORANGE SALAD

CALORIES	302
CHOLESTEROL	0
VEGAN CALORIES	302
POLYUNSATS	★★☆
ANTIOXIDANTS	★★★
CALCIUM	★★☆
IRON	★★☆
B VITAMINS	★★☆

2 oranges, peeled and diced
4 lychees, peeled, halved and pitted
2 dates, pitted and sliced
2 mandarins, peeled and sliced

1 banana, peeled and chopped
1 tbsp cashew nuts
2 tsp maple syrup
approximately 2 tbsp almond milk

Divide the oranges, lychees, dates and mandarins between two glass bowls. Blend the banana with the cashews, maple syrup and enough almond milk to make a smooth cream, pour over the fruits and serve.

357 ▼ HOT WAFFLES WITH FRESH FRUIT

CALORIES	464
CHOLESTEROL	0
VEGAN CALORIES	464
POLYUNSATS	★★☆
ANTIOXIDANTS	★★☆
CALCIUM	★★☆
IRON	★☆☆
B VITAMINS	★★☆

4 small waffles
2 mandarins, peeled and chopped
1 banana, peeled and sliced

1 pear, halved, cored and sliced
1 tbsp chopped walnuts
2 tbsp maple syrup

Toast the waffles and place them on two dessert plates. Pile the fruit on top, sprinkle with walnuts and maple syrup, and serve immediately.

CITRUS FRUIT SALAD

⭐❤️💧⬛️❌▢

CALORIES	94
CHOLESTEROL	0
VEGAN CALORIES	94
POLYUNSATS	★☆☆
ANTIOXIDANTS	★★★
CALCIUM	★☆☆
IRON	★☆☆
B VITAMINS	★☆☆

1 orange, peeled and sliced
1 pink grapefruit, peeled and sliced
1 clementine, peeled and sliced
maple syrup to taste

Place the fruit in a glass bowl. Drizzle with the maple syrup and serve.

WINTER FRUIT SALAD
WITH CREAMY DATE SAUCE

⭐❤️💧⬛️❌▢

CALORIES	306
CHOLESTEROL	0
VEGAN CALORIES	306
POLYUNSATS	★☆☆
ANTIOXIDANTS	★★★
CALCIUM	★★☆
IRON	★★☆
B VITAMINS	★☆☆

1 papaya, peeled, deseeded and
  sliced
2 kiwis, peeled and sliced
1 banana, peeled and sliced

6 dates, pitted and diced
1 tbsp lime juice
100ml (3½fl oz) apple juice
1 tbsp rum (optional)

Arrange the papaya slices on two dessert plates and top with the kiwi
and banana slices. Blend the dates with the lime juice, apple juice and
rum (if using) to make a sauce. Then heat the sauce in a small casserole
dish and pour over the fruit. Serve immediately.

FRUIT FLOWERS

⭐❤️💧⬛️❌▢

CALORIES	237
CHOLESTEROL	0
VEGAN CALORIES	237
POLYUNSATS	★☆☆
ANTIOXIDANTS	★★★
CALCIUM	★★☆
IRON	★★☆
B VITAMINS	★★☆

2 oranges, peeled and horizontally
  sliced
1 banana, peeled and diagonally
  sliced
2 kiwis, peeled and horizontally

sliced
1 papaya, peeled, deseeded and
  sliced lengthways
2 tsp maple syrup (optional)

Arrange the fruit in layers on two flat plates, beginning from the middle
and making flower-petal and leaf shapes with the fruit slices.
Drizzle with the maple syrup (if using) and serve.

AFRICAN FRUIT SALAD

⭐❤️💧⬛️❌▢

CALORIES	343
CHOLESTEROL	0
VEGAN CALORIES	343
POLYUNSATS	★★☆
ANTIOXIDANTS	★★★
CALCIUM	★☆☆
IRON	★☆☆
B VITAMINS	★★☆

1 avocado, halved, pitted, peeled
  and sliced
1 guava, peeled, deseeded and
  chopped
1 mango, peeled, deseeded and
  chopped

1 pear, quartered, cored and sliced
1 tangerine, peeled and chopped
1 tbsp lime juice
100ml (3½fl oz) apple juice
1 tsp honey
1 tbsp grated coconut

Mix the fruit in a glass bowl and sprinkle with lime juice. Heat the apple
juice in a saucepan and dissolve the honey. Allow the sauce to cool a little,
pour over the fruit and gently mix. Garnish with coconut and serve.

362 ▶ PEAR TART

CALORIES	452
CHOLESTEROL	0
VEGAN CALORIES	452
POLYUNSATS	★★★
ANTIOXIDANTS	★★☆
CALCIUM	★★☆
IRON	★☆☆
B VITAMINS	★☆☆

1 packet ready-made shortcrust pastry, rolled out
2 tbsp flaked almonds

2 large sweet, ripe pears, peeled, halved and cored
approximately 55g (2oz) marzipan

Preheat the oven to 200°C/400°F/gas mark 6. Place the rolled-out pastry in a 20cm (8in) square, ovenproof pie dish, leaving a generous rim hanging over the edge of the dish. Sprinkle with almonds. Place a knob of marzipan in the hollow of each pear half, then arrange all four pear halves in the pastry shell, stalk ends meeting in the middle. Fold the pastry into the centre to cover the base of the pears and bake for 30 minutes until golden. Serve with plain or soya yoghurt, crème fraîche or soya cream.

363 FRUIT AND NUT SALAD

CALORIES	393
CHOLESTEROL	0
VEGAN CALORIES	393
POLYUNSATS	★★★
ANTIOXIDANTS	★★★
CALCIUM	★☆☆
IRON	★★☆
B VITAMINS	★★☆

1 banana, peeled and sliced
1 apple, cored and chopped
1 pear, cored and chopped
1 handful raisins

5 almonds, chopped
4 Brazil nuts, chopped
2 tbsp chopped walnuts
2 tbsp sunflower seeds

Mix the fresh fruit in a glass bowl. Add the raisins, nuts and seeds and gently toss. Serve with yoghurt or soya yoghurt and maple syrup.

364 APPLE SALAD WITH CASHEW CREAM

CALORIES	345
CHOLESTEROL	0
VEGAN CALORIES	345
POLYUNSATS	★★☆
ANTIOXIDANTS	★★☆
CALCIUM	★☆☆
IRON	★☆☆
B VITAMINS	★☆☆

2 dessert apples, cored and grated
2 mandarins, peeled and chopped
4 dates, pitted and chopped

50g (1¾oz) cashew nuts
2–3 tbsp apple juice

Mix the apples, mandarins and dates in a bowl. Blend the cashews with the apple juice to make a thick cream. Divide the apple salad between two dessert glasses, top with the cashew cream and serve immediately.

365 WINTER SUNSHINE SALAD

CALORIES	260
CHOLESTEROL	0
VEGAN CALORIES	260
POLYUNSATS	★☆☆
ANTIOXIDANTS	★★★
CALCIUM	★☆☆
IRON	★☆☆
B VITAMINS	★☆☆

½ pineapple, peeled, cored and cut into chunks
2 mandarins, peeled and divided into segments
1 sharon fruit, sliced

½ papaya, peeled, deseeded and sliced
100ml (3½fl oz) orange juice
seeds from 1 pomegranate
1 dash maple syrup (or to taste)

Divide the pineapple, mandarins, sharon fruit and papaya between two small glass bowls. Sprinkle with orange juice, pomegranate seeds and maple syrup, and serve.

FOOD
FACTS

This chapter helps you to check how many calories you need each day and provides tables showing how much of each vitamin, mineral and trace element you need for maximum health, followed by the top ten primary food sources of each micronutrient. Recommended daily amounts vary from country to country, and also evolve as our understanding of micronutrients grows; so, in reality, it is not possible to say precisely how much of a given nutrient an individual needs because we are all different and have different absorption rates and metabolisms. These figures, therefore, should be taken as guidelines for average needs of the population as a whole and not as hard and fast measurements.

Obtaining micronutrients from food is usually more efficient than taking nutritional supplements, because food provides nutrients in a steady stream as it is digested, thus making absorption more efficient. The top ten tables show you which foods to eat more of if you feel you need to increase your intake of a particular micronutrient and are intended as a guide to help you change your diet and improve health and well-being naturally.

VITAMIN A (retinol and beta-carotene)

Estimated Average Requirements
*6 micrograms of beta-carotene is equivalent to 1 microgram of retinol

AGE	MICROGRAMS RETINOL EQUIVALENT* PER DAY
0–1 year	250
1–6 years	300
7–14 years	375
From 15 years onwards	500
Pregnant women should add 100 micrograms/day	
Breastfeeding mothers should add 350 micrograms/day	

Top Ten Foods
micrograms per 100 grams of food
*6 micrograms of beta-carotene is equivalent to 1 microgram of retinol

BETA-CAROTENE* FROM PLANT SOURCES

1. Paprika	36250
2. Carrots	12472
3. Sweet potato	8910
4. Spring greens	8295
5. Parsley	4040
6. Red pepper	3780
7. Spinach	3535
8. Curly kale	3145
9. Watercress	2520
10. Cantaloupe melon	1765

RETINOL FROM ANIMAL SOURCES

1. Liver	17300
2. Liver pâté	7300
3. Butter	958
4. Double cream	779
5. Margarine (average)	665
6. Crème fraîche	388
7. Cheese (average)	300
8. Single cream	291
9. Eggs	190
10. Greek style yoghurt	115

VITAMIN B1 (thiamin)

Estimated Average Requirements
amount needed per 1000 calories eaten

AGE	MILLIGRAMS PER DAY
0–12 months	0.23
From 1 year onwards	0.30

Top Ten Foods
milligrams per 100 grams of food

1. Yeast extract	4.10
2. Wheatgerm	2.01
3. Sunflower seeds	1.60
4. Breakfast cereals (average)	1.20
5. Peanuts	1.14
6. Pork	0.98
7. Sesame seeds	0.94
8. Oatmeal and wheat bran	0.90
9. Peas	0.74
10. Brown rice	0.59

VITAMIN B2 (riboflavin)

Estimated Average Requirements

AGE	MILLIGRAMS PER DAY
0–3 years	0.5
4–10 years	0.8
From 11 years onwards	1.0
Pregnant women should add 0.3 milligrams/day	
Breastfeeding mothers should add 0.5 milligrams/day	

Top Ten Foods
milligrams per 100 grams of food

1 Yeast extract	11.90
2. Liver (average)	3.00
3. Breakfast cereals (average)	1.20
4. Crab	0.86
5. Almonds	0.75
6. Wheatgerm	0.72
7. Venison, duck and goose	0.60
8. Tempeh	0.48
9. Eggs and cheese (average)	0.45
10. Oyster mushrooms	0.40

VITAMIN B3 (niacin)

Estimated Average Requirements
amount needed per 1000 calories eaten

AGE	MILLIGRAMS PER DAY
From birth onwards	5.5
Breastfeeding mothers should add 2.3 milligrams/day	

Top Ten Foods
milligrams per 100 grams of food

1. Yeast extract	71.0
2. Wheat bran	32.6
3. Liver	19.4
4. Peanuts	19.3
5. Paprika	18.4
6. Breakfast cereals (average)	15.0
7. Game	12.0
8. Sesame seeds	10.4
9. Wheatgerm	9.8
10. Tempeh	4.7

VITAMIN B5 (pantothenic acid)

Estimated Average Requirements

AGE	MILLIGRAMS PER DAY
0–1 years	1.7
From 1 year onwards	3.0

Top Ten Foods
milligrams per 100 grams of food

1. Broad beans	3.8
2. Liver	3.8
3. Breakfast cereals (average)	3.8
4. Peanuts	2.7
5. Cod roe	2.6
6. Wheat bran and wheatgerm	2.2
7. Sesame seeds	2.1
8. Mushrooms	2.0
9. Eggs	1.8
10. Trout	1.6

VITAMIN B6 (pyridoxine)

Estimated Average Requirements

AGE	MILLIGRAMS PER DAY
0–3 years	0.7
4–6 years	0.9
7–10 years	1.1
From 11 years onwards	1.5
Pregnant women should add 0.2 milligrams/day	
Breastfeeding mothers should add 0.3 milligrams/day	

Top Ten Foods
milligrams per 100 grams of food

1. Wheatgerm	3.30
2. Tempeh	1.86
3. Muesli	1.60
4. Yeast extract	1.60
5. Wheat bran	1.38
6. Sesame seeds	0.76
7. Salmon	0.75
8. Walnuts	0.67
9. Venison	0.65
10. Turkey	0.61

VITAMIN B12 (cobalamin)

Estimated Average Requirements

AGE	MICROGRAMS PER DAY
0–12 months	0.1–0.5
1–6 years	0.7–0.9
From 7 years onwards	1.0
Breastfeeding mothers should add 0.5 micrograms/day	

Top Ten Foods
micrograms per 100 grams of food

1. Liver	58.0
2. Mussels	35.0
3. Dried seaweed, nori	27.5
4. Yeast extract	13.3
5. Kippers, sardines, anchovies and cod roe	11.0
6. Prawns	8.0
7. Salmon, trout and mackerel	5.0
8. Duck, rabbit, beef, lamb, turkey and goose	2.5
9. Eggs	2.5
10. Cheese	2.0

FOLATE (folic acid)

Estimated Average Requirements

AGE	MICROGRAMS PER DAY
0–3 years	50
4–6 years	75
From 7 years onwards	150
Pregnant women should add 100 micrograms/day	
Breastfeeding mothers should add 60 micrograms/day	

Top Ten Foods
micrograms per 100 grams of food

1. Yeast extract	2620
2. Chicken liver	1350
3. Black-eye beans	630
4. Soya flour and soya beans	345
5. Wheat bran	260
6. Lambs liver	250
7. Purple broccoli	195
8. Chick peas, mung and red kidney beans	180
9. Asparagus, parsley, Swiss chard and Savoy cabbage	170
10. Beetroot	150

BIOTIN

Estimated Average Requirements

AGE	MICROGRAMS PER DAY
All ages	15–100

Top Ten Foods
micrograms per 100 grams of food

1. Chicken liver	216
2. Peanuts	110
3. Hazelnuts, almonds and soya beans	65
4. Tempeh	53
5. Plaice	47
6. Wheat bran	45
7. Wheatgerm	25
8. Eggs	20
9. Oatmeal	17
10. Mushrooms	15

VITAMIN C (ascorbic acid)

Estimated Average Requirements

AGE	MILLIGRAMS PER DAY
0–10 years	20
From 11 years onwards	30
Pregnant and breastfeeding women should add	
20 milligrams/day	

Top Ten Foods
milligrams per 100 grams of food

1. Guava	230
2. Blackcurrants	200
3. Parsley	190
4. Spring greens	180
5. Green, red and chilli peppers	120
6. Brussels sprouts	115
7. Curly kale	110
8. Broccoli	87
9. Watercress	62
10. Papaya	60

VITAMIN D (cholecalciferol)

Estimated Average Requirements
with daily exposure of the skin to sunshine
or skyshine no dietary vitamin D is needed

AGE	MICROGRAMS PER DAY
0–6 years	10
From 7 years onwards	2.5
Pregnant and breastfeeding women should add	
7.5 micrograms/day	

Top Ten Foods
micrograms per 100 grams of food

1. Herring	19.0
2. Cod roe	17.0
3. Trout	9.6
4. Kipper and mackerel	8.1
5. Salmon	7.1
6. Sardines and tuna	4.0
7. Eggs	1.8
8. Pancakes (made with whole milk)	1.3
9. Liver	1.1
10. Butter and pork	0.9

VITAMIN E (tocopherols)

Estimated Average Requirements

AGE	MILLIGRAMS PER DAY
All ages	4

Top Ten Foods
milligrams per 100 grams of food

1. Wheatgerm oil	136.7
2. Sunflower and safflower oil	45.0
3. Sunflower seeds	37.8
4. Almonds and hazelnuts	24.5
5. Sun-dried tomatoes	24.0
6. Wheatgerm	22.0
7. Corn oil	17.2
8. Brazil nuts	7.18
9. Fresh mint	5.00
10. Avocado and walnuts	3.50

VITAMIN K

Estimated Average Requirements

AGE	MICROGRAMS PER DAY
0–1 year	10
From 1 year onwards	1/kilo body weight

Top Ten Foods
micrograms per 100 grams of food

1. Curly kale	623
2. Parsley	548
3. Spinach and spring greens	394
4. Watercress	315
5. Cabbage	242
6. Broccoli	185
7. Brussels sprouts	153
8. Lettuce	129
9. Safflower oil	113
10. Asparagus	52

CALCIUM

Estimated Average Requirements

AGE	MILLIGRAMS PER DAY
0–3 years	400
4–10 years	450
11–18 years	800
From 18 years onwards	700

Breastfeeding mothers should add 500 milligrams/day

Top Ten Foods
milligrams per 100 grams of food

1. Parmesan cheese	1025
2. Sesame seeds	670
3. Tofu	510
4. Cheese (average)	450
5. Anchovies and sardines	420
6. Dried figs, almonds and yoghurt	250
7. Purple sprouting broccoli	200
8. Spring greens, spinach and curly kale	170
9. Okra, chick peas and Brazil nuts	160
10. Cow's milk	130

MAGNESIUM

Estimated Average Requirements

AGE	MILLIGRAMS PER DAY
0–1 years	40–60
1–3 years	65
4–6 years	90
7–10 years	150
11–14 years	230
From 14 years onwards	250

Breastfeeding mothers should add 550 milligrams/day

Top Ten Foods
milligrams per 100 grams of food

1. Brazil nuts	410
2. Sesame and sunflower seeds	380
3. Almonds, cashews, pine nuts and wheatgerm	270
4. Walnuts	160
5. Beans and brown rice	110
6. Swiss chard, spinach and okra	75
7. Anchovies, sardines and prawns	50
8. Brown bread and rye bread	46
9. Cheddar cheese	39
10. Meat and fish (average)	25

IRON

Estimated Average Requirements

AGE	MILLIGRAMS PER DAY	
	BOYS/MEN	GIRLS/WOMEN
7–12 months	6.0	6.0
1–6 years	5.0	5.0
7–10 years	6.7	6.7
11–18 years	8.7	11.4
19–50 years	6.7	11.4
From 50 years onwards	6.7	6.7

Top Ten Foods
milligrams per 100 grams of food

2. Wheat bran	12.9
2. Liver	11.3
3. Sesame and pumpkin seeds	10.4
4. Fresh mint	9.5
5. Kidney	9.0
6. Beans, chick peas, lentils and wheatgerm	8.3
7. Parsley and black-eye beans	7.7
8. Dried peaches, soya flour and mussels	6.8
9. Venison, shrimps, cashew nuts and pine nuts	5.1
10. Anchovies and dried figs	4.1

POTASSIUM

Estimated Average Requirements

AGE	MILLIGRAMS PER DAY
0–3 years	800
4–6 years	1100
7–10 years	2000
From 11 years onwards	3100

Top Ten Foods
milligrams per 100 grams of food

1. Yeast extract	2100
2. Dried apricots	1880
3. Wheat bran and wheatgerm	1050
4. Beans, peas and lentils	1000
5. Dried fruit	900
6. Nuts (average)	750
7. Sweet potato, avocado, greens and cabbage	450
8. Banana	400
9. Potato, chicory (Belgian endive) and courgette	360
10. Meat and fish (average)	350

ZINC

Estimated Average Requirements

AGE	MILLIGRAMS PER DAY	
	BOYS/MEN	GIRLS/WOMEN
0–3 years	3.8	3.8
4–6 years	5.0	5.0
7–10 years	5.4	5.4
11–14 years	7.0	7.0
From 15 years onwards	7.3	5.5
Breastfeeding mothers should add 5 milligrams/day		

Top Ten Foods
milligrams per 100 grams of food

1. Wheatgerm and bran	17.0
2. Liver	15.9
3. Nuts and seeds	5.3
4. Soya beans and lentils	4.0
5. Venison	3.9
6. Kidney, meat and cheese	3.5
7. Cod roe, lamb and turkey	3.3
8. Wholemeal flour and pasta, beans and chick peas	3.0
9. Anchovies and bacon	2.5
10. Sardines, prawns and mussels	2.3

SELENIUM

Estimated Average Requirements

AGE	MICROGRAMS PER DAY	
	BOYS/MEN	GIRLS/WOMEN
7–12 months	12	12
1–3 years	20	20
4–10 years	25	25
From 11 years onwards	40	30
Pregnant women should add 5 micrograms/day		
Breastfeeding mothers should add 10 micrograms/day		

Top Ten Foods
micrograms per 100 grams of food

1. Brazil nuts	254
2. Kidney	209
3. Lentils	105
4. Tuna	78
5. Squid, lemon sole and lobster	62
6. Liver	50
7. Sunflower seeds	49
8. Mussels	43
9. Sardines, plaice, kipper and mackerel	39
10. Cashew nuts	34

IODINE

Estimated Average Requirements

AGE	MICROGRAMS PER DAY
0–1 years	50
1–6 years	90
7–10 years	120
From 11 years onwards	150
Pregnant and breastfeeding women should add 50 micrograms/day	

Top Ten Foods
micrograms per 100 grams of food

1. Dried seaweed, kombu	448670
2. Dried seaweed, arame	84140
3. Dried seaweed, hijiki	42670
4. Dried seaweed, wakame	16830
5. Dried seaweed, dulse	5970
6. Dried seaweed, nori	1470
7. Cockles and mussels	140
8. Cod and lobster	100
9. Kipper, yoghurt and eggs	63
10. Salmon, butter, milk and cheese	31

INDEX